mahabharata

mahabharata

by William Buck

with an introduction by
B. A. van Nooten

illustrated by
Shirley Triest

University of California Press
Berkeley   Los Angeles   London

University of California Press
Berkeley and Los Angeles
University of California Press, Ltd.
London, England

Copyright © 1973 by
The Regents of the University of California

First California Paperback 1981
ISBN 0-520-22704-2
Library of Congress Catalog Card Number: 70-153547

Designed by Theo Jung

Printed in the United States of America

09 08 07 06 05 04 03 02 01 00
9 8 7 6 5 4 3 2 1

Lovers call again to their minds old gentleness and old service, and many kind deeds that were forgotten by negligence. For like as winter rasure doth always arase and deface grene summer, so fareth it by unstable love in man and woman. For in many persons there is no stability; for we may see all day, for a little blast of winter's rasure, anon we shall deface and lay apart true love for little or nought, that cost much think; this is no wisdom nor stability, but it is feebleness of nature and great disworship, whomsoever useth this.

Morte Darthur

contents

pUBLISheR's pRefAce

In 1955 Bill Buck discovered an elaborate nineteenth century edition of *The Sacred Song of the Lord, the Bhagavad-Gita of Lord Krishna*, in a state library in Carson City, Nevada. Immediately captivated, he plunged into a study of Indian literature which has resulted in this rendering of the *Mahabharata*, one of the *Ramayana*, and an unfinished manuscript of *Harivamsa*—unfinished because of the death of Bill Buck in 1970 at the age of 37.

His discovery of the *Bhagavad-Gita* moved Bill Buck to read the *Mahabharata*, and he would be satisfied with nothing but the full translation, an eleven volume set of which was then being reprinted in India. So determined was he that he subsidized the reprinting when it became apparent that the publisher had insufficient funds to complete his task.

Midway through his reading of volume 3, Buck decided the *Mahabharata* should be rewritten for a modern English-speaking audience. In his own words, *"Mahabharata* was about 5,000 pages, and *Ramayana* much shorter. When I read these translations I thought how nice to tell the story so it wouldn't be so hard to read. We talk about all the repetition and digression of the originals, but as you read all that endless impossible prose a very definite character comes to each actor in the story, and the land and times are most clearly shown. I wanted to transfer this story to a readable book."

To this end, Bill Buck began years of reading and rereading the translations, studying Sanskrit, planning, and writing. One of his approaches to his task was to decipher all the elaborate appellatives used for heroes and gods, kings and princesses which were used in the original text, often in place of names. These were qualities related to the characters, of which Buck compiled lists. He later used the adjectives interlaced with descriptions to preserve the mood and meanings of the characters in his own renderings. He also read all available English translations and versions of the two great epics, later saying of them, "I have never seen any versions of either story in English that were not mere outlines, or incomplete, except for the two literal translations." He was always aware that the epics were originally sung, so reading aloud both the original translations and his own work became part of the Buck family life. But the writing was done in seclusion, many hours at a time, with only finished chapters presented to the family.

During the course of his work, Bill Buck grew to love the characters of the epics, above all Krishna. He loved, too, the friendship between Krishna and Arjuna, the ancient bond of which Krishna could remember all the incarnations, although they were obscure to Arjuna. It was a theme Buck intended to enlarge in his *Harivamsa*. He had also a great respect for Duryodhana and felt that without an understanding of this character one would miss the meaning of the story and "of Life."

Buck's vision of his task was firm, with a balanced form that remained clearly in his mind as he worked. He said, "It is always apparent just what is the thread of the story—the great story that was told at the Horse Sacrifice—and what are later interpolations. It is stuffed with preachments, treatises of special interests, doctrines of later caste systems, long passages of theological dogma, but these are in chunks, and only slow the story." His great goal was to tell the tales in such a way that the modern reader would not be discouraged from knowing and loving the stories as he did. He wanted to convey the spirit, the truth, of the epics.

In answer to a critic of his manuscripts he replied, "I've made many changes and combinations in both books, but I wish to have them considered as stories which they are, rather than as examples of technically accurate scholarship, which I told you they weren't. I'd be more than willing to make any changes that could help the internal structures of the books, but I wouldn't want to change anything to conform to the 'real story,' either in details of the stories or, more subtle, in some of the places where I have given the people some of the characteristics that we admire today, and which make a story we can read today. One thing however is true. Read the stories and you get the real spirit of the original once you're done, and if they're entertaining that's all I ask." And to a friend, "I have changed my *Mahabharata* from the original in a few little ways besides length. I got a good story out of it, but what will a professor think of its use or its scholarly fidelity? Still, if you read it you know the *Mahabharata*.'

That was his aim—to make it possible for the modern reader to *know* the *Mahabharata* in a way meaningful in terms of modern life, as well as in terms of its origins. Of the finished manuscripts he wrote, "My method in writing both *Mahabharata* and *Ramayana* was to begin with a literal translation from which to extract the story, and then to tell that story in an interesting way that would preserve the spirit and flavor of the original. The *Mahabharata* especially is a case of a good story lost among an overgrown garden of digressions, interruptions and no few sermons. My motive is therefore that of the storyteller. I'm not trying to prove anything and I have made my own changes to tell the story better. Here are two great stories just waiting for people to read them. Based on the words of ancient songs, I have written books. I tried to make them interesting to read. I don't think you will find many other books like them."

introduction
by
B. A. van Nooten

The *Mahabharata* is an Indian epic, in its original Sanskrit probably the largest ever composed. Combined with a second great epic, the *Ramayana,* it embodies the essence of the Indian cultural heritage. William Buck, a young American whose untimely death at the age of thirty-seven occurred only months after he delivered manuscripts for both epics to the University of California Press in Berkeley, has retold these classics, as many poets have before, in a language and at a length that make them available to the contemporary reader.

The *Mahabharata* is the story of a dynastic struggle, culminating in an awesome battle between two branches of a single Indian ruling family. The account of the fight between the Kurus and the Pandavas for the fertile and wealthy land at the confluence of the Yamuna and Ganges rivers near Delhi is enhanced by peripheral stories that provide a social, moral, and cosmological background to the climactic battle.

We do not know exactly when the battle took place. The

Mahabharata (pronounced with the stress on the third syllable: mahabhárata) was composed over a period of some four hundred years, between the second century B.C. and the second century A.D., and already at that time the battle was a legendary event, preserved in the folk tales and martial records of the ruling tribes. The Indian calendar places its date at 3102 B.C., the beginning of the Age of Misfortune, the Kaliyuga, but more objective evidence, though scanty and inferential, points to a date closer to 1400 B.C.

At that time Aryan tribes had just begun to settle in India after their invasion from the Iranian highlands. The land from western Pakistan east to Bihar and south not farther than the Dekkhan was occupied by Aryan tribes whose names are often mentioned in records much older than the *Mahabharata*. The tribal communities varied in size and were each governed by the "prominent families" (*mahakulas)* from among which one nobleman was consecrated king. The kings quarreled and engaged in intertribal warfare as a matter of course, their conflicts were sometimes prolonged affairs, sometimes little more than cattle raids.

It is in this context that the Bharata war took place. The Kurus were an ancient tribe who had long been rulers of the area in the upper reaches of the Yamuna River. The Pandus, or Pandavas, were a newly emergent clan living in Indraprastha, some sixty miles southwest of the Kuru capital, Hastinapura. According to the *Mahabharata,* the new aristocrats were invited to the court of the ancient noble house of Kuru to engage in a gambling contest. There they were tricked first out of their kingdom and then into a promise not to retaliate for twelve years. In the thirteenth year they took refuge at the court of the Matsyas, where they allied themselves with the Kurus' eastern and southern neighbors, the Pancalas. Together in a vast host they marched up to Hastinapura, where they were met on Kuruksetra, the plain of the Kurus. Here the Kurus and their allies were defeated.

In bare outline that is the story of which the bard sings. But the composer of the *Mahabharata* has portrayed the actions of the warriors in both a heroic and a moral context, and it should be understood as a re-enactment of a cosmic moral confrontation, not simply as an account of a battle. Unlike our Western historical philosophy, which looks for external causes—such as famine, population pressure, drought—to explain the phenomena of war and conquest, the epic bard views the events of the war as prompted by observances and violations of the laws of morality. The basic principle of cosmic or individual existence is dharma. It is the doctrine of the religious and ethical rights and duties of each individual, and refers generally to duty ordained by religion, but may also mean simply virtue, or right conduct. Every human being is expected to live according to his dharma. Violation of dharma results in disaster.

Hindu society was classed into four castes, each with its own dharma. The power of the state rested with the *ksatriyas:* kings, princes, free warriors and their wives and daughters. Their dharma was to protect their dependents, rule justly, speak the truth, and fight wars. The priest caste was not socially organized in churches or temples, but consisted of individual *Brahmans* in control of religion. Among their other duties, they officiated at great sacrifices to maintain the order of the world and accomplish desired goals. They were also in control of education, could read and write, and taught history according to their outlook on life. The *Mahabharata* in its final form was largely the work of a Brahman composer, so we find in the peripheral stories an emphasis on the power and glory of the Brahman caste, although in the main story of the epic there is not one powerful Brahmin. The *Vaisyas,* of whom we hear little in the *Mahabharata,* were merchants, townspeople, and farmers, and constituted the mass of the people.

The three upper castes were twice-born: once from their mothers and once from their investitures with the sacred thread. The lowest caste, the *Sudras,* did menial work and served other castes. They were Aryans, however, and their women were accessible to higher-caste men: Vyasa was the offspring of a ksatriya and a sudra, and so was Vidura. Outside the caste system were the "scheduled castes," the tribal people of the mountains, such as the Kiratas, as well as the Persians and the Bactrian Greeks.

Besides their caste dharma, people had a personal dharma to observe, which varied with one's age and occupation. So we find a teacher-student dharma, a husband-wife dharma, the dharma of an ascetic, and so on. One's relation to the gods was also determined by dharma. The lawbooks specify the various kinds of dharma in detail, and these classifications and laws still govern Indian society.

The Hindu system of eschatology is often expounded in the *Mahabharata.* In brief, it is the doctrine of the cycle of rebirths *(samsara)*, the doctrine of the moral law (dharma), which is more powerful than even the gods. The moral law sustains and favors those creatures that abide by it, while thwarting those that trespass. Its instrument is *karma,* the inexorable law that spans this life and the afterdeath, working from one lifetime to another, rewarding the just and making the evil suffer. In this Hindu universe those in harmony with dharma ultimately reach a state in which rebirth is not necessary any more. If, however, the forces of evil are too strong, the moral law reasserts itself and often uses forceful means to restore harmony where it has been lost. To accomplish that, often a being of a higher order, a god, who in his usual manifestation has no physical body, takes birth among the people and becomes an *avatara,* a "descent" of his own power on earth. Often the physical manifestation is not aware of his divine antecedents, but discovers them in the course of his life on earth. Therefore an avatara has many human qualities, including some that by our own standards would be less than divine: hostility, vengefulness, and an overweening sense of self-importance. These qualities are necessary for him to confront confidently the forces of evil, the *asuras,* who have taken flesh also and appear as bitter enemies committed to a battle to the end.

The emphasis on morality in the *Mahabharata* brings with it considerations of the nature of the divine. There are many gods; the Indian pantheon is overwhelming in its diversity and vagueness. At the highest level of creation are the gods *(devas),* who are in continual conflict with the demonic forces, the asuras. Among the gods, Visnu, Siva, and Indra are especially important. Visnu is mainly manifest through his incarnation as Krisna. He is a supreme god worthy of love and devotion. Siva is also a supreme god, but represents the ascetic side of Indian religion. He dwells on a mountain, dresses in a tiger skin, and wears a characteristic emblem, the trident, still carried by Indian mendicants. The third eye in the middle of Siva's forehead scorches his enemies. Indra is in name the king of the gods, but in fact his importance had declined by the time of the *Mahabharata*, although he remained a principle god. In the *Mahabharata* he is the god of rain and father of Arjuna, a Pandava.

Less powerful are the elemental gods of fire (Agni), wind (Vayu), water (Varuna), sun (Surya), and moon (Soma). Kama is the god of love. Unlike the gods in Western mythologies, the prominent Indian gods are difficult to characterize. Although they are assigned obvious functions as powers, their spheres of power and their characteristics overlap because they are ultimately all manifestations of the universal principle, Brahman, the universal soul or being to which individual souls will be reunited after the illusion of time and space has been conquered.

At a lower level, still divine but progressively less lofty, are the hosts of the Gandharvas, Apsarases, Siddhas, Yaksas, and Raksasas. The first three classes are usually benevolent to mankind. Gandharvas play heavenly music to which the nymphs, the Apsarases, dance. Indra also uses the Apsarases to seduce ambitious ascetics who, by their severe self-castigation, have accumulated so much spiritual power that it becomes a threat to Indra's supremacy; as a result of seduction the anchorite loses his power. Yaksas are sprites, dryads, and naiads. Raksasas are malevolent demons who prowl around the sacrificial altars or in other ways disturb human beings.

Humans look at the gods as powers to be appeased or controlled, with the exception of Visnu, who is simply adored. Gods often interact with humans, marry them, give them weapons, invoke their assistance or aid them. At times gods interact with men through the intermediary of wise old men, sages whose advice was obeyed by prudent warriors who would not violate the will of the gods in order to avoid incurring the sage's curse. Upon his death, the ancient hero expects to go to Indra's heaven, where there is feasting and rejoicing.

Rivers and other landscape features are personified and function as both divine or semi-divine beings and as natural phenomena. In the *Mahabharata* gods communicate with men, animals talk and are sometimes real animals, sometimes human beings or gods. The story often moves into an idealized land where heroic feats, deeds of valour and physical strength are regarded with awe and fear. These incidents foster a sense of marvel in the reader: we are transported into an idyllic world where illusion and reality cannot be separated.

The *Mahabharata* should be understood as a moral and philosophical tale as well as an historical one. Only in this way can we appreciate the significance of the *Bhagavadgita*, the Song of the Lord, which is part of the *Mahabharata*, but which is usually excerpted and read as an independent religious work. In India, the *Mahabharata* as a whole has been regarded for centuries as a religious work, to the extent that a medieval poetic theoretician characterizes its main sentiment *(rasa)* not as heroism but as tranquillity *(santi)*.

Between the time of the events described in the epic and the time the *Mahabharata* was composed, social conditions had changed considerably. India was no longer a set of tribal communities; it had become subdivided into large regions *(janapadas)* ruled by kings who had become absolute monarchs. The conquests of King Asoka and Candragupta Maurya, which united large areas of India under one ruler, had paved the way for the emergence of a national consciousness. "Dear to all men is Bharata-land, as it was to the god Indra, Father Manu and the mighty warriors of old," says the poet. And although the Indian world was by now interacting with the world around it, the most important part of the world was still Bharata, the land of the Aryans, which was now concentrated south of the Himalayas and north of the Vindhya Mountains, between the desert in the west and the swamps of Bengal in the east.

The *Mahabharata* did not remain an exclusively Sanskrit work. Within a few centuries of its composition it was translated and paraphrased into other Indian languages: the Dravidian languages of South India, and the Indo-Aryan languages that succeeded Sanskrit historically in the north. Stories were adapted for dramatization, folksingers composed ballads in their own tongues, preachers and politicians made use of its philosophy. Thus the Great Epic gradually spread by word of mouth from village to village, from kingdom to kingdom, from region to region. It was recited in courts during great festivals and sacrifices honoring a king (indeed, even as the *Mahabharata* is told as a story heard by the bard at a great sacrifice.) Jains and Buddhists found a place for it in their non-canonical literature, and as the Indian empire expanded from the first years of the Christian era onward, the *Mahabharata* and its sister epic, the *Ramayana*, accompanied the itinerant merchants. On the trade routes to Europe, to Burma, to Thailand and Vietnam, to the spice islands of the western Pacific the bards followed the traders, and later, when colonial kingdoms were established in these tropical countries, they found a place at the kings' courts. The profound moral message of the *Mahabharata* became identified with the power of the ruling dynasties, and the epics were often translated into the languages of the colonized countries. Gradually the *Mahabharata* became part of the literature of the receiving country: the epic was reworked, rewritten, condensed and phrased in contemporary terminology and in terms of the adopting culture.

It is in this tradition that we find the present English rendition of the *Mahabharata*. It is not a translation. The author, William Buck first became acquainted with the *Mahabharata* through a chance reading of the Bhagavad-gita during a vacation in Nevada. Inspired by the poetry of this work he subsequently read the whole *Mahabharata* and the *Ramayana*. He then set out to make his own renderings. It is a retelling based on a translation of the Sanskrit original published by Pratap Chandra Roy, published in the beginning of this century. The slow and forceful pace of the Sanskrit original, its honest, wise, and totally convincing outlook on the state of the world, its descriptions of awesome battles and gruesome deaths as tragic yet natural events in human experience, these are just a few of the features that have found response in the hearts of millions of Asian people. Most Western renditions have obscured the brilliance of the Sanskrit poetic constructions, but we have all of this in William Buck's work. It is remarkable that a Westerner has been able to uncover the nuggets of this Indian epic with such sensitivity. Like the original, it deserves reading, rereading, and even reciting aloud, for it will affect the reader at various levels of his awareness.

William Buck has, of course, condensed the story. The old translation from which he worked covers 5800 pages of print, while his own book is less than a tenth that length. But by and large, Buck's rendition reflects the sequence of events in the Sanskrit epic, and he uses the traditional techniques, for instance, of stories within stories, flashbacks, moral lessons layed in the mouths of principal characters. In detail, however, there are differences between the two, which makes it unwise to use this book as an exact reference work. William Buck has excerpted passages without trying to be complete, so many passages have been left out or altered to fit the shortened version. One of the parts omitted is the Bhagavad-gita.

One feature that will strike the reader of this work is its abundance of names, sometimes long difficult words, sometimes names that look alike except for a single letter. But to learn the characters' names is an inevitable hurdle that has to be overcome before the *Mahabharata* can be appreciated, and William Buck has smoothed the way by regularizing many of the names, making them sound more like English and omitting the tedious diacritical marks. Also at times he has altered the names of rivers and mountains, as the Javanese have done.

There are other English versions of the *Mahabharata*, some shorter, some longer. But apart from William Buck's rendition, none have been able to capture the blend of religion and martial spirit that pervades the original epic. It succeeds eminently in illustrating how seemingly grand and magnificent human endeavors turn out to be astoundingly insignificant in the perspective of eternity.

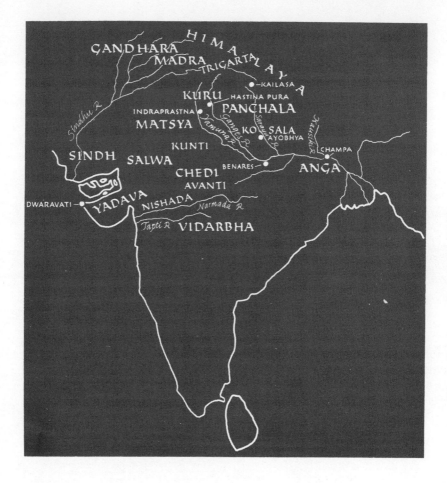

PART ONE

IN THE BEGINNING

OM!

I bow to Lord Narayana,
To Nara, the best of men,
And to Saraswati,
The Goddess of words and writing:

JAYA!
Victory!

MAY this ancient *Bharata* become a jewel garland that will never leave you. Duryodhana causes all creatures to be slain and wastes the Earth; he fans the flame of hostility that at last consumes all. But in my opinion life is taken with every breath, what do you think?

Bhima's wrath is unappeasable: he will never let this story be lost in the empty world. Arjuna is the prince of all bowmen: with spells of bewilderment he guards these pages embellished with elegant expressions and conversations human and divine. Nakula is dark and Sahadeva is fair: they guard Arjuna's chariot wheels; in this whole world of men they have not their equals in beauty and strength and excellence of conduct. Yudhishthira is the embodiment of all manliness: he is kindhearted; cease to fight him, do not court defeat.

Karna disdains to fight except alone; he wears a cape fastened at his shoulder by a round clasp; he looks at me with hard eyes. But if love has any cause, he is my ancient friend from another life, angry at me after a little quarrel. Vyasa the poet tells you, Oh beware, beware of Reality, beware of Justice, enough of waiting and waiting, you are in danger. Once hearing this *Bharata,* who can bear listening to other stories, which sound like the braying of an ass?

The world is beautiful everywhere I look. Look, see the lights and the happiness, the singing and all the fine presents. Victory, victory to the great king; no loss to you. But the images perspire in the temples, the ways of Dharma are subtle and hard to find. After this I am still alive . . . I think I have no death. Forgive me, I will go into the forest.

1: a mine of jewels & gems

Sauti the storyteller told this tale to his friend Saunaka in Naimisha Forest. Bending with humility, Sauti came wandering through the wood in the evening and saw before him the glowing fire that burnt by day and night to guard Saunaka's forest home.

Saunaka asked him, "Lotus-eyed Sauti, from where do you wander?"

Sauti answered, "From Hastinapura, from the snake sacrifice of the Kuru king Janemejaya. There I heard Vyasa's *Mahabharata*, that was first written down for the poet by the elephant god Ganesha."

"How was that?"

Sauti answered, "I will tell you what happened."

❖

Listen—

For three years Vyasa composed the *Mahabharata* in his mind, and when it was finished, he summoned Ganesha to be his scribe. 召唤

Shiva's son came and asked, "Why call me?"

Vyasa replied, "Do you not remove all obstacles and barriers? You are the god of thieves and writers. Write down my book as I tell it to you."

Ganesha swished his trunk around. "OM! But there are books and books. Is yours a very good one?"

"Yes."

Ganesha laughed, and his huge belly shook. "Well just let me get rid of all these things . . ." He set down the conch shell and lotus, the discus and axe that he held in his four hands. " . . . and I shall write for you; but if once you stop the story, I will leave and never return."

Vyasa said, "On this condition: if you don't understand what I mean, you must write no more until you do."

"Done! The very day I was born I made my first mistake, and by that path have I sought wisdom ever since."

⚜

Listen—

I was born fullgrown from the dew of my mother's body. We were alone, and Devi told me, "Guard the door. Let no one enter, because I'm going to take a bath."

Then Shiva, whom I had never seen, came home. I would not let him into his own house.

"Who are you to stop me?" he raged.

And I told him, "No beggars here, so go away!"

"I may be half naked," he answered, "but all the world is mine, though I care not for it."

"Then go drag about your world, but not Parvati's mountain home! I am Shiva's son and guard this door for her with my life!"

6

"Well," he said, "you are a great liar. Do you think I don't know my own sons?"

"Foolishness!" I said. "I was only born today, but I know a rag picker when I see one. Now get on your way."

He fixed his eyes on me and very calmly asked, "Will you let me in?"

"Ask no more!" I said.

"Then I shall not," he replied, and with a sharp glance he cut off my head and threw it far away, beyond the Himalayas.

Devi ran out, crying, "You'll never amount to anything! You've killed our son!" She bent over my body and wept. "What good are you for a husband? You wander away and leave me home to do all the work. Because you wander around dreaming all the time, we have to live in poverty with hardly enough to eat."

The Lord of All the Worlds pacified her; looking around, the first head he saw happened to be an elephant's, and he set it on my shoulders and restored me to life.

"Parvati was happy again, and that is how I first met my father," said Ganesha, "long, long ago."

"Alright," said Vyasa, "now I will begin." And he began to tell his story to Ganesha, who wrote it on leaves.

❀

"And many times Vyasa would compose lines that would make Ganesha pause, so he could use the time to think out the next part," said Sauti.

Saunaka replied, "Yes—that *Bharata* is a mine of gems like the deep Ocean. Whoever hears it, and understands

7

even a small bit of it, escapes the chains he has forged by deeds of good or evil; he finds high success, for *Mahabharata* is excellent, and holds the power of victory! The one who tells it to one who has asked to hear gives him as a gift the whole Earth with her belt of seas. Stay with me and tell me that tale."

Sauti answered, "Yes—I will."

❖

Listen—

Long ago, when the sea was milk, Narayana said to the gods of heaven, "Churn the ocean, and she will yield amrita, the nectar of immortality, and precious gems, and all manner of illusion and revelation."

So they placed the snow mountain Mandara in the middle of the milk sea. Its deep-striking roots rested on the ocean floor; its summit rose high above the surface. The great serpent Sesha, whose hood is an island of jewels, stretched himself across the sea, his body wrapped endlessly round the mountain in the center. On one shore his tail was held by the Asuras, the dark, olden gods; on the other shore his neck was held by the devas, the mortal gods of heaven. They each pulled in turn, so that the mountain spun first one way, then the other, while his trees and stones were thrown off into the foaming sea.

First the mild Moon rose from the milk sea; then the Lady Lakshmi, bearing good fortune to men; then the smooth jewel adorning Narayana's breast; then Indra's elephant Airavata, white as clouds; then Surabhi, the white cow who grants any wish; then Parijata the wishing-tree of fragrance; then Rambha the nymph, the first Apsaras; and at last

9

The first head he saw happened to be an elephant's

Dhanwantari the physician, robed in white, bearing a cup filled with amrita, the essence of life.

Suddenly poison burst fuming from the sea, and the milk became salt water. Shiva, the Lord of Mountains and Songs swallowed the poison to save the worlds. He held it in his throat and his neck turned blue, iridescent as a butterfly's wing.

Shiva put the crescent moon in his hair as an ornament. Narayana became a woman, beautiful with desire, and bore away the cup of life.

Now thousands of rivers rush swiftly to the sea as rivals for his love. In the ocean are the palaces of the serpent kings who rule the rivers of Earth, and far from land, in the heart of the deep, roars the red submarine fire that boils the water into rainclouds.

The changes of the moon make the ocean rise and fall with the slow rhythms of Time. Wherever land ends, there the sea dances with the uplifted hands of his waves—wide as space, vast as Time.

The holy Ganges runs from the hills into the sea, and the Yamuna runs into the Ganges. Between the two rivers lies Kurujangala, that is ruled from the Elephant City of Hastinapura by Parikshita's son Janamejaya.

Yudhishthira the Pandava was the Kuru king before Parikshita, but when he received Arjuna's letter—*Come to me*—he made the newborn Parikshita king, then left with his brothers and their wife for the Silver Mountain Kailasa and was never seen again. Parikshita ruled his kingdom well for sixty years, but then one day in the forest, angry that a deer had escaped him, the king mortally wounded a serpent who meant him no harm. Before he died that Naga touched water and said, "Within seven days Parikshita shall die of snakebite for his cruelty; there is no hope for him!"

A woodsman heard and told the king, who left his palace and began to live night and day in a house supported by a single column, well guarded by warriors. Parikshita had but entered his retreat when an old man, dusty and torn, was seen approaching. Sometimes he was visible to the eye; sometimes he faded away as he walked and again slowly reappeared. He walked up to the guards and joined his hands in greeting, and his form shimmered and danced like heat waves in the air.

Then he narrowed his eyes and spoke, "I am Takshaka the Naga prince; warn the king that I shall burn him!" The soldiers rushed at him, but he laughed and vanished on the spot.

Now, my friend, there was no way to enter or leave Parikshita's house save by a ladder, and none could climb up or down who was not a loyal friend to the king. So with his court the king stayed there until the end of the seventh day. At sunset, when the ladder was about to be drawn up for the night, Parikshita saw a tiny copper-colored beetle crawling over a mango, and with a smile he picked it up.

"Now I have no more fear of Takshaka than of this insect!" said the king, and his court laughed as Parikshita held up the tiny beetle and set it on his shoulder. Even thus was Takshaka disguised! Instantly, the Naga prince became himself and bit the king.

Parikshita's courtiers and ministers fled down the ladder

in fear, and as they ran in every direction they saw Takshaka fly away through the blue sky of evening like the vermillion streak that divides a woman's hair through the center.   ⚜

Janamejaya then became king, and he planned a snake sacrifice to burn Takshaka. I heard of it and went to watch. There, at the proper time, brahmanas dressed all in black set afire a great stack of buttered wood. They repeated, over and over, all the names of Takshaka; they poured butter into the fire from great wooden ladles and the flames became deep red and the smoke grew heavy and black. Their eyes were red and tearful from the smothering smoke. All around them the spectators watched the air above the fire, waiting to see Takshaka appear.

When Takshaka felt himself being drawn to Janamejaya's fire he fled from his jeweled palace in the underworld and sought refuge with Indra, the Lord of Heaven. Indra gave him his protection, so the brahmanas spoke their mantras and poured their butter in vain and Janamejaya grew restless in the hot afternoon.

Then a young man came to the king's side and knelt beside him. His name was Astika, and he was born of a Naga woman. His father had hesitated to marry, yet wished for a wife, and once in the still forest very faintly asked for a woman to marry him. There a Naga girl heard him, and he married her, true to his word.

Astika looked upon the world of men with an even eye. He bent his head, touching his brow with hands joined in namaste, and said, "Majesty, I am Astika. I wander here and there throughout your kingdom of Kurujangala. Let those we cherish be happy! Let our kings and our princes live Long! Janamejaya—know that Takshaka is in heaven with Indra!"

The king replied, "Welcome to you!" He called his brahmanas and told them where Takshaka was hiding and said to Astika, "For this, ask of me any gift and I will give it!"

Astika answered, "Be patient, Majesty. Soon I shall ask."

The brahmanas began to call down Indra and Takshaka both, and in a few moments the Lord of Rain appeared in his chariot, drawn by misty grey horses, hanging in the air over the fire; there was no sign of the Naga. The brahmanas cried out, "Lord of heaven, give us the Naga prince or we will cast you both into the flames!"

Indra looked down with unblinking eyes and a flashing thunderbolt appeared in his hand. He took deadly aim at the brahmanas and raised his arm to destroy them. But the mantras and spells had overcome Takshaka as soon as Indra turned his attention from him, and he was hanging in midair above the fire, between Indra and the brahmanas. Seeing this, Indra vanished, for there was nothing more he could do for the serpent.

But the brahmanas still could not make the Naga prince fall into the flames, because Astika whispered softly, "*Stay . . . Stay . . .* " Then he turned to Janamejaya and said, "Majesty—stop the sacrifice."

Janamejaya smiled. "Astika, instead I will give you gold and silver," he said.

"Gold and silver I do not want, but half my blood is of the Naga race."

"Beautiful women and white cattle I will give you instead."

"Majesty, women and cattle I do not want, but the Naga prince is dear to me."

"Then I give you his life! You have saved him from me, and you have done it well!"

"And this in return, Majesty: have no fear of any serpent, but think—*Serpents of good fortune, live in peace here with your dear ones.*"

"Let it be so for all my people."

Astika said, "It will be so, Majesty, for all your people," and Takshaka vanished from our sight.

❀

When he entered his palace, Janamejaya Raja found waiting for him a dark man, dressed in deerskin and bark, who bore his one hundred and fifty years with calm and dignity and sparkling eyes.

"Vyasa!"

"Sit beside me, Janamejaya. The jeweled Naga escaped you, and you bear him no malice. That is good."

The king called for water and washed Vyasa's feet. "I bow to you," he said, "you who knew my ancestors. Will you not stay and tell me your story? Will you not untie the knots of my heart?"

"I am old, Bharata. With my dark blue skin I am like a thundercloud holding the memory of lightning, of love and terror and the deeds of heroes. But I have not come alone, and I have told my story in the forest to my companion Vaisampayana, who waits outside. He is young, and fair, and wears one silver earring in the shape of a moonbeam. I will stay while he tells it to you, and I myself will listen."

14

Janamejaya and Vyasa found Vaisampayana outside in the spreading shade of an old tree. Janamejaya bowed to him with joined hands.

Vaisampayana in his white robe said, "Excellent, Majesty! I shall be pleased to tell you! Let Vyasa sit with his back against the tree, and let all who wish to hear gather round us now."

Then Janamejaya, and Astika, and myself, and many of the Kurus sat down under that old tree. Vaisampayana sat beside Vyasa and said, "Welcome! Now hear from me the *Mahabharata.*"

Listen, Majesty—

You are born in the Lunar race, descended from the Moon, descended from Bharata and Kuru; you are Arjuna's grandson.

I begin my story with the Kuru king Pratipa. In his old age he was still childless, so with his queen he left Hastinapura and lived in the forest near the Ganges. There he hoped fortune would favor him with a son.

At that time the dead king Mahabhisha sat in heaven, listening to Lord Brahma explain the riddles of all Creation to a large audience of the faithful. But Mahabhisha was bored. He sat on the edge of the group, and his attention strayed here and there until he saw Ganga the beautiful River Goddess walk by. White as moonbeams, her silken robes flowed over her body as she moved, concealing little and suggesting much, as though she walked through silver water. The Queen of Rivers felt his glance and their eyes met.

Mahabhisha began to perspire, and this never happens in

15

heaven until one is ready to be reborn. He removed his heavenly garland, which had remained fresh and fragrant for centuries, and watched the jasmine and ginger flowers fade and turn brown. He smiled at the Goddess and vanished from Heaven.

The beautiful Ganga wishfully followed his soul with her heavenly eyes as it fell back to Earth and entered the womb of Pratipa's Queen.

※

Pratipa sent his wife and his son Santanu back to the city, but to give thanks for Santanu's birth he himself remained in the forest as before. One evening he was sitting on a rock under a tree by the river when a wonderfully beautiful lady arose from the water and walked over to him. She smiled down at him and sat on his lap.

Pratipa asked, "Whoever you are, how can I help you?"

Ganga brushed the wet hair from her smooth forehead and said, "I am in love, Majesty."

Gently the king put his arm around her. "When a woman asks, one cannot ignore her," he said. "But you sit on my right thigh, where a daughter belongs."

"Yes," said Ganga, "I have loved him since before his birth to you."

Pratipa answered, "When he is grown I will tell Santanu that you are waiting for his love."

"Blessed be you, Pratipa! I will meet him by the river many years from now." Then Ganga dove into the flowing water and was gone. She swam upstream, through the gate where the Ganges falls from heaven, and was again in the realm of the gods.

16

There she lay on a warm stone, drying her long, dark hair in the sun, smiling to herself, when the eight Vasu gods, who are Indra's attendants, came to see her, looking downcast and guilty.

"What is it?" asked Ganga. "What's the matter with you?"

Prabhasa, the shining spirit of dawn, shuffled his feet uneasily and said, "Ganga, we have a favor . . . I mean . . . look here, would you be our mother?"

Ganga laughed. "You'd better tell me what you've done, first."

Prabhasa gave her a crooked smile. "Brahma's son Vasishtha has cursed us to be born on Earth!"

"Well, that's not so bad. But what did you do?"

"My wife talked me into stealing Surabhi, the cow of wishes. Vasishtha thinks more of that cow than of all heaven and Earth, and even though he wasn't around I didn't want to do it. My wife has a friend on Earth and she wanted to let her drink some of the magic milk and so be free from disease and old age. I wanted just to take the milk, but my wife looked hurt, and at the same time innocent as the cow herself. We were all of us there, and the other women joined in, wondering aloud why I didn't love my wife enough to . . . well, you know . . ."

Ganga had a wide smile on her face. "I am polite enough not to laugh," she said, "even though you would, if it had happened to someone else. How could you fall for something like that?"

"Ganga! I refuse to explain what you know very well yourself," said the Vasu. "It is enough to say that we in turn spoke to Surabhi and talked her into coming for a visit with us, down to Earth. While we were gone Vasishtha returned, discovered us with his magic insight, and gave us his curse for our trouble."

"And why come to me?" asked the goddess.

"Well, we knew you had plans . . ."

"Say no more! You will all be born to the wife of Santanu the Kuru king!"

❀

When Santanu was a young man, Pratipa told him, "When you were very young, a fair maiden came to me and told me of her love for you. If you should meet her secretly near the Ganges, ask not who she is, nor whose, nor from where she comes, but take her for your wife by my word."

Soon after this Pratipa died and Santanu became the Bharata king. One day as he rode alone beside the Ganges he met there a maiden shining with beauty, dressed in transparent watery blue silk trimmed with gold, and wearing a belt of pearls. Each looked and looked into the other's eyes, and each longed to look there forever.

Softly the king said, "Beautiful One, of whatever race you are, goddess or Naga, Asura or Apsaras, or human being as myself—return with me now as my Queen."

Ganga smiled at him and lowered her eyes. "I would like to do this," she said, "but if I become your lady you must never ask my name, nor speak to me unkindly, nor interfere with anything I do, or I will leave you."

"I promise; come sit behind me."

Here in this city they were married, and every year Ganga bore a son to Santanu. But for seven years she threw each

18

child into the Ganges and drowned him there, saying, *"This is for your good,"* and so freed all the Vasus but Prabhasa.

Santanu said nothing to her about this, for he loved her and remembered his promise. Seven princes died at Ganga's hands; but when she carried her eighth son to the river and held him over the water, smiling into her baby's eyes, the king cried out, *"Stop! Do not kill him!"*

"Then take him as my gift," said Ganga. "I shall not free him from life." Then the Goddess stepped into her river that flows from heaven to beneath the sea. "My Lord, I am Ganga, and I leave you now with your son!"

Santanu held his child at his breast and turned away without a word. He was a good king, he kept the Kurus in peace, and by the touch of his hand he could remove old age from any man. ❧

Bharata, to the south lies the land of Chedi. When Santanu was a boy, the Chedi king Uparichara once left his palace to hunt in the forest. It was springtime, and every tree and vine of the forest was in flower. Bees swarmed over the blossoms, birds sang and called to each other, and a fragrant breeze sighed gently through the wood.

When he had gone a little ways, Uparichara sat down to rest under a flowering tree. He closed his eyes and fell asleep, and he dreamt of his beautiful Queen who waited for him at home. When he awoke, he found that his vital seed had left him and fallen on a leaf nearby.

The king summoned a hawk to carry that leaf to the Queen. The hawk flew away with it into the sky, but

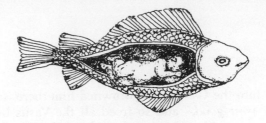

He found in her belly a baby girl

another hawk attacked him, thinking that he carried food, and the leaf fell into the Yamuna, where a mother fish swallowed it as it touched the water.

That fish made her way upstream to Santanu's kingdom and was netted from the river many months later. When the fisherman cut her open he found in her belly a baby girl, whom he raised as his daughter, naming her Satyavati. She grew up to be very handsome, but had always about her the smell of fish. She spent her days sculling a shallow boat along the Yamuna, helping her father tend his nets.

One day the wandering minstrel Parashara came to the riverside, and when he saw Satyavati he said to her, "Accept my love today, beautiful one."

Satyavati blushed. "Now it is broad daylight," she whispered, "and there are people all up and down the riverside."

"But leave your boat and sit by me," answered Parashara. When she was by his side, he sang a magic song that made thick fog cover the river and the land, concealing everything. They went in her boat to a little island, and while the boatmen on the river called out to avoid collisions all around them, Satyavati gladly gave herself to her lover. In return he removed the smell of fish from her and instead made her fragrant as flowers.

20

On the river island Satyavati gave birth to the poet Vyasa. Parashara took him away into the forest, and Satyavati returned to her father.

⚜

King Santanu named his son Bhishma. It was his great happiness to see him grow to manhood, strong and intelligent, with broad shoulders and fair skin. Once near the Yamuna the king caught the fragrance of flowers in the season when there are no flowers. Following his nose, Santanu discovered Satyavati, took her up on his royal chariot, and carried her to Hastinapura as his Queen.

Bhisma was pleased to see his father so happy, and as his marriage gift he told him, "Let your child by Satyavati rule the kingdom after you, and I will protect him and his children as long as I can."

"Why do you offer this to me?" asked Santanu.

"Majesty," replied Bhishma, "I care not to be king, nor to marry, but I would rather make our race the strongest in all the land by my energy."

Santanu said, "Then take these words as my gift, Bhishma: *Death will never come to you, so long as you wish to live. He will dare to approach you only when you have given him permission.*"

Santanu's son by Satyavati was named Vichitravirya; when he was a youth, Santanu made him king and retired alone to the forest. There by the Ganges, in the hermitage where he had been born, he lived all alone until he died.

⚜

Bhishma heard that the three daughters of the king of Banaras were to hold their swayamvara, the self-choice ceremony, where each would choose her husband from among the kings and princes assembled there. He wanted Vichitravirya to marry, but the king was too young to stand any chance of being chosen. So Bhishma himself went in a light chariot to Banaras.

Once there he told no one who he was and did not enter the open arena with the other kings. Bhishma had no weapons with him, nor any sign that he was a warrior. His four swift horses were covered with dust and no one gave them a second glance as he waited while the royal guests assembled. Then the three princesses, named Amba, Ambika and Ambalika, arrived; the Banaras army surrounded the area, ready to make peace among rejected kings; and Bhishma spoke softly to his horses.

Without the weight of armor his light chariot leapt forward; he broke through the king's army from behind, where they kept no watch, and scattered them from his path. In the wink of an eye he had stopped and caught up the three maidens before anyone could realize what had happened.

Bhishma smiled at the powerful kings and princes gathered from every land and said, "Know that the Kurus do not compete with your kind, and know also that the wife is most dear who is stolen by force! You now have my permission to go home!"

Biting their lips in wrath, the suitors slapped their armpits with cupped hands and roared in anger, calling out to Bhishma, *"Stay!—Wait!"* They called for the Banaras army; they drew their swords, aimed their arrows, ran to find their chariots and armor. Bhishma laughed and was gone in a cloud of dust, while ten thousand arrows and darts buried themselves deep in the Earth behind him. The thunder of his horses and the rattle of his car were soon gone in the distance, and none could hope to overtake him.

In Hastinapura Bhishma gave the three captives to Satyavati until their marriage. She was kind to them, and they spoke openly to her. Ambika and Ambalika were willing to marry Vichitravirya, but the eldest princess Amba said, "In my heart I have already chosen King Salwa, who rules in the west, and he has chosen me as his wife. Now do what should be done for me."

Satyavati understood, and sent Amba to her husband. Her sisters married Vichitravirya, but the Kuru king stood in the shadow of death from consumption and soon died, leaving behind his kingdom and all who loved him.

"My son had no child," wept Satyavati. "The kingdom is dead without a king. How have I done wrong, that he has died so young?"

Bhishma said, "Queen, blame not yourself. Have you not another son, the island-born Vyasa? Bring him here and ask him to father sons by Vichitravirya's wives."

"He lives in the forest," answered Satyavati, "and I may call him to me by my thoughts."

Then, Bharata, Vyasa came at his mother's call and fathered three sons. For one change of the moon he lived with Ambika; then for a month with Ambalika; then after with one of Satyavati's maidservants. When he had sown those sons in Vichitravirya's fields, Vyasa left for the forest. When the children were born, Bhishma raised them as his own. First was born Ambika's son Dhritarashtra, who was blind, but whose bodily strength had no equal among men. Next was Ambalika's son Pandu; and the youngest brother was Vidura, the maidservant's son.

Now the wonderful world is born,
In an instant it dies,
In a breath it is renewed.

From the slowness of our eye
And the quickness of God's hand
We believe in the world.

2: the RING & the well

Majesty, because Dhritarashtra was blind, Bhishma made Pandu king; and when Pandu had grown to manhood he looked about for a Queen.

To the south of Kurujangala was the kingdom of Kunti, and there lived the princess Kunti with her father the king. She welcomed anyone traveling through the kingdom who requested food and lodging at the king's palace. In this way she met the hermit Durvasas, clad in rags and ashes, and so pleased him by her kindness that as he left he taught her a magic spell. By this mantra, he told her, she could call on any god in heaven to make love with her and receive a son from him.

Was it true? wondered Kunti. She stood in the sun, running over the magic words in her mind, and stared down at her shadow. She thought, "Durvasas has played a joke on me!" and frowned. Then she thought, "Or he has not . . . "

The sun was warm on her back. Surya of a thousand rays shone down on her. Kunti thought of him, "All the world sees him in the day. But at night, he would be mine alone." Was he as handsome as the statue in the Sun Temple?

That night Kunti lay awake in bed until it was midnight. Outside, the Earth lay in silence; the palace was dark. She went to her window and softly spoke the mantra of Durvasas.

There was light, the smell of hot metal, a wind, hot and dry as the desert, singing in her ears. It was so bright that Kunti shut her eyes, but the wind made colors behind them. She trembled and fell, lying on the carpet like a broken vine on the forest floor.

Surya the Lord of Light carried her to her bed and stood smiling over her, lighting the room with his presence so there was no shadow anywhere. He wore a tall golden crown, whose designs shifted and changed as he breathed. A band of brilliants and jewels fell across his bare chest from over his left shoulder; loops and pendants of light-bearing gems hung from his belt, from his necklace and bracelets of brass, from his long heavy gold earrings; all their lights swept about the room in thousands of colored arcs. He took off his crown and his golden hair curled round his face like a helmet of dull bronze.

"Princess—awake!"

Kunti opened her eyes. "You called," said Surya, "and I have come."

Kunti found her voice. "Lord of Day—forgive me—but I called only to test my new mantra."

"I know why you called, and now I am yours alone. Do you want me to go?"

"I have no husband, Lord Surya."

"Soon you will marry. The children of the gods are born in one day. May I not stay?"

29

There was light

"The light . . . my father will see."

"No one else can see this light, Princess. Children may command the gods; I will go if you wish, and you will see me again only in the far blue sky."

"So soon!" sighed Kunti. "But stay a moment, you have come so far to see me here."

The next evening Surya's son was born, wearing earrings and hard golden armor. Kunti set the child adrift in the Yamuna in a basket made waterproof with wax. As he floated away she said, "May all your ways be happy. Blessed is the lady who will find you and be your mother, and watch you crawl on the ground covered with dust, and first hear you try to speak." And she wept softly at losing him.

The Yamuna carried the child into the Ganges, and Ganga washed him ashore at the feet of Adhiratha the charioteer and his wife, who had come to bathe in the river, in the Anga land, early in the morning.

Adhiratha gave the boy to his wife and said, "This is a great wonder, my lady—a child of the gods, sent to us who are childless! Earrings brighten his face, and he wears armor shining bright as the sun. Though I am a charioteer I shall make him the best of those who bear arms. I name him Karna!"

When Kunti's father thought it time for her to choose a husband, Pandu came to her swayamvara ceremony, and there she chose him by placing round his neck the white flower garland that she carried. When Pandu returned with Kunti, he found that Bhishma had given gold to the Madra king Salya, and had brought back from the north Salya's sister Madri to be Pandu's second wife.

Pandu and his wives lived happily in Hastinapura for many months; then he wanted to retire into the forest for awhile with Kunti and Madri. His attendants built a forest home for the king, and Dhritarashtra daily sent food to them from the city.

One day Pandu left his wives and rode off alone into the forest to hunt. Soon he saw two deer, joined in copulation, and pierced them with sharp arrows. The doe fell dead, and her mate beside her, fatally wounded.

When Pandu drew near, the stag looked up at him and with tears in his eyes asked, "Why have you done this?"

Pandu replied, "Kings may hunt deer, it is no crime."

"Not for hunting do I blame you," answered the deer. "But for your cruelty in killing us while we made love I curse you! You have brought me grief when I was happy; you have made my love useless—and yours shall be the same. Death will strike you down when you next make love."

Then the deer was dead. Pandu told his wives, "Go back to Hastinapura, for I am under a curse and now I must live alone in the forest and be at peace. Then joy and sorrow will not stick to me, nor fear dare be in my presence."

Madri wept; and Kunti said, "We must share your curse and stay with you; for if you cast us away we shall soon die with broken hearts."

"I would not do you harm," said the king. "We will be

31

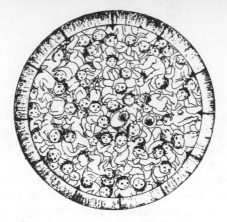

"Here are your hundred sons"

three." He called his servants and gave them the royal jewel to give to Dhritarashtra, then sent them away. And Pandu began to live with his wives in a far hidden valley of the Himalyas, beneath the snow-covered Hundred Peak Hill where stars rest at night, like flowers of light in the deep lake of the sky.

Hot tears ran down Dhritarashtra's face when he learned Pandu had left Kurujangala, and he would not eat or sleep.

Bhishma said, "Take this jewel and rule the kingdom. Someday he may return."

"He will never return, Bharata!" answered Dhritarashtra.

"Who knows the future, Majesty? Take it, and stop your sorrow."

"Why?"

"This is why: I have sent messengers to the mountain kingdom of Gandhara, and even now the king's daughter comes to be your wife—and she comes to wed a king, not an ascetic."

"A king who is blind!"

32

"Now you are the Kuru King Dhritarashtra, whose wisdom is his only eye. Her brother Sakuni brings Gandhari with her marriage gifts. Already she loves you, and has blindfolded her own eyes for life."

"This she did from love for me, whom she has never seen?"

"That is the truth, Majesty. Take this jewel now, for she is not many days from here."

Dhritarashtra lost his sorrow in Gandhari's love, as a river is lost in the sea. She became pregnant by Dhritarashtra, but a full year passed by without her giving birth, and longer, until Dhritarashtra sent for Vyasa in dismay.

Vyasa came to the king and said, "Gandhari carries one hundred sons. She will give birth at the end of two years. Be patient and know that there is no danger to her, and I will return when it is time."

Vyasa then spoke with Bhishma, so that when Gandhari gave birth there were a hundred bronze jars filled with clear butter, ready and hidden in the palace garden. From her womb came a hard ball of flesh that Vyasa took from her and washed in cool water.

"Here are your hundred sons," he told Gandhari, "but there is more to do before they are formed."

Vyasa divided that ball of flesh into pieces. As he worked in the garden, Bhishma put each piece into a jar and sealed it. At the end there was an extra piece. Bhishma brought another jar and Vyasa said, "There are now one hundred sons and one daughter. See that the jars are not opened for two more years; then they will be born."

Bhishma took from his robes a short arrow wrapped in

golden cloth and stuck it in the Earth. "I will. I have placed my ward arrow; none can see these vessels but myself."

❖

After two years Gandhari opened the jars, one every day for a hundred and one days. The first of Dhritarashtra's sons was Duryodhana. After his birth, on the same day, a maidservant bore Dhritarashtra's son Yuyutsu. The next day Duhsasana came from his jar, and then all the other sons, and last of all Dhritarashtra's daughter Duhsala.

Pandu, too, had had sons, just previous to the birth of Duryodhana. He had been sad at heart because he could have no children, so when Kunti saw this, she told him of her mantra. Pandu smiled happily and said, "Call Lord Dharma, the god of justice."

Dharma came from heaven down to Hundred Peak Hill in his chariot and at noon gave Kunti her son Yudhishthira. "He will know truth," said Pandu. "Now call Vayu the wind god and bear me another."

The Bearer of Fragrance came to Kunti riding a red deer and gave her the Pandava Bhima. "He has great strength," said Pandu. "Now call for Indra!"

Madri asked him, "May I not also give you sons? Ask Kunti if I may use her mantra."

Kunti told Madri the magic spell of love. Pandu said, "If you each use it once more, it will be enough," Indra's son by Kunti was Arjuna, who was your grandfather, Majesty.

Madri called to her the Aswins, the twin horsemen and physicians of the gods, the lords of light and darkness. They are young and very old; together they came to Madri, in the twilight of dawn, the morning after Arjuna's birth. Then Madri bore Pandu twin sons, Nakula and Sahadeva.

As Pandu watched his five sons grow up he felt his own strength return to his arms anew. Yudhishthira and Bhima were fair; Arjuna was dark; the twins were lighthearted and handsome: and all were a joy to him. Slowly, as the years passed, Pandu lost all memory of the deer's curse; he felt carefree and young once more. He kept no guard against the five flower-tipped arrows of Kama the love god, who holds the most powerful bow in the world, though it is made but of sugarcane and strung with only a line of bees as a bowstring.

So in the spring beneath the snow mountains, as Madri went alone to bathe, he stalked her through the forest and seized her; and though she tried to resist him, he entered her in love and instantly died with a cry in her arms. Madri held Pandu's body and wept that he had died without satisfying his desire till her own heart was broken and she too was dead, gone to Heaven to finish that lovemaking with her husband Pandu.

Two Nagas found them, and taking the guise of mountain men, wearing tigerskins, they came to Kunti and said, "Leave the children and come apart from them a moment."

They told her, "Because they have died desiring each other, we will burn them here together and lead you with your sons to Hastinapura."

Kunti cried to herself, and answered, "She was more fortunate than I, to have seen his face alive again." When she arrived at the Elephant City with her five sons, Bhishma

35

and Dhritarashtra bowed to them at the gate, and the escort of Nagas gave Vidura the ashes of his brother and Madri.

❁

Majesty, I have now told you of the birth of Bhishma; of the blind king Dhritarashtra and his hundred sons; of the poet Vyasa who sits beside me; of Pandu, and the golden-eyed Yudhishthira, the terrible Bhima, and the silver prince Arjuna; and of Karna, the best of warriors. Now again I return to the days of Santanu, and tell of Kripa, whose name means Compassion; and of Drona, who was born in a waterbowl.

Deep in the forest near a bell-heather bush, a Kuru soldier found twin children abandoned, a brother and sister, and brought them to Santanu.

"What was there with them?" asked the king.

"They lay on a deerskin, Majesty, with a strung bow and an arrow. The boy holds the arrow and will not let go of it."

"They are the children of a brahmana well skilled in weapons," said Santanu. "I name the boy Kripa, and his sister Kripi. Let them be raised in my palace, for they are cast away and have no other home."

❁

At the Gate of the Ganges to the north, in the kingdom of Panchala, lived the recluse Bharadwaja. One day he saw an Apsaras bathing in the river, proud in her beauty, and at the sight of her his vital seed left him and fell into his waterbowl. From that fluid was born his son Drona.

As Drona grew up in his father's retreat he became friends with the Panchala prince Drupada, whose father sent him to be taught what he might learn by Bharadwaja. Then his father died, and Drupada became the Panchala king and came no more to the forest. Next Bharadwaja ended his life, Drona lived on alone, learning all the weapons of heaven and Earth.

When he had mastered them, Drona came to Hastinapura and asked Kripa for his sister in marriage. Kripa gave her gladly, and Kripi was delighted to marry Drona. Together they returned to Panchala and lived in poverty in a small village; and to them was born Aswatthaman their son, born with a blue jewel in the center of his forehead.

When Aswatthaman was young he ran home crying one day because everyone in the village but he had milk to drink. Drona told him that they were very poor and had no cow, and Aswatthaman understood and was comforted. But soon after Drona saw some older boys give his son water made white with rice powder. Aswatthaman danced in joy, believing that at last he had tasted milk, until the others mocked him and laughed.

Drona's dark face hardened as his heart was torn. A long time he stood still where he was. At home he found Kripi holding their son to her breast as the boy wept, and he heard her say, "The shame is theirs, who make sport of your father for his poverty. They are blind and cannot see where he is rich; and their children take after them because they know no better."

Then Drona went to Kampilya, the capital of Panchala, and went before King Drupada in his palace. He said, "Majesty, I am Drona."

Drupada replied, "Do I know you from somewhere?"

"But I am your friend; we grew up together in my father's retreat."

Drupada frowned in anger. "Don't be a fool! You are lazy and unlucky, but not my friend. All that has faded. Now I am king, and I must have friends and enemies from among my equals. Time leaves nothing true forever."

❧

Now when the Bharata princes were young men, Kripa began to teach archery to the Pandavas and to Dhritarashtra's sons. Drona and his family had lived with Kripa for many years, but no one knew they were there.

One day the five Pandavas were playing with a ball outside the city when it fell into a deep dry well. They could not get it out by any means; then they saw a lean, dark brahmana approaching.

He smiled and said, "Shame to your royal strength and skill!" He took a gold ring from his finger and threw it into the well. "Promise me a dinner tonight, and I will bring up your ball with blades of grass, and my ring with an arrow."

Yudhishthira said, "You ask for very little. I promise."

Over a handful of long grass Drona spoke a mantra of illusion; then leaning over the well-curb he threw one blade and pierced the ball; and a second, that pierced the end of the first blade; and a third that stuck in the end of the second; and so he made a chain of grass many blades long. When it was long enough, Drona pulled up the ball.

"Now a bow and an arrow," he said. Arjuna gave him his, wide-eyed with wonder and delight.

The arrow sped into the well and returned to Drona's

hand bearing his ring. He gave the bow and the ring, still on the arrow, to Arjuna.

"Teach us to do this," said Yudhishthira, "and when you need us, we are yours!"

Drona gently told him, "Take this ring from the well to your grandfather Bhishma."

When he heard the Pandavas speak, Bhishma quickly went to Drona and said, "Welcome to you! This is the fruit of our good fortune! Why have you come to Hastinapura?"

Drona said, "Because many years ago Drupada refused me even food and shelter for one night; I have determined to do what I shall do soon enough."

"Arjuna keeps that arrow as a treasure. Here is your ring. Drupada is a fool."

"It is because I look like a poor man," smiled Drona. "But what can I do for you?"

Bhishma said, "String your bow, Brahmana!"

"And what on the bowstring? The hurricane winds, the snow and the sleet, the shattering rain, the hot fire—the illusions of war that burn and drown?"

"This only: with Kripa, teach the Kuru princes, and your own son with them, what each one may learn. And to the best of them reveal what weapons you wish."

⚘

So Drona lived in a house full of rice and gold. Every morning he gave each prince a jar with a narrow neck and sent them all to bring him water from the river. To Aswatthaman he gave a wide-mouthed jar, and in the time before the others got back he taught his son in secret. But on the second day Arjuna began to fill his jar by the water weapon, and so together with Aswatthaman he learned more than the others, all except for that first day.

Drona told the palace cook, "Never let Arjuna eat in the dark." But one night at dinner the wind blew out Arjuna's lamp. His tent was plunged in black darkness, yet he found himself still eating, his hand went to his mouth by habitual skill. Later Drona heard Arjuna's bowstring in the night; he went outside and told him, "Prince, if it is to be you, I will first teach you how to regard other men."

When he had finished all his teaching, Drona called his students, one by one, apart from the rest. High in a treetop was a bird of straw and cloth for a target; he called Yudhishthira and said, "Take your bow, and aim an arrow to cut off its head."

While Yudhishthira stood aiming at the bird, Drona asked, "What do you see?"

Yudhishthira answered, "The tree and the bird, the bow and the arrow, and my arm, and you."

Drona said, "Stand aside." He called Aswatthaman, and received the same answer; and Duryodhana and his brothers, who answered the same; and Bhima and the twin Pandavas, but he let none of them release their arrows.

Then he called Arjuna. "Take aim at the bird's head and shoot when I tell you." Arjuna stood with his bow drawn into a circle. "Tell me what you see."

"A bird."

"Describe him to me."

"I cannot, I see only his neck."

"Send that arrow!" Arjuna's bowstring sang, and the target's head fell to Earth.

Drona embraced Arjuna and said, "I have made you the

40

best bowman in all the world. But you must promise me one thing."

"What?"

"That if ever I come against you, alone or with many, you will fight to win."

"I promise."

Drona told the Kuru princes, "The time has come for you to pay me for your lessons; and this is the payment: bring Drupada the Panchala king here to me."

At once they drove in their cars to Kampilya, but Drupada came out to meet them like a wheel of fire rolling over the Earth. He was alone in his white chariot, but he seemed to be everywhere at once. Thousands of arrows flew flaming from his bow; and he drove away Duryodhana and his brothers, and four Pandavas, who ran before him like sheep.

Drupada turned back laughing, but Arjuna was between him and his city, racing towards him. Drupada put an arrow on his bow, but the bow was broken; he drew his sword, but another arrow shattered it in his hand. Then the chariot was upon him, a strong dark arm caught him up, and Arjuna tumbled him into his car without stopping.

"Hang on!" cried Arjuna over his shoulder. "Yield to me and do not fear for your life!"

"I yield," answered Drupada. "Who are you? You have no flag."

"That is because I have not yet paid my teacher. I am Arjuna, and we go now to Hastinapura, Majesty."

Drupada stood next to Arjuna and shouted in his ear as the chariot crashed and shook on its way. "What for? You are Pandu's son, and he was my friend."

"You are Drona's price, Majesty."

"Ah! And After?"

"You fight well, Drupada, and I will guard your life."

When Arjuna and Drupada stood before him, Drona smiled and said, "Majesty, now I take half your kingdom, so we may be equals and you may recognize me when you see me. Now you may be my friend or my enemy, just as you wish."

"And my capital?" asked Drupada.

"It is yours," answered Drona. "I shall take the northern half, where once I lived."

"That is very kind."

"Brahmanas are forgiving. Their hearts are made of butter, not of stone, and their happy memories are long."

"Mine also shall be long," said Drupada. "With your character you will make a very good king, Majesty. With your permission, I will now leave you."

⚜

Next Drona chose a day of the light half of the month, with a star of promise ascendant, when his students might demonstrate their skill in arms for all to see. He chose the land, clear of trees, with springs of cool water, and measured it out by throwing a heavy stick. There at Dhritarashtra's command were built covered pavilions and gates, and walls to enclose the ground, and open tents and platforms for all the spectators, and high flagpoles for the long colored pennants of the festival.

On the day appointed, when the king had taken his place and the Queen sat with the women, Kripa first came in by the main gate that faced the east. Over his left shoulder fell strings of pearls and blue stones set in gold, and over the crowd fell silence.

Kripa stood before the king. "Dhritarashtra! Give us permission to show the Kshatriyas—the warriors and the kings—what is the strength of the Kurus, and let brahmanas and tradesmen and all your people know how they are protected and let live in peace."

Dhritarashtra answered, "I give!"

The old music of the Cherished King Bharata began, and Drona came through the gate, like the moon from the sea, dressed all in white. His long hair and beard were white; his robe and his flower garlands were white; and over his dark body was white sandalwood paste. With him was Aswatthaman, and after them came the Kuru princes: on foot, on elephants painted with colors, on two-wheeled war chariots and on horseback.

Swords flashed from thundering horses, and the best swordsmen were Nakula and Sahadeva. Chariots wheeled and turned, and the best car driver was Yudhishthira. Bhima and Duryodhana maneuvered their heavy maces at targets moving and still; they were so evenly matched that the crowd took sides, and would have provoked them to combat, but Drona told his son, "This is no competition. Stop them."

Flushed with excitement, Bhima and Duryodhana had already turned from mere targets to each other, feinting and dodging for position, but Aswatthaman without a second thought stepped between them and calmly said, "That is enough, now. Your turn is over."

Breathing quickly, Bhima said, "It has just begun!" and his hand tightened on the mace-grip.

Duryodhana spoke through clenched teeth, "Away, Brahmana, lest harm fall on weakness!"

The blue jewel between Aswatthaman's eyes flashed fire—the princes could not move, he took Bhima's mace in one hand and Duryodhana's in the other, and threw them to Kripa's feet, and the crowd cheered.

Aswatthaman smiled. "Hear them! Arjuna has strung his bow releases but one arrow and a hundred fly through the sunset cloud filled with rainbows and lightning! Look—his bow released but one arrow and a hundred fly through the air, and none miss the mouth of the swift iron boar. See the fearless spectators duck! I too know many mantras . . . come away, Kshatriyas, we are in danger here."

Drona cleared the arena for Arjuna. Dhritarashtra leaned over and asked, "Kripa, what struck the Earth near us?"

Kripa looked up and answered the king, "Two iron maces, Majesty, thrown together at my feet by Drona's son."

"Where does Aswatthaman stand?"

"Far across the way, Dhritarashtra."

"Why do the people cheer?"

"For Arjuna."

"I am well favored, well protected, by Pandu's sons," said Dhritarashtra.

Arjuna shot roaring flames from his chariot, then fountains of water to put them out; he hid himself in silver clouds, he drove the dust away with wind; he called up a mountain from the Earth, he spoke to an arrow and the hill was gone. In his car, on the ground, with sword and shield, bow and arrow, mace and dart, Arjuna surpassed everyone who had gone before.

Then Drona made ready to end the exhibition; the crowd was ready to leave when from outside the wall came the sharp crack of an armpit slipped with a cupped hand—the Kshatriya challenge, loud as a great whip snapping—and the people fell back wondering, "Is the Earth breaking and splitting apart? Or where is there thunder in the cloudless sky?"

Aswatthaman looked at his father.

"Man or god or demon, let him in!" answered Drona, and Aswatthaman opened the gates.

⚜

Karna entered the arena like a golden lion, wearing the earrings with which he was born, and the golden armor bearing the sun wheel upon the breastplate, and in deep, red-gold, the lines of falling sunlight over his back. Splendid as the sun and handsome as the moon, he bowed his head very slightly to Drona, like a tall golden palm tree nodding in a gentle breeze.

Karna turned gracefully to Arjuna and said, "I shall do all you have just done, so that you too may be amazed." Drona gave his permission, and Karna did it all, and easily did it better; he was quicker, he was more gracious, and his skill was effortless.

Kripa walked up to Karna and said, "Tell us your name, and the name of your father and mother, and your royal family."

Karna turned pale as a white lotus torn in the rain. But in an instant Duryodhana was at his side, and he told Kripa, "We know that this list is open only to royalty. Oh Kripa—who was your mother, who was your father?" He led Karna apart and asked, "Where do you live?"

"In Anga."

"I am Duryodhana, eldest son to the king." He raised his voice. "Here and now I make this man king of Anga."

"And what have I to give you in return?" asked Karna.

"Your friendship."

"It is given. I am Karna, Majesty!"

Then with parched rice and flowers, with water and gold, Duryodhana made Karna a king and held over him a royal parasol, while his brother Duhsasana fanned Karna with a yaktail fan.

Adhiratha the charioteer, perspiring and trembling, leaning on his staff, walked haltingly to his son, his robe worn and loose; and the new-made king knelt before him, his hair still wet over his shoulders from the water used to make him king. Adhiratha touched his head, and Karna rose, and led the old man to sit beside him.

Bhima laughed scornfully. "What good is this," he asked Duryodhana, "to make a chariot driver's son a king? Let this Karna put down his arms, and work with a driver's whip!"

Karna asked Duryodhana, "Who is this one?"

Duryodhana said, "Bhima the Pandava, Majesty."

"Adhiratha my father," said Karna, "taught me the weapons used by the warriors that he drove in chariots in his youth. These you have seen! In my heart I have always searched for my home, and this Duryodhana has given me. At sunrise I face the east and sit quietly until there is no shadow behind me and my back is warmed by the sun; and so I have learned many things without your approval, Bhima."

Kripa stepped between Karna and Bhima with a lighted lamp. "It is evening," he said, "the day is closed."

Duryodhana led Karna way by the light of a thousand lamps, and Bhima left with Drona and Aswatthaman. Yudhishthira stood alone in the empty field, and he knew then that there was no other warrior on Earth equal to Karna.

What is this life flowing
In our bodies like fire?
What is it?

Life is like hot iron,
Ready to pour.
Choose the mold,
And life will burn it.

3: fIRE & fLAME

Majesty, in the court of the Kurus Duryodhana made his voice sweet as honey, hiding the poison in his heart as one hides a razorsharp knife in his hair. And he asked Dhritarashtra, "I wonder, who will rule Kurujangala after you, myself or Yudhishthira?" Then he left, as though the question had just crossed his mind, and was really not important.

But Duryodhana came again in the evening, when Dhritarashtra was alone, and said, "Karna is my friend, so I do not fear the Pandavas, but they are favorites with the people. Pandu gave you the royal jewel, but the people are restless because you were not chosen king at first, and they look at Pandu's sons and think them heirs to the kingdom. The people should not be divided, or think you unfit. The people say Yudhishthira would look after us as you care for Bhishma."

Dhritarashtra frowned. "The people say! Am I already dead? I will send the Pandavas away for awhile, and I will give you this kingdom or I won't, or I will divide it. Ask Yudhishthira to come to me."

Dhritarashtra said to Yudhishthira, "You are like your father. Do you want to inherit this kingdom from me?"

Yudhishthira answered, "That is a bad question, Majesty! My brothers and I serve you; what you decide we will not let anyone put aside."

"Then do this for me, Bharata: go to Varanavata for the festival of Shiva—and, if you like, for yet awhile longer. I shall also send Duryodhana and Duhsasana somewhere for some other reason while you are gone."

Yudhishthira said, "Yes, I understand. We will go tomorrow with our mother."

Duryodhana and Duhsasana that very night told their private minister, "Go quickly to Varanavata; build a house for the Pandavas—such a house that will burn at the touch of fire, but such that no one can tell this by looking. Make but one door, and a room for yourself right next to it. Call it the *Blessed Home*—this is no lie, for it will surely lead them to heaven! Welcome them and wait for word from me."

The minister Purochana hastened to obey. The next morning the Pandavas prepared to leave Hastinapura, and in the afternoon they set off on horseback, with Kunti riding in a litter on an elephant.

Vidura rode with them a little way and spoke to Yudhishthira in the barbarian tongue, "All sharp weapons are not made of steel. But what dries the dew will not disturb the wild dogs, whose homes have many secret doors underground. The blind one sees not his way; the blind one has no knowledge where he goes. By wandering, one may know paths; by the stars he may know direction; by taking care, none shall oppress him."

In the same tongue Yudhishthira replied, "I have

52

understood you." Then Vidura turned back to Hastinapura.

After they had made camp in the evening they went away from their servants and Kunti asked, "What did Vidura say in those words?"

Yudhishthira answered, "The house we go to is inflammable. The way to escape is a tunnel."

⚜

When Purochana saw no sign of suspicion in the Pandavas, he installed them in their home at Varanavata, waited on them, and waited for Duryodhana's order.

In their bedroom, Bhima said, "Smell how the flame is hidden in the ceilings and floors of pitchy wood soaked in butter. Smell the walls of lac covered with plaster. Smell the oil and hemp resin and wax hidden in the dry bamboo and straw of the roof. Why do we stay here in a death trap?"

Yudhishthira answered, "We are waiting. We know nothing. Duryodhana has money and rank and power."

Kunti went out often with Purochana so he could show her the festival, and while he was gone a man came and told Yudhishthira, "I am a miner. Vidura spoke as a barbarian. Beginning at the door, in fourteen nights the sun will gleam at midnight. Tell me what to do."

"Begin by the river," said Yudhishthira, "and finish . . . here." He put his foot down on the hall floor.

The miner said, "In the afternoon of the last day, raise those boards."

On the thirteenth day, Yudhishthira said to Nakula and Sahadeva, "We need six people. Get them for us."

The twins smiled, and Sahadeva said, "Corpses: five handsome men and one old woman."

"From the cemetery and from nowhere else."

"Yes, burned—partly burned; they will be ready."

After dinner the next night, Purochana retired to his room, and Yudhishthira opened the mouth of the tunnel. Nakula and Sahadeva pulled up the bodies they had gathered and put one in each bed.

A strong wind began to rise in the night. Bhima said, "Get in the tunnel. I'll be along in a minute." When the others were gone, he walked noisily up to Purochana's room and banged on the door.

Purochana opened it, rubbing his eyes as though he had been asleep.

"I hate to disturb your rest," said Bhima. "But the outside door is locked."

"I always lock it," replied Purochana, "and sleep here so none may enter and rob us."

"I know."

"It is very late, Bhima, and . . . "

"And it might not be a good idea for me to go out?"

"Yes, that's it," smiled the minister.

"Even though the house is going to burn to the ground tonight?"

Purochana stepped backwards and fell onto his bed, where he sat watching Bhima, who said, "Duryodhana's orders must not be made false. Must you not set the fire here by the only entrance?"

"Yes . . . I am an old man, Bhima . . . -'

"And from inside or outside?"

"He did not say."

Bhima picked up a burning lamp and held it out to Purochana. "That was careless of him. But you do not think it safe to go out."

"Bhima, as a favor . . . "

"I will," said the Pandava. Purochana threw the lamp against the front door, and before it had become a wall of flame an instant later, he lay again on his bed with his neck broken.

Bhima ran for his life and jumped down the tunnel as fire swallowed the house. It burned for the rest of the night in the wind, and in the morning the miner came with the people of Varanavata who were looking through the ashes and covered over the entrance to his tunnel from above, and later from below.

When Dhritarashtra heard that the bodies of the Pandavas had been found he called Kripa and said, "I will question two men. Hide yourself somewhere in this room. Whoever lies to me must die."

"I will kill him, Majesty," replied Kripa. "I will bring my bow and two arrows."

Then Dhritarashtra summoned his sons Duryodhana and Duhsasana. "Now Pandu has truly died," he said, "and it cannot be undone. Purochana was your minister. Was that fire an accident?"

Duryodhana did not hesitate. "No."

"Duhsasana?"

"No accident, Majesty," replied Duryodhana's brother.

"You may go." When they left Dhritarashtra sighed, and thought, "With kindness we could have lived like a grove of tall trees in the sunlight. But now Duryodhana is alone, to be worshipped like a single tree in a village." He called, "Kripa!"

"I am here."

"That is my son! Now my path is clear. There is no more choice to make. But—how much have we lost!"

Bhima overtook his brothers and Kunti in the tunnel, and together they ran under the walls of Varanavata. Bhima pushed some brush away and they stepped out into the windy night. The light of the Blessed Home shone in the sky, inside the walls, and danced red on the Ganges lapping at her sandy banks. While Bhima hid the mouth of the tunnel again, Yudhishthira saw a boat waiting on the river and went over to it.

The boatman said, "I come from Vidura, who spoke to you outside Hastinapura in the barbarian tongue. He embraces you; he tells you that wandering will bring you good fortune; he warns you not to be careless. Let none know who you are, this is his message. Tell me what to do."

Yudhishthira answered, "Tell him we obey, our lives are his! Now take us aboard."

With all her flags flying in the dark midnight, that boat went downriver until at dawn the Pandavas and Kunti stepped ashore in a wild forest, far from any town, in the guise of wandering brahmanas.

Bhima broke a path for them through the forest as an elephant does, pushing over trees in his way and pressing fallen ones into the ground; and his mother and brothers followed behind in a shower of falling leaves and vines. He

Bhima overtook his brothers and Kunti in the tunnel

carried them when they were tired, under his arms and on his back; and for a day and a night they went to the south, guided by the sun and the stars.

Then late at night the forest became less desolate; they saw where men had gathered wood or hunted game. To go quietly they followed a deer trail past lakes and hidden valleys and came at daybreak to the gates of the village of Ekachakra. When the gates were opened they entered, and from kindness and charity and for the love of the gods, a brahmana gave them lodging in his home. Every day they read aloud the holy Veda and begged for their food throughout the village. And every evening they divided what food they had received; and Bhima ate one-half, and the rest was divided into five for the others.

One day Kunti and Bhima were alone at home when a heart-rending cry came from the brahmana's rooms. Kunti ran to find out what was wrong, as a cow runs to her calf, but at the doorway to his bedroom she stopped. She saw him sitting there with his wife and daughter, all three weeping in great sorrow, and she did not want to intrude upon their private grief.

But the brahmana saw her and said, "Shame to this life, which is hollow as a reed, and as fruitless! It is based on sorrow, built up of bondage and misery, and adorned with disease! I believe no more in Salvation! And I regret ever having loved anything or any person, for now their loss is mine! Too late . . . now it is too late to escape!"

Kunti asked, "What is it? Tell me, so I may remove your grief."

He said, "Those are good words, and worthy of you! But

there is no hope; there is nothing to do. Not far from here lives the man-eating Rakshasa king Vaka. He protects Ekachakra from harm, but as tribute every year we must send a cartload of cooked rice, two buffalos, and a human being, to a field outside the village. Each year we draw lots—and I have drawn it for tomorrow!"

"Have you no human king?" asked Kunti.

"He is afraid of the demon and is always away, never near. But we knew all this and stayed here anyway, thinking how seldom the lots are drawn and how many houses there are in Ekachakra. Not even a demon king can prevent a brahmana from wandering where he will. He is free, and cares nothing for the boundaries of states and kingdoms. But now I am not free! The lot is drawn; Vaka would never let me pass."

The brahmana's wife stopped crying and said, "We have no money to buy a substitute, my Lord, but I will go in your place. Perhaps Vaka will not slay a woman."

The daughter said, "My little brother will die without his mother; we all will perish without my father. Let me go, and have another child after me."

Just then the brahmana's little son came in from outdoors, dirty and smiling, holding a blade of grass. He touched each one of his family and told them, "My father, do not weep. My mother, do not weep. Do not weep, my sister." He laughed and said, "For with this grass sword I will kill that evil Rakshasa who eats people!"

His mother gathered him into her arms and held him, and despite their sorrow they smiled. The brahmana turned to Kunti and said, "You see? We love each other so that we shall all die together tomorrow. Live in this house when we are gone. There is no other way; we can never bear to send one of ourselves to death alone."

Kunti said, "One of my sons will take him his food."

"You don't know!" said the brahmana. "Your sons are my guests, and under my protection, little as it is. I cannot send them to Vaka, any more than I could kill them if they asked me to!"

Kunti sat next to the brahmana, "Listen—and tell no one. Not my son, but Vaka, will die. This is the truth."

"But how?"

"Brahmana, had I five hundred sons and not five, still each would be as dear to me as your children are to you. Why would I send him to death? After long years of secret study and impossible penance, my son learned from his preceptor many mantras and spells. But do not ask to learn his mantras of death. If they are revealed, all the virtue and power of the words vanishes instantly and forever."

"Swear this is the truth?"

"Brahmana, favors are never lost upon a true man. You have been kind to us, we who have no home; whom shall we kill to show you the power of his mantras?"

The brahmana was silent.

"Then prepare the rice and animals, and give your word of secrecy."

"I give it. It will all be ready for him by tonight."

When Bhima heard Kunti's plan he grinned happily and said, "This is wonderful! I've never yet had enough to eat here!"

That night Yudhishthira took one look at Bhima's face and

asked Kunti, "What does the Son of the Wind think to do now?"

She answered, "It's my idea. He's going to kill that Rakshasa king."

Yudhishthira threw down his foodbowl, and Bhima caught it. But Yudhishthira's face was sharp and he said, "We have heard of that Vaka all day! Everyone is very sorry, and so we have much food! But this is murder; see how thin Bhima is."

Bhima smiled up at his brother and said, "As befits a poor brahmana, Yudhishthira!"

"Then it's not murder, it's suicide—except that you're mad."

"It is against the Veda, in any case," said Arjuna in a solemn voice.

Yudhishthira was furious. He turned to his mother and yelled, "Kunti Devi, you tell me: how on Earth can he win?"

Kunti said, "Sit by my side and calm down. Do you think my wits are gone from old age? When Bhima was one day old and lying on my lap a bright orange tiger pushed his head through the branches so near to my face that I felt his warm breath. Without thinking I stood up, and Bhima fell on a round stone and broke it to bits. Must not a Kshatriya put his strength at the service of the weak who are threatened? And here this brahmana is our host, helping us hide from Duryodhana's spies, this whole village lives in fear of a miserable demon, and you would do nothing! Bhima will take Vaka his food, and that's that. And he's going alone."

"We don't even have a kitchen knife between us," said Yudhishthira.

"Alone, and unarmed, and not another word about it!" answered Kunti.

❖

In the morning, before it was light, Bhima drove off in the buffalo cart to the clearing in Vaka's forest. First he built a fire and roasted the animals and ate them. Even as he ate, his body filled out again, and when the meat was gone he set to work on the rice, sitting on the ground and calling out between mouthfuls, "Ho! Vaka! Come and get it, you ugly monster!"

Vaka came striding out of the forest. He smelled man, and his mouth watered at the thought of fresh human blood, hot and foaming. The Rakshasa king was broadshouldered and tall as a cliff; his hair and beard and eyes were flaming red; his mouth opened from ear to ear; his ears were long and pointed like sharp arrowheads. His skin was green; his great belly could hold an elephant; his limbs were thick as giant trees; he licked his brown lips and showed his long pointed fangs and teeth. He was horrible. Then he saw Bhima sitting there eating his rice.

Vaka's mouth dropped open and his eyes popped in surprise. He scowled and shouted, *"What fool eats the King's food before his very eyes?"*

Bhima cast him a single glance, smiled at him, and turned his back, still madly eating the rice, which was already half gone.

Vaka's face grew dark. He ran at Bhima with his arms

over his head and struck Bhima's back with both fists. But Bhima didn't even look up. He just kept on eating away. He had made himself hard.

Vaka watched his rice disappear and tore up a tree for a club. But now the rice was gone. Bhima stood up and pulled the tree from Vaka's hand. Then he threw it at the demon, who ducked out of the way. Bhima had made himself huge.

"By the gods, you are ugly!" taunted Bhima, while dodging the trees that Vaka was throwing. "And stupid as well. Don't you know it's bad manners to hurry guests at mealtime—not to mention eating them? But you've grown fat and greasy for nothing. You've got a belly like a baby, or else you're pregnant and . . ."

The root end of a heavy tree struck Bhima full in the face. It split into splinters and branches, but Bhima didn't move even a hair. He had made himself heavy.

Bhima turned around to spit the dirt out of his mouth. Vaka had run out of trees, so he quickly caught Bhima from behind and squeezed him in his arms. He might as well have caught a whirlwind in that death grip. The Pandava twisted and broke free, and with a lion-roar he lifted Vaka high over his head and dashed him to the ground, where he died with his back broken.

Just at sunrise Bhima dragged the body to one of the gates of Ekachakra and left it there without being seen. When the villagers awoke and found the great Rakshasa slain, mangled and covered with blood, they were struck with awe and wonder. They trembled and their skin turned cold, and when they remembered whose lot had been drawn, hundreds of them went to the brahmana's house where the Pandavas lived.

He came out and told them, "A certain brahmana, well skilled in the mantras of death from the holy Veda, took Vaka his tribute in my place. He told me not to fear for him, and left with the buffalos and rice, saying that he would never return, for his vows forbid that he enter the same village twice. And more than this I do not know."

Then all the village gave a great celebration and dedicated a big tree in the honor of an unknown brahmana, a hero and master of his art. The Pandavas lived as before, and one evening a dark beggar stood at their door and said, "There is a space in the forest with torn trees scattered about like straws in the wind."

Yudhishthira rose and joined his hands. "Vyasa!"

Vyasa returned the salute and sat down with them. "I have been looking for all of you," he said. "I have something to tell you."

Listen—

After that battle where he was captured for Drona, King Drupada left his palace and his Queen and wandered over the wide Earth, gathering power. He passed by all the joy of life and lost the sorrow that clouded his strength. No one knew him, nor where he was, and every day he asked Shiva for a son who would defeat Drona.

In a dream Shiva told him, *"Now is the time."* Drupada built a fire in Shiva's name and poured clear butter into two cups, as the dream had told him—one for a son, one for a daughter.

The Panchala king said, *"For the Death of Drona!"* and poured one cup of ghee into his fire. The flames shot up, and out from them came a young man in a tall crown and armor, holding a drawn sword. Drupada spoke as his son's armor cooled and hardened on his body, "Welcome, I name you Dhrishtadyumna." *"For the wife of the burned bowman!"*

Then Draupadi stepped from Shiva's fire, her dark hair fell to her bare feet and her dark body bore the scent of a blue lotus. Her eyes were black and as large as lotus petals; her nails were bright as copper; she was handsome and warm and affectionate. Drupada saw her and said, "Excellent, my Lord!" And he took his two fire-born children to Kampilya.

"Now you must go to Drupada's city," said Vyasa, "to Draupadi's swayamvara. Let none know you till you win her, for you are burned and dead to all the world."

⚜

As the Pandavas and Kunti drew near southern Panchala they fell in with many brahmanas on the road, and one of them said, "Come along with us to Kampilya! Drupada will give us food and gifts, and we will see all the kings of the world assembled there! He will have actors and singers and dancers, there will be stories to hear, and—you all look strong—you may win a prize against the king's athletes."

Yudhishthira smiled, his golden eyes sparkled, and he said, "Yes, we will come and see."

The city was dusty and crowded and filled with music. Magnificent heralds tried to make way for the chariots of kings; creaking square oxcarts with solid wheels tall as a man brought in food; through every gate came wanderers and vagrants and royalty and showmen and farmers and craftsmen and artists and merchants and all their families and relatives and friends and enemies to witness the choice of Draupadi born of the fire.

The Pandavas found lodging in a potter's house and went every day to Drupada's silk-shaded arena, where food was given free to all; they mingled unknown with the brahmanas, standing around in the shadow of the high white palaces where the royal guests were staying. They felt the coolness from the water scented with sandalwood that kept the dust down for the kings; they smelled the flowers and the black aloeswood; they saw the gleam of gold and diamonds from within the mansions white as the neck of a swan; they turned back again into the swarming city to wait.

Drupada had never suffered defeat in battle except from Arjuna, so he wanted Arjuna to marry Draupadi. He thought of that when she was born, and he thought it now. He did not believe that Arjuna was dead, because he did not want to.

He had a bow made, so stiff no one but Arjuna could pull it, even in a dream. In the sky over the arena he strung a hollow cow's horn, swaying in the air. Then it was time: the kings took their places; the brahmanas sat on the ground; and Dhrishtadyumna, carrying that bow and five long arrows, led his sister into the arena. Draupadi held the garland that she would give her husband.

Dhrishtadyumna lit a fire for a witness and all were silent. He looked at the kings and said, "Here. Let someone string this bow and send these arrows into that horn. Then if Draupadi wishes him she will choose."

As each king was named, he came and tried to string the bow. But none of them could do it. Some were thrown by the bow and covered with dust; some fell to their knees exhausted; others did not want to try. The brahmanas tried their best not to laugh, and the kings grew short-tempered, thinking Drupada had tricked them. Duryodhana tried but, though he pulled till his muscles burst the bronze armor down his back, he failed.

Then there were no more kings to call. Karna had not come there; he knew Draupadi would not love a charioteer. Dhrishtadyumna cast his eye over the royal guests, and turned his back on them. "Is there no man here?" he asked. "Let anyone in this audience come!"

Arjuna stood up from among the brahmanas and walked over to the bow. The brahmanas shook their heads and began to argue, some saying, "Stop him. What can a slender, dusty wanderer with restless eyes do except make us look foolish?" while others answered, "There is nothing a brahmana cannot do!"

The kings began to stir angrily and there was the slipping sound of swords being drawn. Dhrishtadyumna turned back to them for a moment and said calmly, "Sit still or my ill-tempered father will grind you all to bits and pieces! He waits in his white chariot for royal courtesy to be forgotten."

He gave Arjuna the bow. Arjuna said, "Take care with them, Dhrishtadyumna!"

Dhrishtadyumna smiled. "They look fierce, all right! But do not fear, brahmana. My men sit among them, and also many peaceful kings who do not wish for Draupadi. No fear to you."

Arjuna strung the bow, and in the wink of an eye sent the five arrows into the horn that spun end over end over end in the air. The brahmanas cheered, Draupadi put her white garland over his head; they were surrounded by brahmanas waving their deerskins and shaking their waterpots of cocoanut shell; the kings rose to leave, Drupada's army came in from two sides and through the middle, and Arjuna threw a dusty robe over Draupadi and the two of them were lost in the crowd.

It was nearly dark when Arjuna and Draupadi arrived at the potter's house. Yudhishthira and Kunti were there, and Bhima with the twins came a few moments later.

Kunti welcomed Draupadi, and Arjuna said, "Princess, this is our mother Kunti. I am Arjuna, that is Bhima, that is Yudhishthira, that is Sahadeva, and that is Nakula!"

The Pandavas all looked at Draupadi, and the Princess of Panchala looked at them. Then his brothers looked at Arjuna, and he said, "Yes."

Draupadi said, "This I will do!"

Someone called from the doorway, "Arjuna!" and they all went to see who it was. Two men stood there, one dark and the other fair. The dark one said, "Let us in, lest any see," and Arjuna let them enter.

"I am Krishna," said the dark stranger, "and this is my elder brother Balarama. Kunti, we were sure you and your sons still lived. Draupadi, you have chosen well. We came to the swayamvara to watch, from our home by the sea."

Arjuna said, "Majesty, I . . . "

Krishna laughed. "Bharata, I am no king! Listen—since long ago have I known you. Those lives I remember, but you do not. But we must go now, so no one will find you here."

Brahma said: "Well, after hearing ten thousand explanations, a fool is no wiser. But an intelligent man needs only two thousand five hundred."

4: INÒRApRAStha

"Dhrishtadyumna, my son! Where has Draupadi gone? Have I thrown a fresh and living flower into a grave?" asked Drupada in the morning. "But that was no brahmana!"

Dhrishtadyumna replied, "That was Arjuna."

"Where are they?"

"Majesty, last night I followed my sister to the humble house of a potter. There she entered with Arjuna, and three others came. Then Krishna and Balarama stepped in and quickly left again, and I waited outside until the lights went out. Then I entered and hid near the door in the dark. I listened and heard voices deep as the rumble of black thunder rolling in the sky. And I learned that there in that house are the five Pandavas, their mother, and my sister. Side by side they slept, the five brothers, and Kunti lay across the line of their heads, and Draupadi lay at their feet."

"I knew it!" cried Drupada. "How could Duryodhana burn them! They shall hide from him no longer — bring them here."

Dhrishtadyumna disguised himself in old clothes and

drove a lumber cart to that house. There he called down from the driver's box, "Oh brahmanas, one has lodging for you. Enter this chariot with me."

Yudhishthira came to the door and said, "What have we to do with him?"

"I am a poor man," answered Dhrishtadyumna. "I'm not paid to talk in the street."

Yudhishthira said, "Yes, we will come," and Dhrishtadyumna drove them to Drupada's palace. Kunti and Draupadi went to the women's apartments, and the Panchala prince led the Pandavas to his father.

Drupada asked, "Haven't we met you somewhere before? May we know your names?"

"No," said Arjuna. "All your questions were answered by that bow and by those arrows."

Drupada smiled. "Oh, Pandavas, welcome to Kampilya! Now, Arjuna, I shall stand guard for your life."

"Thank you, Drupada! There is one thing — Draupadi chooses us all for her husbands."

"She is a woman, I will follow her heart," answered the king. "Dhrishtadyumna, take off that disguise and go as my messenger to Dhritarashtra. Tell him — from the King of Panchala to the King of Kurujangala — *I have found five sons, somehow lost by you. Where will they live?*"

❖

Draupadi married Yudhishthira first, and the next day she married Bhima, and in five days she had wed them all in her father's palace.

Dhrishtadyumna rode like the wind to Hastinapura. Near

the city he passed by Duryodhana without a word and went straight as an arrow to Dhritarashtra.

"Majesty, I am Dhrishtadyumna," he said. "Good fortune has come to your house."

Dhritarashtra asked, "Has Duryodhana won Draupadi?"

"Better yet — the Pandavas have married her."

"We have won again," said the king.

"Majesty," said Dhrishtadyumna, "you have but found what you cast away; now regain your good name by giving them half your kingdom. They will be your friends if you will permit it. Wash away the stain of fire and never change your mind."

Dhritarashtra said to Vidura, "That will be my wedding gift. Go to Kampilya and invite them here."

Then Duryodhana entered, and said, "What do we need with the Pandavas? If the whole world is against you, you will keep your kingdom if that is your destiny, although you exert yourself only to breathe air! And if you are destined to lose a throne — do what you will, with all your strength, you shall fall."

Dhritarashtra said, "Vidura, go to Kampilya and say what I have said. My grief at the Pandavas' death is dead, let this be the last death among us."

⚜

Vidura greeted the Pandavas and smelled their hair, as though they were his children. "Come back with me," he told them. "Everyone awaits you, and the women all want to meet your wife."

Yudhishthira answered, "You have given us our lives, Bharata! Whatever you wish done, we shall do for you!"

Vidura said, "Dhritarashtra speaks honestly. You belong in our land; he will give you a place to build your own city and half the kingdom."

"We are yours," said Arjuna. "Tell us what to do."

"No," answered Vidura, "you are not mine, I give you back. Go where the king says, near Khandava forest on the Yamuna. Cherish your people; be as the rainclouds and the wide fields are to the grain, as the spreading tree is to the birds — be a refuge and a support to all the Kurus."

Bhima asked, "And Duryodhana?"

Vidura said, "It is very hard to overcome Duryodhana, even when he stands carelessly alone! But now, Dhritarashtra and Bhishma will not take sides with him, nor Drona, nor Kripa. Now you should return and make yourselves secure."

⚜

Near Khandava forest the Pandavas built the city of Indraprastha with a wall as high as heaven and as white as silver. And within, mirrored lotuses began to grow in the ponds; people came to live in the city, and songbirds came to live in the gardens and parks.

Arjuna asked Yudhishthira, "Majesty, who is Krishna, who met us in Panchala?"

Yudhishthira said, "He grew up among the cowherds of the Yamuna with his brother. Then they moved to Dwaravati, the City of Gates, on the shore of the Western Sea, ruled by the Yadava king Ugrasena. Krishna's father is Kunti's brother; that is why he came to see us."

Arjuna said, "I asked Kunti if I had ever seen him before,

as a child. He is familiar — but a stranger. She said we never met."

"That's a strange feeling," answered Yudhishthira. "I feel that way about Karna."

"Karna! Duryodhana's friend?"

"Yes. I saw him and I knew what he would do."

"I am going to that city by the dancing sea, if I may," said Arjuna.

Yudhishthira said, "Yes, Bharata. Go and find out."

❧

In two months Arjuna walked to the ocean, then he followed the shore to the south. Without knowing, he drew near Dwaravati, and Krishna met him there, in the evening, on the ocean path. The two stood alone, facing each other in the sea wind, and were silent for a moment.

Krishna spoke first, "Nara, this is how we meet — by the water that was milk. Welcome to you."

Arjuna gave namaste and said slowly, "I remember . . . you are . . . Lord Narayana! — That's what you meant!"

Krishna smiled and embraced Arjuna. "You and I have been friends since — do you remember the tree?"

Arjuna remembered. "Narayana's Tree! It is high, and it . . ." The memory was gone.

"It has its roots in a silver mountain; it has its leaves and branches in the day and night. Come with me now. My chariot is nearby."

In Dwaravati Arjuna met Balarama, in his blue robes and his garland of wildflowers, who told him, "Welcome. And also Peace!" and took a long drink from a great earthen winejar he carried everywhere.

"While you were on your way here," said Krishna, "Balarama was in Hastinapura and Indraprastha, teaching Bhima and Duryodhana how to use a mace better."

Balarama was swaying on his feet, but he drank again and said slowly, "And! And I once moved . . . with my! Plow! A city wall. Goodnight, Bharata."

"Goodnight," said Arjuna, and Balarama was gone, slanting his way home.

"He likes you," said Krishna. "He is my brother, and the plow is his weapon, and he means to tell you — *peace, or else!*"

Arjuna had lived in Krishna's house for awhile, when one day he saw there a handsome girl who captured his heart with her slow stolen glances. He told Krishna, and Krishna said, "Can a wanderer's heart be so easily stricken with love? That is my sister Subhadra."

"To get her," said Arjuna, "I will do anything man can do."

Krishna smiled. "Our custom is the swayamvara. But there she might choose anyone at all! Listen — I have lived with her for years, and even I don't know her mind. So take her by force. Who can tell what she will do on her own?"

"How? When?"

"Take my chariot, but don't put any weapons on it. In a few days Subhadra will go for a picnic outside the city. Carry her off, and I shall meet you in Indraprastha."

Arjuna waited impatiently until Subhadra went into the country. Then in Krishna's chariot he scattered her armed attendants and caught her up. He held her close to him while the chariot sped away.

Her servants ran into Dwaravati and told Krishna and Balarama what they had seen. Balarama drank a huge bowl of hot spiced flower-wine and reached for a long golden trumpet that hung by his door.

"What will you do?"

"Call my bowmen!" cried Balarama. "This one, made welcome as your guest, has stolen your car and our sister! Why do you stand there quietly dreaming?"

Krishna said, "I lent him my chariot. Why should there be doubt where love is concerned?"

Balarama refilled his wine bowl and sat down. "Words!" he said, and drank. "This time. If they will be happy."

"Transferred from one clear lake to another, like a lotus," answered Krishna.

Arjuna and Subhadra drove slowly to Indraprastha. They walked by the sea gathering pearls and along the banks of river islands where the silver water rushed past over the round stones. They lay near smiling blue pools of flowers, by lakes where animals came to drink, in cool green caves hidden from the world. The paths they followed through the glens were roofed over by arching trees; the hillside roads were open to the sun's eye. Subhadra grew more and more beautiful, while Arjuna thought her a treasure worth more than a kingdom, or the whole world, or himself.

When at last they reached Indraprastha, Arjuna dressed her in the simple dress of a farm girl and led her to where the women lived.

"Why bring her here?" asked Draupadi. "Go somewhere away with her, for the second tie round a bundle always loosens the first!"

Subhadra did not reply, but went to Kunti and knelt before her. Kunti smelled her hair and smiled and said, "Welcome to our house. My blessings to you both." Then to Draupadi she added, "And my son is no bundle of sticks for the fire."

Subhadra bowed low like the full moon to Draupadi.

Krishna came with marriage gifts for Subhadra and for Draupadi, and there were golden chests filled with bars of silver, and milk cows, and white horses; and from Balarama he brought a thousand elephants with faces like mountains, with blankets and bells and thrones on their backs.

"May you grow and prosper like the soul in a happy body," said Krishna. He sent his escort back to Swaravati and remained in Indraprastha as the Pandavas' guest.

❈

One day, in the heart of summer, Krishna and Arjuna were walking along the Yamuna near Khandava forest after bathing in the water. They were laughing together when a woodsman came towards them, dressed in black rags. He was tall and thin; his skin was like gold; round his face spread his shaggy blond hair and beard, and his mouth was smeared with butter.

He smiled at them, showing golden teeth, and said, "My lords, I am a hungry wanderer. Please feed me."

Arjuna answered, "Of course! We will give what we can. What do you want to eat?"

The woodsman said, "The forest of Khandava." He held out his open hand. In his palm flickered a tiny flame. "I am Agni the Fire God," he said, "and this dry forest must be my food!"

Arjuna greeted him with joined palms. "Why?

"I am dull and weak," answered Agni, "because I have eaten too much butter from the sacrifices of kings. I am sick, and only this will revive me. But I have tried seven times to burn Khandava and always failed, for each time Indra comes and protects it with soft rain."

Krishna said, "Tell me if any people live in this desolate wilderness of Khandava."

"No one," said Agni.

"Or animals?"

"A few. They will run before me and escape, Krishna."

"And the bright birds and tangled trees?"

"The birds will fly; the trees have their roots beyond my reach. This is a strange forest. None of those under your protection will burn."

Arjuna said, "Then give us the means, and we shall hold off Indra."

"I give!" Agni gave Arjuna the bow Gandiva, two quivers of arrows that could never be exhausted, and a many-colored chariot with white horses and a flag showing an angry ape. The god said, "These are for you, Bharata, until I take them back from you. In the chariot there is an iron discus for Krishna."

"This is enough," said Krishna. "You are generous to us, Agni."

"Lord Narayana," replied the god, "that heavy Chakra —

that discus, razorsharp round its rim, with a thousand spokes, with an iron rod through a hole in its center to throw it — that has been yours since you created it. I have but kept it for you."

The deep Earth shook and trembled, and there was a tearing sound like the straining of a great tree in the wind: Arjuna had strung Gandiva bow. He jumped into the chariot with Krishna and said, "We are ready."

From all the worlds, fire then departed. All the fires went out, one by one: leaving kitchens and lamps and firedrills and stones; leaving the palaces of kings and the huts of farmers; leaving all heaven and Earth and the underworld of the Nagas. Seven tongues of flame appeared on Agni's brow. His hair caught fire and a hot wind blew through Khandava. Dust clouds darkened the sky; branches were torn from the trees and sent crashing down.

Agni bent and touched the dry underbrush with his finger; and then the smoke-bannered Lord of Fire vanished into a sheet of flame that struck Krishna and Arjuna with its heat and forced the chariot horses back. Burning leaves and sticks were blown into the trees and the fire shot up to heaven.

The gods asked Indra, "What is Agni doing? Has the time come to destroy the three worlds?"

Indra looked down upon Khandava. He saw the trees explode and twist and fall, showering sparks into the wind like a river of fire.

Rumbling thunderclouds fell low over the forest and hid the sun, pouring rain like a thousand waterfalls. Lightning flashed angrily among the flames; smoke rose and blackened

82

the clouds; the darkness became blacker; the rain fell steaming and boiling.

Then, quickly as the moon covers the sky with fog, Arjuna covered the fire with a roof of arrows. He struck down Indra's thunderbolts before they could break his arrows. But the weight of the rainwater crushed the roof. Water fell as though Khandava were to be buried under an ocean, and the flames hissed and wavered.

A fire-mouthed arrow sped from Gandiva bow into the clouds and they were destroyed, dried out and blown away. The sun shone down and the fire roared again through the forest.

When Indra saw his rainclouds torn and scattered by the wind weapon, he appeared in the sky on his white elephant, holding a thunderbolt; and with him were other gods of heaven, all tall and still as mountains. Varuna, God of the Ocean, rode on a fish and held his noose; Yama, Lord of the Dead, with his green skin and red robes, sat on his buffalo with a deadly mace; Skanda the war god sat on a peacock, pointing his long lance, motionless, his six faces all turned straight at Arjuna; Vaishravana the Lord of Treasure was in his car with a spiked club; Surya the Sun held a bright dart; the twin Aswins stood holding green plants of poison.

Thunder rolled across the sky; meteors whirled across heaven in bright streaks and fell smoking on the Earth.

Krishna saw the gods surrounding Indra, protected by armor of gold and tough leather. They stood without fear, down near the horizon, not far away, all looking at Arjuna and Krishna. Their eyes never blinked and their weapons shone like a second sun.

"Stand still," said Krishna. "This will be my work."

Indra raised his thunderbolt and threw it at them with all his strength. But as it sped crackling through the air Krishna threw his Chakra against it, and the two met in the sky.

"Those two are slain!" cried Indra, as the sky and Earth shook with a great explosion and shock.

But the Chakra was back in Krishna's hand; the thunderbolt lay in angry pieces on the Earth. Krishna called, "Indra! Have you not heard of us in heaven?"

"I have heard," answered the Lord of the Gods. "Blessings to you both! We go now. Who can fight against the soul of all life and his friend of old?" And the gods vanished and were gone.

Krishna laughed. "Bharata, THIS is the world. There is no other!"

Arjuna looked around them. The forest was nearly consumed and Agni was visible again as a man, but strong and swift and bright. His eyes were blazing scarlet; his crimson tongue flaming; his hair all fiery — and he was chasing someone.

It was the Asura Maya, the architect of the olden gods, who ran from the flames. Then Maya burst out of the forest and cried, "The protection of Arjuna! Run to me quickly!"

Arjuna called to him. "No fear!" and the chariot raced toward Maya. The flames turned back and died away. Agni joined his hands in namaste and vanished; Maya the Asura jumped into Arjuna's chariot. It was evening, and only burning coals showed where Khandava forest had been. Arjuna drove along the river for awhile and then those three — Arjuna, Krishna, and the Asura Maya — got down from the chariot and sat on the delightful riverbank.

All looking at Arjuna and Krishna

Maya said, "Cherished King, let me repay your kindness. Let me make something for you. Bharata, I am a great artist, and can create whatever you wish for."

Arjuna answered, "Then build us a palace — such a palace as cannot be imitated, even after careful examination."

Maya leaned back against a tree and smiled. "Yes . . . yes!" he said. "I will. On the northern slope of the Himalayas there is a place filled with flat posts set in the Earth that shine like the gods; they are bordered with gold, and decorated with golden flowers and set with jewels. I don't know who put them there or what they mean, for they are left from long ago, before my time. But nearby I have stored my own gemstones, roughly hewn to size for a building. I shall go there and return with my supplies. And also, for you, Arjuna, I have the conchshell trumpet named Devadatta that came from the sea into my hands somehow. I've saved all this for the right person for a long time."

Krishna lay down alongside the river, and said, "Ages ago I set out those markers, one by one, to ornament that mountainside and show that I was never far away. Now no one lives there. But I have put my signs in the rest of the world just as clearly. They are all around, if a man will see them — all around him, wherever he goes."

Maya smiled at the river flowing by, and said to himself, "It is true, then, that nothing living can even blink its eye without you."

Arjuna asked, "who used to live there?"

"You did," said Krishna.

"I don't remember it."

"No. We lived there a long time, and it was your home. There you found love and sorrow, and happiness and death. But you remember nothing at all."

⚜

Maya began to build his palace, keeping it hidden and invisible until he had finished. Upon a thousand columns of gold he built a magic building of white marble set with pearls. He worked day and night, by sunlight and moonlight and the dancing rays of pearls and jewels. He covered the open windows with networks of gold. He set lamps of softly shining gems in the rooms and hallways and arcades, gems that flowed after he once touched them. He set fine carpets on the floors and furnished the rooms and laid down the wide flights of stairs.

By the front door Maya put a tree of lights. Its leaves were cut from thin sheets of emerald and beryl, with veins of gold. Its tall trunk and long branches were encrusted with every known jewel, and from it came the fragrance of high mountain forests. It rang musically in the wind; it flashed and gleamed bright in the sun as though its broad leaves had just been wet. Scarlet and pink flowers of coral opened and closed with the day and night.

Then Maya carried full-grown trees and made parks in the courtyards; and brought songbirds and put them in the trees. He made ponds and pools of water and filled them with fish and flowers. He made the palace cool in the heat and warm in the cold; and when he had finished he was very pleased, and a broad smile made his face shine.

Maya stood by the main door and removed his spell of

illusion; and he called the Pandavas and Krishna to see what he had done.

"It is so beautiful," said Arjuna, "that it hardly seems real. Is it not an illusion, Maya?"

Maya said, "I don't know. I was very tired — I worked like a demon building this — but now my aches and pains are gone, like a cloud disappearing from across the face of the moon. Now if the palace vanished also, what could I say?"

Krishna laughed. Maya bowed low, and said, "Goodbye, Pandavas. Now I return to where I came from. Goodbye, Krishna." He stood up and disappeared.

"Now take care," said Krishna. "Maya mixes his blessings. Let me lead the way."

The Pandavas followed Krishna up the stairs. "Is it dangerous?" asked Arjuna.

Krishna replied over his shoulder, "Not exactly, but . . ." With a crash Krishna walked straight into a closed door of clear crystal, and stood back rubbing a bruise on his head. "See? That's the sort of thing not to do . . ." Krishna was pushing at the door. Then he gave up and went to a smaller doorway next to it. "I'll get in, or else!" He stepped up, pushed, and fell right through.

Krishna lay on the beautiful floor. "Well, come in. There is no door here, just empty air."

❖

After the rains, after Krishna had returned to Swaravati, Yudhishthira received a message from Duryodhana: "*I am*

escorting Sakuni from the hills to visit my mother in Hastina-
pura. We pass close by you and ask to visit your city."

"I would not let him in!" said Bhima. "There is danger in
such innocent words."

"No, but let him see how we live," said Yudhishthira,
"and he will plot no more against us."

Bhima smiled unpleasantly. "He already has a plan or he
would not come. But you must act the king: do what you
want, in haste, without thought — and above all, do not
consider the consequences."

Arjuna said, "We dislike him, but how can we refuse? If
we quarrel among ourselves he has already won. Let
Yudhishthira decide."

"I have," answered Yudhishthira. "He will be our guest
for one day."

So, Bharata, Duryodhana came to Indraprastha, and there
seemed to be no danger to his coming. But in an inner court
Maya had set a pond of water clear and still as the air. A
flight of stairs led into the pond, and on the bottom grew
magic flowers, so that the pond looked empty. Duryodhana
was walking there, and started down the steps without
thinking, and when he got his feet wet he was so startled
that he slipped and fell, splashing in the water.

And someone laughed at him — a devilish laugh.

Sakuni helped him change his robes, and together they
went to find Yudhishthira in another garden court, where a
stream of crystal that seemed to be water had to be crossed.
Duryodhana was already angry, and when he saw that glass
rivulet, with glass fish, looking alive, and glass water lilies,

he carefully watched his foot, and stubbed his toe on the hard crystal.

Duryodhana cried, "Yudhishthira, one of your servants has insulted me in this house of treachery."

Yudhishthira smiled. "That is not as serious as arson, prince! Tell me what outwitted you this time."

"You resemble a young maiden prancing over rain puddles," said Bhima. "You are a great actor."

Sakuni stepped forward. "Majesty," he said to Yudhishthira, "the Kuru prince has been mocked in your house. We require an apology."

Yudhishthira leaned forward and said, "We have none, for you or your client."

Duryodhana replied, "*Yudhishthira, I challenge you!*"

Quickly Yudhishthira turned on him. "To what?"

"Let me speak," said Sakuni. "Do you accept?"

"Yes."

"To a game of dice."

"Very well," answered Yudhishthira. "In Hastinapura, when the moon is full."

"It will be done, Majesty," said Sakuni politely. "We wish for no more trouble here."

Arjuna said, "Sakuni, you think you have saved Duryodhana from risking his life, but it is not so."

"I think," said Sakuni, "that Duryodhana is a fool to be jealous of such as you. But there are no weapons hidden in dice. You are like the tiny bird that picks meat from the lion's mouth, and tells others: *do not gamble!* If you are afraid, do not play."

"I speak plainly," said Arjuna. "Think what will happen, see what you have done, do not only pretend to see."

"You speak plainly," said Sakuni, "because that is your nature."

"And?"

"And it is not everyone's, Arjuna!"

Yudhishthira said, "Like a brilliant planet cast down from the sky, reason is overthrown, and man bows to his fate. Leave us now, and we shall follow."

❦

In Hastinapura, Vyasa came and spoke to his mother Satyavati, and to Ambika, Ambalika and Vidura's mother, "The world is grown old, do not stay here only to see the death of the Kurus. Leave this city before all happiness leaves it, come away with me." He took them to live with him in the forest, and there they still live in a hidden retreat.

I am the King;
My wealth and my treasure
Are too great to be counted.

Yet I have nothing.
If all my City burns to ashes,
Nothing of mine will be harmed.

5: the falling sand

Majesty, at the full moon the Pandavas came to Hastinapura with Draupadi and Kunti. They left their wife and their mother with the Kuru women and went into Dhritarashtra's assembly room. The king was not there, but Duryodhana and his brothers and Sakuni were waiting for them. And as at an assembly, all present left their weapons without and entered the room.

Karna was there, and Bhishma, and Drona, and Vidura. Sakuni stood by the square dice-cloth on the floor, next to Duryodhana, and the Pandavas went over and sat down opposite them. Duryodhana said, "Let us begin." He held out two sets of long ivory dice with six sides and two ends. "Take three, Yudhishthira."

When the Pandava had chosen, Duryodhana gave the other three to Sakuni. "He will throw for me," said Duryodhana.

"Is this permitted?" asked Bhima.

"It is nowhere forbidden," answered Sakuni with a smile.

"The high number wins. I will play, using Duryodhana's wealth against yours."

Arjuna said, "Duryodhana, take care. A river in flood will overturn every tree that grows beside it. Not one can escape it."

Duryodhana laughed. "Not one! Come, let us play!"

Yudhishthira said, "I stake all my pearls, which fill one hundred jars, each tall as a man," and threw his dice on the cloth.

Sakuni replied, "I stake the same number of pearls from Duryodhana's treasury." He threw, and said, "See—I have won them!"

Yudhishthira said, "Do not be proud; let us stake thousands and thousands!" When they had both thrown, Sakuni said, "Look—I have won!"

Yudhishthira said, "I throw for many beautiful jars of gold and my royal chariot."

Sakuni took his turn, and said, "I have won!"

"My elephants and my warriors."

"I have won!"

"My Gandharva horses, and my jewels mined by Nagas."

Again Sakuni threw and said, "I have won all!" The mountain king had pale blue eyes, and he smiled kindly at Yudhishthira. "Majesty, you have lost much. Do you have anything left to wager?"

Yudhishthira answered, "Now I throw for all the untold wealth that is mine in Indraprastha."

Sakuni said, "I stake all of Duryodhana's treasury." The mountain prince threw, and said, "See—I have won it all!"

"I stake my cattle and sheep!"

"I have won!"

"My city."

"I have won it!"

"Then I stake my brother Nakula."

"I have won him!"

"Sahadeva."

"I have won!"

"Arjuna is my wealth; I stake him."

"Majesty, see—I have won!"

"Bhima."

"I have won him, Bharata!"

"I stake myself, against my four brothers."

"I have won you! What now?"

"I stake Draupadi against all five of us."

"Ah!—Yudhishthira, I have won her!"

The assembly sat in breathless silence; Bhishma and Drona were soaked with perspiration. Then Vidura held his head in his hands and sighed like a snake.

Duryodhana went over to Vidura and said, "Bring in Draupadi of slender waist and wide hips so we can put her to work in the kitchen."

Vidura looked up. "*What?*"

"You heard me," said Duryodhana.

Vidura stood up, angry as a lioness driven from her prey. His face grew dark, and Duryodhana drew back from him as though he had been pushed away.

"You blockhead!" said Vidura. "You are binding yourself with cords the gods themselves could not undo! Tigers are eating your feet, deadly snakes lie coiled on your head, and you are standing on the edge of a cliff telling me to push

97

you over! Yudhishthira already lost himself, he had no right to stake Draupadi. Stop this, for you have your hand on the door to Hell itself!"

"If you will not go. . ."

"Oh, I will go! I will have nothing more to do with this!" Vidura turned and left the room.

Duryodhana sent a servant instead, but the man returned alone and asked Yudhishthira, "Draupadi asks you: *Who stakes his wife in a dice game?*" He got no answer; Yudhishthira sat dazed, staring at the dice on the carpet.

"Go get my prize," ordered Duryodhana.

"But what am I to say?"

"You are afraid of her? Duhsasana, you go. Our slaves cannot hurt us."

Duryodhana's brother went to the women's quarters, and when Draupadi tried to run from him he caught her hair and pulled her along behind him to the gambling room. He shoved her roughly through the door and caught the corner of her robe to pull it off.

In that instant Draupadi thought of Krishna, to whom nothing is impossible, nothing unknown, nothing unbearable. From Dwaravati he came to that room before her thought was fully formed and hid behind a pillar. Duhsasana ripped off her dress, but he saw that she wore still another robe beneath it. And Krishna vowed his death when it was time.

Duhsasana pulled away that other robe, and another under it, and yet another, and Draupadi raised her eyes and watched the pile of clothing grow. She saw the fine robes of every color spread over the floor, and when twenty or thirty

Dusasana pulled away another robe

of them lay strewn about, and Duhsasana stopped to catch his breath, Draupadi struck him. She didn't slap him, Majesty; she hit him with her fist like a boxer and he dropped down like a swatted fly, which suddenly ceases buzzing. He was out cold and blood ran from his mouth.

Duryodhana's eyes were wide with rage. He felt for his sword, and it was not there. He started to go to Draupadi but Bhishma stood in his way.

"Let me by!"

Bhishma pierced Duryodhana with his grey eyes under his silver hair, and his hand fell on Duryodhana's shoulder with all the weight of Time. There was no expression on Bhisma's face, but with that one hand he forced Duryodhana back, though the prince resisted with all his might. One step back, then another, then in silence Duryodhana fell to his knees panting for breath.

Bhishma spoke to the assembly. "Now have respect for age and wisdom. Answer! You must answer. Has Draupadi been won or not? Yudhishthira first lost himself, but yet a wife is said to be always in her husband's service."

Karna stood up and said, "We don't have to answer you at all. This Draupadi with five husbands deserves to be won or lost at dice!"

Bhishma said to Draupadi, "These Kurus, my lady, are under some curse, as I heard long ago. What the strong say is right holds fast; though the weak speak truth, who will listen? So let Yudhishthira say what must be done."

But Yudhishthira still sat in a trance and did not know what was happening. Duryodhana uncovered his graceful thigh that was strong as ironwood, and said laughing, "Let

100

Draupadi choose another husband—someone who is not a slave and will not gamble her away!"

Bhima looked at him, blazing in anger, and said, "I will break that thigh!" Sparks of fire swirled about Bhima, like those that in the dark come from every crack and crevice of a burning tree. Duryodhana stared at him in amazement, and at that moment Vidura returned, leading Dhritarashtra by the hand.

"Majesty," said Vidura, "even now your son argues over a royal lady in public. Flames of wrath fill the room. He thinks he has won Draupadi—but he has himself been won by Death."

Dhritarashtra held out his hand and said, "Duryodhana, you have won great wealth in a dream; give me the dice." Duryodhana obeyed, and the blind king crushed the ivory in his hand and gave the pieces back to his son. "Now sit down," said Dhritarashtra. "Come here, Draupadi."

Draupadi came and said, "Majesty, your hand bleeds."

"Bandage it for me." Draupadi tore a piece from her new robe and tied it round his hand. Dhritarashtra said, "Ask of me something in return."

"Set Bhima free, Bharata."

"He is free. Ask something more."

"Free his brothers."

"They are free. Ask something more."

"I cannot ask more than twice, Majesty."

"Then do not," answered Dhritarashtra. "I set you free and restore to the Pandavas all they have lost."

Karna looked closely at Draupadi, and at Yudhishthira and his brothers, and said, "Draupadi, you have saved them as a raft saves drowning men. Blessings and good fortune to you—you have surpassed your beauty."

Dhritarashtra asked, "Bhishma, what do you think of this?"

"I cannot approve of it," answered Bhishma. "I have no favorites; your sons and Pandu's are equal to me."

"Drona?"

Drona said, "I think the same. Let's have peace here."

Vidura told the king, "Your two best and oldest friends speak what is in my heart also."

Karna said, "But these pampered old men only talk. They are unable to do more."

Dhritarashtra said, "If you disagree, tell us something better."

"*I* will tell you," said Duryodhana. "My challenge is still undecided. I have angered the Pandavas, they will never forgive me."

"Let it go," answered Dhritarashtra. "Have you not done enough?"

Duryodhana said, "I am what I am. As water flows down and not up, I follow my own nature. Peaceful kings are eaten up by others. Only discontent leads to happiness."

"What do you want?"

"There are no rules about who is an enemy. It all depends on how one feels. I must gamble for the destruction of the Pandavas. Let them get out of my kingdom! Why should they rule half of it? Let us throw the dice again—just once— and let the loser go into the forest."

"Then you will leave them alone, whatever happens?"

"Yes."

"You will cast your own dice?"

"Yes."

"Yudhishthira, what do you say?"

"I cannot refuse a challenge," said Yudhishthira. "But why should he leave us alone if he wins?"

Duryodhana said, "Because we will no longer be rivals. If I lose, let Duhsasana and Karna and Sakuni and me go for twelve years into the forests, wherever we wish, and let us pass the thirteenth year in some city in disguise. If you lose, you do this with your brothers. And whoever is discovered during the last year must return to the forest for as many years again, and again pass the thirteenth year in disguise."

"And after?" asked Yudhishthira.

"The loser may ask for his kingdom again."

"Success or misfortune will come to me whether I play or not," said Yudhishthira. "I am not afraid."

Duryodhana got more dice and cast this three.

"Seven!" said Bhima. Yudhisthira threw his down.

Duryodhana whispered, "Six."

⚜

The Pandavas made ready to leave. Vidura said to them, "Kunti will live with me as my guest. When you return from the forest, you will be stronger than you are now. May the moon give you happiness and the Earth give you patience; and do not forget what you learned from wandering before."

Kunti said, "Yudhishthira, take care of your brothers." Then she said, "Sahadeva, stay here with me," but he replied, "I cannot."

Arjuna sent a message to Indraprastha telling Subhadra to return to Dwaravati. Then the Pandavas and Draupadi left Hastinapura, walking to the south gate.

Vidura watched them go, and Dhritarashtra asked him, "Tell me what you see."

Vidura said, "Draupadi, beautiful as the full moon, goes first; she weeps and covers her face with her hands that close like the lotus at night, then open like the night-lotus after dark. Then follows Yudhishthira, his face covered with a cloth; then Bhima, who is restlessly squeezing his arms. Sahadeva walks behind him with white ashes on his face, and his brother Nakula has covered his body with powdery dust. Last of all walks Arjuna, lightly casting grains of sand all around him with both hands."

"Why do they do this?"

"They face in the direction of death, Majesty. Yudhishthira does not wish to burn anyone by his glance. Bhima thinks of his strength. Nakula does not want to break the hearts of any women watching him leave. Draupadi is first in all their hearts, and Sahadeva does not want to be recognized. And Arjuna, whose skill is dark and whose deeds are silver, scatters sand as he will scatter arrows in battle. Listen: the Kurus are crying out against you by their dreadful silence. The sun has been eclipsed, and white lightning flashes noiselessly like mirrors in the empty sky."

Duryodhana saw this and went to Drona, who told him, "I shall not abandon you. Be patient, wait awhile, and when danger threatens I shall protect you. But Duryodhana—don't lose a moment; quickly do what you wish, for your happiness is short-lived as the light dew of summer."

That evening, Dhritarashtra sat alone with his charioteer Sanjaya. Sanjaya said, "Majesty, madness may overtake a man, and in a strange light evil seems good to him. He desires folly and follows its path. He joyfully welcomes his destruction and it crushes him. Who but your son would dishonor Draupadi?"

Dhritarashtra said, "Sanjaya, we have insulted Lakshmi herself, the gentle goddess of good fortune born from the milk sea. Had she let fall a single tear to Earth we would be destroyed now. Bhima will return; Arjuna will return, and Krishna, and Draupadi will never forgive us. The wind is rising in the night and has blown out all our lamps and fires, and outside the palace all the war-chariots have burned to the ground and their flags have fallen down. Oh, Sanjaya—why have I such affection for Duryodhana as to draw down disaster upon us all?"

Outside the city, the Pandavas got in their chariots, and by nightfall they reached the banks of Ganga, where they spent the night. The Kurus who lived there welcomed them and lit their fires all up and down the river in the dark. The Pandavas bathed in the cool water and talked among themselves in the fresh night air.

In the first pale light of dawn, Arjuna slipped into the forest to hunt for food. He was walking silently among the trees when he heard the sound of a side-blown flute, soft and low—and the flute-song was first the call of the calm sea, then it was the song of the Bharata kings, played very slowly.

"Arjuna. Cherished prince, come here."

"Good morning, Krishna."

"Good morning. What are you doing here?"

Arjuna sat beside his friend. "Hunting...We lost our kingdom and have to live in the forest for twelve years."

Krishna said, "When I was young I lived in Vrindavana on the Yamuna river, and I used to call the women to me in the forest with this flute. Shall I take my chakra and soak the Earth with the blood of Duryodhana, and of the radiant Karna?"

"It's not time and it's not your affair."

Krishna smiled. "Remember: you are mine and I am yours. And who strikes you, strikes me also. You come from me, and I from you, and there is no one who can understand the difference between us."

Arjuna soon killed a deer and Krishna helped him carry it to the camp. The Pandavas welcomed Krishna as a gentle breeze is welcomed in the still, hot summer. But Draupadi wept when she saw him, and her tears fell burning on her deep breasts.

"How could it be," she cried, "that I was dragged by Duhsasana like an animal? I was born from the fire of Shiva! Krishna, you are my only protection."

Krishna said, "Princess, we are now on the wheel of life that turns and turns, we wander forever from one birth to another. Here we are kings, there we live out all our life on the tip of a blade of grass. But we always live. Nothing can stop that wheel. Nothing and no one will make us lose that life, whatever happens. Draupadi, when a great happiness comes to you, do you never wonder and hesitate to believe it to be real?"

"I do that often."

"Then do not accept this misfortune without testing it. For all you know, it may go away again, it may not be true."

"Can't you do anything at all?"

"What?"

"Tell Arjuna to show Duryodhana we are not his slaves!"

"Wouldn't you rather have a husband? Karna would kill him."

"Kill Arjuna?"

"Yes," said Krishna. "With the armor he was born in, Karna is the best of warriors."

Arjuna heard them talking and said, "I will wander alone for awhile in the hills and see what I find. Be patient and wait for me to return."

Draupadi held Arjuna's hand and said, "You will carry all our hearts with you, and I shall miss mine the most. Every morning and evening I will pour butter on our fire so you will be safe from harm. . .Oh, return soon or we will lose all pleasure in life."

"Here we are kings, there we live out all our life on the tip of a blade of grass"

107

Arjuna took his bow and sword and walked through the forest until he was near the great snow mountains and began to climb the foothills. He walked through a shining grove of golden trees, and a forest of stone trees with stone leaves that sang in the night wind. Farther above these were trees with branches of gems and silver-lace leaves, and not far beyond them Arjuna found a shabby old man sitting under a common pine, noisily sipping wine from a clay cup.

The old man smiled with his few black and broken teeth, and said, "Only peaceful people live beyond this tree, but you won't see them if you go on because they will be invisible to you. Those golden trees you passed and left behind can grant any wish, go back to them and get what you want."

Arjuna looked serious and said, "Those trees aren't worth a straw."

"Here is no place for bearing weapons," said the old man. "Throw them away and live here in peace."

Arjuna replied, "I am not so poor that I must wander here to find peace."

"If you go on with your bow and your sword you will find only barren ice ringing in the endless wind. You will be lashed by driven snow where no bird can fly."

"All this I fear not."

"Good lord!" The old man scratched his leg. "Then what do you want?"

"A drink will do fine."

"Here, you are welcome." Arjuna took the cup and drank it down, and when he looked again the old man was gone.

Arjuna threw the clay cup as far as he could uphill. When

it hit the ground it exploded like a thunderbolt; it shook the Earth and cracked the mountain peaks; the trees on the slopes above loosed a shower of black-green leaves and golden flowers that looked like a dark cloud laced through with lightning.

Arjuna thought, "That's a delicate wine, my Lord Indra," and continued on his way. In the afternoon he stopped to drink from a deep blue stream that ran slowly through a high meadow. There were living crystal flowers growing there, and when Arjuna brushed against one it broke off and fell onto the soft moss beneath, and shattered with the musical sound of thin glass breaking.

That small sound hung in the air, for a silence had fallen all around. The flowing stream made no sound; all the birds and animals were still; the wind blew through the trees in silence; and Arjuna heard no sound from his own movement.

Without a sound in the silence a wild boar broke from the brush and charged at Arjuna across the meadow, as in a dream. He quickly brought down the animal with an arrow, and when he fired the arrow his bowstring snapped and rang, the arrow slammed home, the boar screamed and fell, and all the world's sounds began again. Arjuna knelt beside the boar. There were two arrows buried half their length in its body, side by side.

"Thief! Get away from my dinner." Arjuna looked up and saw a mountain man standing nearby, tall and fair, dressed in a white tigerskin, holding a short bow. The hunter said, "This is my home. You have no business here at all."

Arjuna stood up. "I'm sorry, We have both hit him."

"You're a sorry sight to me!" cried the stranger.

Arjuna reddened under his dark skin. "Be calm. You can have him and I'll go my way."

But the mountain man glared at him. "Words, words, and words! *Can* have him! You sound like a coward!" And with that he put an arrow on his bow and sent it flying at Arjuna, so swiftly that his hands were only a blur. The arrow missed Arjuna's head by half a finger's breadth.

The Pandava smiled, and sent a shower of arrows back. But the hunter laughed at him as the arrows broke against his body until he was standing in a litter of splinters. He shot just as many arrows back at Arjuna, and called to him, "Use your best arrows!"

Arjuna said, "Excellent! Good!" He cut those arrows down in their flight, some into two pieces and some into three. They stood for awhile shooting at each other until Arjuna had no more arrows. Then the smile left his face— the inexhaustible quivers of Agni were empty!

The hunter picked up up some dust and spoke some words over it. Arjuna knew it was a mantra and reached for his sword to ward it off. But the sword handle broke away and the blade stayed in its sheath. Arjuna saw the hunter blow dust at him from his open hand, and the world began to spin around him; he felt his breath fade and float away, and he fell after it, down and down like a feather onto the soft Earth where he lay fast asleep.

When Arjuna awoke it was evening, and he was near the stream. He splashed water on his face and made from mud a simple image of Shiva and stuck a flower on top of it. But the flower disappeared. Arjuna looked around and saw the

111

Arjuna looked around and saw the mountain hunter

mountain hunter sitting by the boar, and in his hair was that same flower.

"*Shiva!*" Arjuna's eyes met the unblinking eyes of the God.

"Arjuna, there is no one else like you! Blessed be you, my friend."

The smell of pines filled the air. The moon-crested lord of wild beasts and green trees shone with light in the forest like the sun, for a forest fire. Shiva smiled and held out his hand. "Come sit by me, Bharata."

The twilight deepened. The cries of birds and animals became louder; darkness fell over the mountains; and a dry wind snapped branches and vines from the dancing trees that rose in the face of the stars.

Shiva said, "Tomorrow, go to Indra's heaven and your father will welcome you, for I am pleased with you. Indra will send his chariot in the morning. Now rest here."

"I will," answered Arjuna.

Shiva stood up. "Farewell, Bharata."

"Farewell, Shiva." And alone in the dark on the mountain's breast, Arjuna fell asleep under the brilliant stars of heaven.

⚜

Ten grey horses pulled Indra's silver chariot down from the morning sky. On the chariot fan blades flashed and wheels spun, swords and winged darts, white cloud-stones and grey thunderbolts and the brightest lightnings all shook and rattled in racks and boxes hung on the sides, and in a swirl of flying dust the heavenly car settled gently to Earth near Arjuna.

Matali the charioteer jumped off the driver's box and

joined his hands together to Arjuna. The horses began to paw the earth impatiently, but Matali calmed them by saying, *"Om,"* under his breath. Then Arjuna got into the chariot and Matali picked up the reins.

With a clatter and crash they sped away into the sky, and Matali shouted, "Now we are invisible as the wind, and on our way to heaven!" Soon they left the sun and moon behind them and drove by the light of the stars that hung like huge lamps in the sky far from Earth.

They passed through the gates of heaven, and the great white elephant Airavata slowly turned his heavy head with his four silver-tipped tusks and watched them pass. And there before Arjuna's eyes was Amaravati, Indra's city, stretching away into the distance before him, filled with shiny chariots that moved by thought, and with the long avenues of lights that make the long starry way we see from Earth crossing above in the summer sky.

Matali drove through the city to Nandana Grove, where every tree bent low under the weight of its blossoms and gently swayed in the air of the gods. There lived the Gandharvas and the Apsarasas, the musicians and the nymphs of heaven, and there the chariot entered through an amber gate and stopped before a silk pavilion where Indra sat with his Queen Indrani.

Dressed in silver and white and arrayed under a seven-tiered white umbrella on a golden staff, Indra rose and embraced Arjuna. With his perfumed hands that bore the thin white scars of thunderbolts he held his son and smelled his hair, and the more he saw him, the happier he was to look at him.

They sat together, and from a leather bag the Rain Lord

113

shook out into his lap many sparkling little bits of brilliant lightning and wove them to make a diadem, and he put the glittering crown on Arjuna's head. They watched the Apsarasas dance to Gandharva music, and saw those beautiful women turn and sway, in any pose able to steal the hearts and minds of all who watched, with their slender waists and smooth skin, their wide hips and flying hair and dark eyes.

When Arjuna had gone to his room in Indra's palace, the king of the gods called Chitraratha the Gandharva chief and said, "While the best Apsarasas danced for us, Arjuna's glance fell always upon Urvasi. Long ago, when Nara and Narayana had gone away from men into the Himalyas together, some Apsarasas of heaven came to disturb them. They thought themselves too beautiful to be ignored by anyone, but when Narayana saw them he only smiled, and as he sat on the Earth he put a fallen flower on his bare thigh. Then from that flower rose Urvasi, whose beauty made the others seem common, and shamed their vanity. Narayana sent her here to me and I gave her a home in heaven. Perhaps Arjuna yet remembers her from that time, so go invite her to him."

Chitraratha was pleased to go and pleased to arrive at Urvasi's side. He delivered Indra's message, and she was happy to hear it, and thinking of the cool sheets on Arjuna's bed she said, "I will go. I have been in love with Indra's son since I first felt his eyes on me. Though he lives in Indra's palace, he has not entered heaven until he holds Urvasi in his arms."

114

part two:

in the middle

OM!

I bow to Narayana,
And to Nara, the best of men,
And to the Goddess Saraswati:

JAYA!

6: nala & damayanti

*Vaisampayana said—Majesty, when Arjuna had gone,
Krishna left the Pandavas near that river in the forests of
Kurujangala.*

Janamejaya asked—What did they do then?

*Vaisampayana said—Then Yudhishthira and his brothers
drove their chariots farther into the forests, where no one
lived, and looked for someplace to wait until Arjuna
returned.*

Listen, Majesty—

It was near the end of winter and they drove through the
forest for many days and halted under a broad tree bent
down with vines, near a spring that gave clear water from
the Earth. There they made their home, and after awhile
Vyasa the poet came to see them.

When he had rested, Vyasa told Yudhishthira, "You think
that there was never anyone more miserable than you, but I
will tell you a story of what happened long ago; the story of
a king far more unfortunate."

Listen, Bharata—

There once lived a king of the Nishada people named Nala, who was strong and handsome, expert at cooking and managing horses, and fond of dice. When as a young man Nala heard of the beauty of Damayanti, the daughter of the Vidarbha King Bhima, from traveling singers in the Vindhya hills, he fell in love with her sight unseen and spent long hours alone in his garden dreaming of her. Indeed, Damayanti was so beautiful that she shone among her maidservants like lightning among summer clouds, and filled the hearts of all who saw her with happiness.

One day in the garden Nala saw a flock of swans with golden wings swimming in a pond. He crept up to the water, and though the swans began to fly away when they saw him, he was quick enough to catch one in his hands.

The swan looked at Nala and said, "Do not hurt me. Let me go, and I will fly to Vidarbha and speak to Damayanti so she will wish to marry no one but you."

Nala released the bird, and the swans flew away to Kundinapura in Vidarbha and landed where Damayanti was playing in a garden with her servants. The girls tried to catch the swans, but every bird ran away in a different direction, and the one Nala had touched led Damayanti away from the others to a quiet corner where he stood still under a rosebush and let her pick him up and stroke his feathers.

"How beautiful you are," she said. "You must be the most beautiful swan in the world."

"I have been in every land," said the swan, "and I have nowhere seen any woman so beautiful as yourself, Princess."

120

"You say that just to be polite."

"No, I do not overpraise you. And it is no kindness to be made so beautiful. Wherever I land people try to catch me and keep me for their own. But who is worthy of me except my mate? She is as handsome as I, and I believe she was created just for me. I could never find another like her anywhere or be happy for an instant without her."

"Ah!—my swan?"

"Yes, Princess?"

"You have seen so much of the world. Have you ever seen a prince who could match the beauty that you say I have?"

"Not a prince," said the swan, "but a king. And only one. He is Nala the Nishada king, living not far from here in these same hills; but who knows when he may marry? Yet out of the hundreds of thousands of kings and princes I have seen, he is the only one who can give any life to your days and years. I think he is Kama the love god, born as a man, living as a king. When the best unites with the best there will be happiness."

Damayanti let the swan go and fell to thinking only of Nala and crying herself to sleep in the night. She grew thin and pale and would not speak nor look at anyone. Her servants told the king that she was ill, but Bhima knew the time had come for her to choose a husband. He invited every king in the land to his city for her swayamvara.

In heaven, four of the gods had seen Damayanti and desired her. They were Indra, and Agni the Fire God, and Varuna the Lord of Seas and Rivers, and Yama the God of the Dead. These four descended to the sky of Earth in their chariots, and on the day before Damayanti's swayamvara they were approaching Kundinapura through the air when they saw Nala below on the road to Bhima's city.

The gods left their cars in the sky and made themselves visible beside the road. Indra stopped Nala's chariot and told him, "I am Indra, and with me are Agni and Yama and Varuna. Will you deliver a message to Damayanti for us?"

"Her father guards her well within his palace," answered Nala.

"But you will be able to see her," said Indra. "Speak with her, and tell her we are here so she may choose a god for her husband."

"I will do it. I would like to speak with her," said Nala. Then Indra picked up a pinch of dust from the road and threw it over Nala, and the gods disappeared.

That evening Nala walked unseen past hundreds of veteran guards in Bhima's palace and found his way into Damayanti's rooms. Damayanti was with her servants, arranging her wedding dress. When they saw Nala the other women stood still and silently thought, "How handsome he is; how gentle; which god is this?"

Damayanti smiled at him and asked, "Who are you? How did you get in here to me?"

"Princess, my name is Nala, and Indra sends me to speak with you, or I could not have come here."

"Majesty—sit here by me."

"To keep my word, I must bring you the message that four gods will be at your swayamvara, where you can choose the husband you want."

"I will remember that," said Damayanti. "But do not stay in danger here. I will see you in the morning."

Nala departed, and the next day Bhima's guests gathered

in a room of the palace like tigers in a cave. When Damayanti entered, everyone's eyes turned to her and followed that part of her body where their first glance fell, without any desire to move or see another part. Damayanti listened to the names and families of all the kings and then carried her white flower garland to where Nala sat. But there were five men sitting there together, all identical.

"These tricky gods cannot defeat *me*," thought Damayanti, and said, "Stand up, Nala."

All five stood up as one. Damayanti looked at them carefully and saw that the eyes of four did not blink, that their garments showed no sign of perspiration, and that their feet did not quite touch the floor. Damayanti smiled and put her garland round Nala's neck.

Indra whispered, "Excellent. Well done!"

"Alas!" said the other kings.

Nala took Damayanti's hand and said, *"I will remain yours forever."*

❧

Glowing with love, Damayanti returned with Nala to his kingdom, and Indra with the other gods returned to heaven. On the way, Indra met Kali, the god of misfortune, on his way to Earth.

"Where are you going?" asked Indra.

That faithless and evil spirit replied, "I have fixed my heart on Damayanti; I will get her at her swayamvara."

"That is not so," said Indra. "Most vile and treacherous god, she has chosen her husband already and is married to Nala."

Kali said, "Since he has been chosen over the gods themselves, I will curse Nala with heavy doom!"

Indra touched one of his thunderbolts and said, "It was done with my permission! And if you curse Nala, you will yourself fall into Hell."

Indra drove away, but Kali could not suppress his anger. He went to Nishada, watched the happiness of Nala and Damayanti, and grew more angry than ever. Then, burning and bitter, he appeared before Nala's brother Pushkara and told him, "I am about to enter Nala's body and destroy him, limb within limb, face within face. Come and play dice with him, and you cannot lose."

Pushkara found his brother with Damayanti and challenged him to a dice game. Nala could not refuse, and did not want to, especially before Damayanti. So he began to play against Pushkara and, possessed by Kali, began to lose whatever he staked. He lost his wealth and his kingdom, little by little, day by day. His friends and his people came to ask him to end the game, but when Damayanti told him they were outside he did not answer her, and with shame and sadness she had to send them away, and they said to themselves, "He is dead."

Still the dice fell always to Pushkara's favor, and at last Nala lost everything he had while Damayanti looked on helplessly. Pushkara said, "You have lost all but Damayanti. Shall we play for her?"

Nala did not answer, but threw his ornaments on the floor and left the palace with Damayanti, each wearing only a single robe. They wandered on foot into the countryside and lived on fruit and wild roots. On the third day they came upon three golden birds, sitting on the earth, that did not fly away when they drew near, and Nala threw his robe over them to catch them. But the birds flew off with his garment, and one of them told him, "We are those same dice, and we did not wish to leave someone like you with even a piece of cloth."

Nala spoke in a strange voice, "See there where the roads meet, going from here to Kosala, to Avanti, and to Vidarbha."

"What are you saying?" cried Damayanti. "I can bear anything but that you should send me away."

Nala answered, "No, I could cast away myself, but never you," and his voice was his own.

"If you want to go to Vidarbha we will go together." Damayanti wrapped half of her robe around Nala. "My father will make us welcome."

"Once I brought you happiness there, but now I would bring only sorrow to your family. We must remain together where we are not known until misfortune leaves us."

That night they came to a rude shelter for travelers in the forest and lay down on the bare earth. Damayanti was soon in a deep sleep, but Nala could find no rest and thought to himself, "What if I do this? What if I do that? Or if I don't do it? Here she suffers for my sake; if I leave her alone she may go to her father instead of wandering miserably after me. After a while she will find happiness again without me."

Outside near the shelter Nala found a sharp sword lying unsheathed and abandoned. With it he cut Damayanti's robe in half as she slept and left her there alone in the forest. But his heart failed him and would not go, and he returned and wept when he saw her again. Then he left again, and again came back, his heart torn in two, driven away by Kali and held fast by love. Departing and still departing, returning and returning again, Nala was at last overcome by Kali and stumbled away into the night alone.

In heaven Indra's wide eyes watched that war between love and madness, and his thunder rolled ominously over that Nishada forest in the darkness. Then wrapped in mist and clouds and rain, Indra bent close to Earth and called his friend, the Naga king Karkotaka. Karkotaka listened to Indra's words and his jeweled hood spread as he answered, *"I will."*

⚜

Damayanti awoke alone in the forest. She searched for Nala, calling out, "I see you—why do you not come to me? How will you pass your days alone without me? How long will you live, tired and hungry, sleeping under the trees alone? There is no comfort like a wife." She called and called to him, and when she realized she was truly alone, she wept and said, "When he was playing at dice he would not even hear my words. His mind is unsettled by madness, and it was not he who did this. Now, in the name of the gods who saw me choose Nala for my own, may whoever brought Nala to this grief bear greater pain than ours and lead a still more miserable life!"

Damayanti walked on through the wild forest singing with crickets, full of lions and leopards and bears and buffalos and deer. Past rivers and hills she went, and met a bushy-cheeked tiger on the path and asked him, "Have you seen in these woods the royal Nala?" The tiger did not answer her, but went on his way to drink from the river. She came to an Asoka tree standing scarlet in the forest, and said, "Asoka, your name means no sadness—where in this wilderness is Nala?" But there was no answer from the tree. Damayanti walked round it three times and went on. She asked the mountain that rose to heaven like a banner over the forest, "I am frightened. Have you seen my husband from your peaks and cliffs? Comfort me and tell me where he is." But the crested mountain knew nothing and could not answer.

Then Damayanti came to a peaceful glen, all quiet and green, where ascetics with controlled minds, lived on water, or on air, or on fallen leaves. They had grown old seeking the way to heaven by faith and worship, and round them monkeys and deer played together with no fear of man. Trees with fruit and flowers grew by a clear river lined with soft grass that bent in the summer wind.

Damayanti hesitated to approach, but an old man dressed in bark with two wild birds on his shoulder saw her, and said, "Welcome. Sit down by me."

Damayanti asked, "Is all well with your life here, and with your trees, and with the animals and birds that live with you?"

"All is well," answered the ascetic. "But tell us who you are and what you seek. Are you the goddess of this forest, or of the mountain or the river? Do not be sad, but tell me."

"I am Damayanti, seeking Nala in the forest."

"Then go to Vidarbha and wait."

"No. That is where he will never be."

127

"We see this by our power," said the ascetic. "Go home; your father will find Nala. You will never find him this way. But you will see him again, and again rule Nishada with him, if you obey us."

Damayanti's eyes filled with tears, and when she blinked them away, that hermitage was gone, and neither ascetics nor animals nor fires nor river remained. The color left Damayanti's face once more, and dark night was near when she saw elephants moving through the wood around her and heard the sound of men.

Lean and wild-looking, pale as the autumn moon, Damayanti saw a caravan making camp for the night beside a river. When she came close to their fires the caravan leader drew back from her and said, "We seek your protection! Rakshasi or Apsaras, do not frighten us in the dark forest."

Damayanti said, "I am human and cannot harm you. Where do you go? Have you seen anyone else in this forest?"

"By the Yaksha king Manibhadra, who protects those who travel about the world, we have met no man or woman but you. We are going to the Chedi kingdom."

Covered with dust Damayanti followed the caravan into the Chedi capital and wandered about the streets. Boys followed her and cried out, "How attractive you are with only half a dress, and deep breasts, and round hips!" She tried to ignore them, but men and women joined the boys and began to throw stones at her.

Then a man in a deerskin with his hair tied in knots stood beside her and said, "I am Sudeva the brahmana. Stand behind me."

Damayanti hid behind Sudeva, who faced the crowd and said, "Get away from here and do not anger a peaceful tender-hearted brahmana."

"Oh great brahmana," said a man, "you want her for yourself!" The crowd laughed. The man went on, "We will drive this lunatic from our city for sport!"

Sudeva said, "I might forgive ignorant children, but not a brave man like you. Spit no more words at me, close your mouth, be gone as I tell you."

"And if not?" The man picked up a handful of sticky mud.

"The small green snake in that mud is very angry," said Sudeva.

The man shook his hand and jumped to the side. Sudeva and the others laughed at him. The man turned to the crowd and said, "Ah, you fools! You heard us—get about your business or I'll break your heads in!"

They quickly went their ways, and Sudeva told him, "Blessings, my son."

"It is nothing, brahmana. I saw a little snake that was not there, but I also saw the gentle sword you wear beneath your deerskin—and it *is* there."

Sudeva led Damayanti away. He rubbed the dust from her forehead and saw a golden birthsign on her brow, shaped like a lotus. "Your brilliance is like a fire wrapped in thick smoke," he said. "The Vidarbha king has sent many seeking you, Damayanti, but I have found you. Why are you hiding yourself?"

"I am looking for my heart that is lost."

"King Bhima's heart is also lost. If you love your father,

go to him and let him find Nala for you with a thousand pair of eyes."

"Yes," said Damayanti, "I am weary of wandering." [tired]

Sudeva took Damayanti to the Chedi king, and the king sent her to Vidarbha in a palanquin with an escort of cavalry. King Bhima rejoiced to see her alive and gave Sudeva land and gold and a thousand cattle, and each man from Chedi received a horse and enough silk for fifty robes. Then Bhima sent the palanquin filled with gold, back to Chedi, on the back of an elephant.

Damayanti went to her mother and said, "I will wear this torn robe until I see Nala again, and if I do not meet with him, soon I will die and leave this body for a better place."

The Queen wept and went to her husband. He sent for Damayanti and told her, "A king has eyes and ears everywhere. My brahmanas and my warriors that have searched for you will look for Nala. In disguise, they will ask in every town and city and village in the world, in every field where even one man stands alone! Tell me what they should say."

Damayanti told him, "Say this: *Beloved gambler, where have you gone? You who are so kind, why are you unkind to your wife?*"

⚜

When he had left Damayanti far behind, Nala found his way blocked by a forest fire. High flames were advancing on him, burning to death the trees and vines and grass, and Nala hurried to escape them. As he ran to one side a voice called out, "Nala, come here!"

Nala looked and saw a Naga lying coiled on the Earth. "I

am Karkotaka," said the serpent, "I cannot move away from this fire unless you carry me. Pick me up, and I will be light in your hands."

Then Karkotaka made himself as small as a thumb and Nala ran with him far away from the fire. Nala would have set him down, but Karkotaka told him, "Walk on a little way, and count the steps." So Nala carried him in his hand, counting as he walked, and on the tenth step Karkotaka bit Nala on the wrist.

Nala dropped the serpent. There was no pain from Karkotaka's poison, but Nala became deformed and twisted and ugly. Karkotaka grew large again and said, "Now no one will know you, and as long as the one who has deceived you stays with you, he will burn with pain within your body. Misfortune will no longer recognize you and my venom will ward away all harm. Now go to Ayodhya in Kosala, and tell King Rituparna: *I am the charioteer Vahuka.* He will be your friend, and you will not be far from victory." Karkotaka brought two pieces of silk out from under a stone and gave them to Nala. "When you wish your true form again, put these on and think of me."

⚜

In Ayodhya Nala told Rituparna, "Hire me to care for your horses and prepare your food."

And the Solar King replied, "Vahuka, stay with me and do all this! I have always loved to be driven fast! Make my horses swifter and faster and I will pay you ten thousand!"

When Vahuka had been in Rituparna's service awhile, the brahmana Parnada sought a place to rest in the king's stables. Vahuka brought him food and water and said,

"Brahmana, a home is better than wandering on dusty roads."

"That is truth," answered Parnaka. "But I have heard an oracle of Shiva in my sleep, and I can have no rest until I discover its meaning. Then I can return to my home."

"What did you hear?"

"Listen. These were the words, and no others: *Beloved gambler, where have you gone? You who are so kind, why are you unkind to your wife?*"

Vahuka sighed. "That could mean many things. That wife was deserted, perhaps in a forest filled with danger, and now she must be dead. It would be better for you to return to your home instead of gambling that you will somewhere discover the meaning to this."

"But think on the words. She must be alive."

"Brahmana, was it long ago that these words came to you?"

"Two months have not gone by," said Parnada.

"That gambler must be waiting for something," said Vahuka. "If she loves him, she must not be angry with someone so weak that even birds could steal from him the last bit of his kingdom."

⚜

Ten days later Parnada stood before Damayanti in Kundina-pura. He said, "Seeking Nala, I came to Ayodhya and spoke your words a hundred times before Rituparna's charioteer answered me behind the palace. After that, I came straight back to you on the fastest horses I could buy. The charioteer is Vahuka, misshapen and bent, as though lame from birth under an evil star. But though his body is ugly, his speech is that of a king. After I left him I returned unobserved and

132

watched him until evening. When he comes to a low passage he does not stoop down, but the passage rises up for him. He made dinner for Rituparna and bowls filled themselves with water at his wish. Grass burst into flame in his hand and he built the cooking fire while it burned and was not harmed. And when the food was done, to garnish the dish he pressed flowers between his hands and they were uncrushed and fresher and more beautiful than before. He looks not at all like Nala, and he cannot be in disguise, but it is he."

Damayanti said, "You have done me the greatest kindness in all the world. I will give you all my gold and silver, and when I recover Nala my father will give you as much again. But now the king must know nothing."

Damayanti called Sudeva and told him, "We hold Nala in our hands. Dress as a royal messenger and ride to Ayodhya. Tell Rituparna that I will choose another husband, and whenever you arrive, say: *It will be tomorrow! Vidarbha's daughter will choose a second husband just after sunrise.*"

When Rituparna heard these words he ran to Vahuka. "Get me to Vidarbha by tonight and you shall have whatever I can give."

Vahuka carefully looked over the horses while Rituparna watched anxiously and tried to get him to hurry. Finally he harnessed four lean horses from Sindh, with wide nostrils and swelling cheeks, and told Rituparna to get in the chariot. The king looked at the horses and asked, "Will these carry us?"

"Majesty," answered Vahuka, "if you dislike them, choose some others."

Rituparna, dressed in his finest robes, jumped into the

chariot. "No, no, Vahuka. I will be quiet. Just get me there."

Vahuka spoke to the horses, and they fell to their knees and jumped into the sky, pulling the chariot behind them, streaking through the air to Vidarbha. Below, the Earth sped by quicker than a flying arrow. Rituparna shouted above the wind, "This is wonderful! I have never gone so fast in my life! You are as good with horses as I am with numbers!"

Vahuka stopped the chariot in the air. "How is that, Majesty?"

"See that nut tree? Altogether, it has fifty million leaves and two thousand and ninety-five nuts, and the leaves and fruit on the ground are greater than those on the tree by the number of one hundred and one."

"Vahuka, do not delay! You are the only charioteer in the world. There aren't any others. Happiness to you forever. How can we stop?"

"Majesty, we are already one third of the way there. It will not hurt the horses to rest if they don't drink."

Rituparna said, "Alright, count them," and the chariot came down to Earth. Vahuka found the king's numbers to be true and was amazed.

"What art has taught you this?" he asked.

Rituparna untied a leather bag from his belt and shook from it three dice. "That's not all," said the Ayodhya king. "With dice I can make any number come up that you call,"

"Twelve."

"How?"

"Six, five, one."

"Now look—there!" Rituparna picked up his dice. "Call again."

"No, that's enough. Just teach me how to do this and we'll be on our way again."

"Will you show me how to drive fast?"

"Rituparna! You have already promised me anything. But teach me the science of dice now, and later I will explain about horses to you."

When Rituparna taught Vahuka how to control dice, that knowledge drove Kali out from the charioteer's body. The evil god was invisible to Rituparna, but Vahuka saw him, fearful and trembling, leaning against a tree and spitting from his mouth the fiery venom of Karkotaka.

Kali spoke so only Vahuka could hear, "Nala, do not curse me! I have been burning within you. I couldn't escape before now. Give me your protection and whoever hears of you will have nothing to fear from me."

Then Vahuka forgot his anger and turned his back on Kali. He and Rituparna remounted the chariot, and again the horses flew through the sky to Vidarbha.

❧

When Rituparna arrived in Kundinapura, he saw at a glance that there were no preparations for a swayamvara. Inside the palace, King Bhima came to meet him, and said, "Welcome! Why have you come to visit me?"

Rituparna thought a moment, and replied, "I have come to pay my respects to you, Majesty."

"You honor me," said Bhima. "Rest now, and stay here as long as you wish." And Bhima thought to himself, "He could not have come so far just to see me, but it is nothing—I will know the reason later."

Damayanti watched from a terrace while Vahuka unharnessed the horses and led them to the stable. Then she sent her maidservant Kesini to speak with him.

Kesini approached Vahuka and said, "Welcome to you. Damayanti wishes to know why you have come here."

"This morning, in Ayodhya, Rituparna heard of Damayanti's swayamvara, so I have driven him here."

"So far in one day! In Ayodhya, have you ever heard of a man deserting his sleeping wife in the forest, after promising her in the gods' presence: *I will remain yours forever?*"

"If some madman did this, who could blame his wife for saying: *I will choose a second husband worthy of me tomorrow*—even though that man lived on, unknown to anyone but himself?"

"He is not unknown, Majesty, and there is no swayamvara. Oh Nala, go to her now."

From under his shirt Nala drew out two pieces of fine blue silk patterned with hollow golden squares in the Naga style. "First I must put these on; then I will follow you to Damayanti."

And when Nala met Damayanti again, the past became a dark night lit at last by the bright cool moon. The Queen told King Bhima what had happened, and he said, "Tomorrow I shall see him with Damayanti by his side."

⚜

In the morning Rituparna could not believe his eyes. "Nala! If I have done you any wrong, forgive me."

"There is nothing to forgive. Now I return to Nishada."

"Ha! Let me go too."

"Rituparna, there is no need. But you have kept your part of our bargain with me, so learn now how to race over the land and through the sky with your horses." Nala taught his friend all he knew about horses and sent him back to Ayodhya.

Then Nala returned to Nishada in a white chariot, with Damayanti by his side. Sudeva the brahmana rode before them, dressed as a herald all in red. When they saw Nala, the Nishadas threw open the palace gates. Sudeva rode in alone, and Pushkara came out to see who had entered.

"Who are you?" Pushkara asked insolently. "And how did you get in?"

Sudeva answered in a hollow voice, "In Lord Yama's name every gate opens. No wall will keep away a red messenger of the Lord of Death."

Pushkara gasped and whispered, "You . . . you are . . . "

Sudeva laughed. "Brave king, I throw a challenge at your feet from Nala. I am Sudeva the herald. You may choose between dueling with dice or weapons."

"Oh, is that so?"

"It is."

"Oh. Well, what does he have to stake at dice anyway? But show him in. I remember my brother all the time because there's no excitement playing dice with anyone else."

When Pushkara saw his brother he said, "Naishada, I will stake all I won from you against whatever you have. I will at last win Damayanti for my own and she will wait on me like an Apsaras."

"Let's begin," said Nala.

Then each threw the dice. And blessed be Nala, who won back his kingdom and his wealth with a single throw!

137

Vyasa continued, "So it was that Nala fell into misfortune through dice as you have done. But do not grieve, for the wheel of fortune also rises as it falls. And this ancient story, of the Naga king Karkotaka and the Princess Damayanti, of King Nala and Rituparna, is poison to evil and misfortune.

"Now, when I was newborn on an island in the Twin River, in the Yamuna, sister to the Ganges, I told my mother Satyavati goodbye and walked away into the forest by the side of my father Parashara. A few years later I arranged the Veda in my spare time, and it says the deceitful may be slain by deceit, and the slayer's honor is not blackened."

Yudhishthira asked, "What deceit?"

"As long as Duryodhana rules alone he gains strength," said Vyasa. "In the Veda, one day and one night, if passed in discomfort, may count as equal to one year."

"Well," said Yudhishthira, "that's a good way to grow old, but I can't go up to Duryodhana and say that. And Arjuna is gone."

"It is not a king's dharma to live in the forest."

"Or to practice misery and discomfort."

"Then," said Vyasa, "if you wish to honor your vow and promise, put aside your fear that someone skilled in dice will summon you, I know the science of dice just as well as did the Ayodhya king in the story, and I will teach it to you. And also, word has come to me from the mountains, on a leaf floated down the Ganges, that the Himalyas are smoking from the heat of a battle between Arjuna and some unknown hunter of the hills."

Listen—
I will speak of honor among men,
and of true love long remembered,
as in the stories of Kings and
Demons that are told to children by
old people.

As Lord Brahma sleeps, he hears
something lost mentioned in his
dream of Life, and he remembers,
and it appears again here among us
as it was long ago.

7: the thousand-petaled lotus

Majesty, every day in heaven is a year on Earth, and eleven years passed for Arjuna's brothers before he met them again.

In heaven, Chitraratha ran to Indra's throne and told him, "Arjuna has refused Urvasi, saying that she looked like his mother! He said he watched her dance because she is as beautiful to him as Kunti!"

"No matter," said the Lord of the Gods.

"But she has cursed him, that for a year he will be a dancer, scorned as a eunuch by all women!"

"Good," said Indra. "Go teach Arjuna the Gandharva music of heaven and the dancing of the Apsarasas. Tell him that Urvasi's curse will strike him in the thirteenth year of exile, bringing an impenetrable disguise to him. And after he has learned from you, I will teach him the deadly weapons of the gods."

Arjuna's brothers lived in the forest for a month, and after that the second month did not seem so long to them. After they had stayed there for a year, the next year passed more

141

quickly; the seasons came and went, with their changes, until ten years had gone by.

Then one night Yudhishthira dreamed that he sat alone in the forest near their home in the first light of dawn when the wild creatures of the day begin to stir. He felt the presence of others around him and knew he was being watched by many eyes just hidden from him in the shadowy forest.

As the sky grew brighter Yudhishthira could see men and women and children standing all around him, every one of them dressed in deerskin, standing in silence and looking at him. Then a man walked out from the trees, making no sound, and knelt near Yudhishthira in his dream.

With the palms of his hands joined on his breast, the forest dweller said, "Bharata, we are the deer of this forest. Majesty, now only very few of us remain, like seed, like broken words; if you do not leave us we shall all perish for your food."

Then Yudhishthira awoke, and it was morning. He told his brothers, "We must move on and let the forest animals recover."

"Yes," said Bhima, "or we will have only grass to eat. Have you never heard of Mankanaka?"

"What happened to him?" asked Draupadi.

"He was an old man," said Bhima, "and a warning on the dangers of a bad diet."

Listen, Princess—

Mankanaka lived for a long, long time eating plants and

weeds in the forest. He had nothing to do with anyone, and just sat, and thought, and was friends with all the animals and birds and the fish in the river.

Of course, he was very strong from living that way so long, but he didn't know it. Then he cut his hand on the sharp point of a grassblade while making a mat, and out of that cut came grass juice, not blood. And Mankanaka was so amazed and pleased with this that he began to dance for joy, dancing up and down, dancing round and round, and over and under, and though he didn't notice it, he had such strength that all the world danced with him. Nothing could keep still; nothing could resist him. All the animals and plants and even the stones and fallen leaves were caught up in his power.

And none of them could stop. The gods looked down and saw the Earth shaking and rolling, the dust rising, the oceans swirling and tumbling, and all created things in danger of dancing themselves to death before Mankanaka caught on to what he was doing. Then quickly they went to Shiva and told him: *"Stop this Man!"* And Shiva dressed as a hermit went down to the Earth, where he stood near Mankanaka, still and quiet while the world danced around him, and said softly: *"Be still a moment and tell me why you dance."*

Mankanaka stopped and smiled at Shiva while the world settled down gratefully. When he could speak the old hermit answered the god, "Something wonderful has happened to me! Look at the sap flowing from my hand! *That's* why I'm dancing!"

Shiva smiled and said gently, "That is very wonderful,

but look . . . " He pressed his fingernail into his thumb, and out came ashes white as the snow, falling softly down.

"So did Shiva save the world," said Bhima, "and that is what will happen if we start eating grass."

"We could knock out Duryodhana that way," said Yudhishthira, "but we have to meet Arjuna again before the year is done, if there's anything left of him after Urvasi."

"Who is Urvasi?" asked Draupadi.

"An Apsaras," answered Yudhishthira. "She caused the birth of Rishyasringa, whose father was a hermit in the wilderness and whose mother was a red deer."

"How could she do that? And who was Rishyasringa?"

Yudhishthira said, "Well, sit down by me, and I'll tell you."

Listen—

It was in the land of Anga, in a lonely forest by the shore of a mountain lake, that the recluse Vibhandaka came upon the nymph Urvasi while she was bathing. When he saw her, Vibhandaka's seed left his body and fell into the lake, and there a red deer swallowed it while she was drinking. And when it was time, that deer gave birth to a boy with velvet patches on his brow that later grew into the antlers of a stag.

Vibhandaka heard the baby crying in the forest and took his son to live with him. He named the boy Rishyasringa, and that child grew up without ever seeing another human being except his father.

When Rishyasringa was a young man there was a deadly drought in Anga. The summer heat burned on, and on, and no rain fell. The Ganges dropped low in her bed, and the streams ran dry, and many wells held only mud; but still the bronze air was heavy, never moving, pressing the life out of Anga like a giant weight in an oven.

At midnight Champa, the Anga capital, was like a furnace, and on a balcony of his palace King Lomapada asked his wisest ministers how to make the rain fall again. They told him, "A man with a pure heart must ask, then it will come."

Then Lomapada sent his messengers all over his kingdom, but they could find no one with an unclouded heart in all the land. Many tried, in the burning days and breathless nights, but there was no rain to fall on the fired Earth.

Then an old man came to Lomapada and said, "The river Kausiki still runs down from the distant lake where long ago I saw a deer give birth to a child. Now that little boy would be a man, and if he still lives there he is as innocent as a deer himself. Seek him out. He has but to show himself in Champa, and the rain will fall."

"I will send the royal chariot to bring him," said the king.

But his ministers told him, "There are no roads."

"Then I'll send my elephant and my army."

"Majesty," they told him, "there is no way through the mountains and forests that will not take months to follow."

"An elephant can break his own way."

"But this man is shy as a deer. He will hide and never be found."

"Ah!—then how will I ever find him?" But no one knew how.

Now after this, the princess Santa came to her father when he was alone and told him, "I will bring him from that forest."

"How?" asked Lomapada.

"Have your men do as I tell them," said Santa. "This thing is not difficult—my handmaidens and I will leave you and return with the deer's son."

"We will start at once," said the king. "What orders shall I give?"

"Take your royal barge, remove all the seats, and fill it with dirt. Leave only the steering oar. Build a forest house on the barge and surround it with trees and flowers and shrubs and grass so no one can tell that it floats on water. When this is done, have men in a boat ready to tow us up the Kausiki."

The floating hermitage was made, and brought up the Kausiki river, and left there by the lake, tied to the shore so it looked like solid land itself. Santa explored the forests and soon discovered that Rishyasringa lived in Vibhandaka's hut. Vibhandaka was often away from home all day gathering food, and one day, after she saw him walk away through the forest, Santa went to his house, dressed in rare silks and carrying a bouncing ball and a basket of fruit and wine. When she reached the house it was empty, and only a full-grown stag, with twenty crown points on his antlers, watched her from the edge of Vibhandaka's clearing.

Santa looked into the hut, pretending to ignore the stag, and said, "Alas! I have come to visit Rishyasringa in vain,

146

and now I shall never get to see him at all!" And she wept as though her heart were broken.

Then Santa felt someone standing behind her, and turned around, and looked straight into Rishyasringa's eyes, which were calm as those of a deer, watching her under the points and curves of his antlers with careful interest.

"Good morning," he said. "I am Rishyasringa and you are welcome to our hermitage."

"Ah," said Santa, "I hope you are well, and at peace here in the forest, and that your father's good works are increasing, and that you follow him on the high roads of religion."

Rishyasringa replied, "How you shine like light! Sit down on these grass mats, and I will bring cold water to wash your feet, and some to drink, and delicious raw roots and acorns to eat. But tell me your name. Where do you live? What religious vows have given you this radiance?"

Santa smiled and said, "My hermitage is not far away, but my vows forbid me to tell my name, or eat your food, or drink your water, or have you bow down to me. By the terms of my religion I must give you food and drink from my basket, and wash your feet, and, since my vows are very strict, I must first of all hold you in my arms and press my mouth to yours."

Santa embraced Rishyasringa and kissed him, and the two of them sat down and ate the sweet fruits she had brought from Champa that Rishyasringa had never tasted, and drank the old wines from her father's storeroom. She taught him the hidden dharma of playing catch with a rubber ball and the veiled mystery of games of tag. And when they were

both tired and laughing and happy, she held him again in her arms, packed up her things, and went away, throwing shy and bashful glances over her shoulder, after telling him, "It is time for the offerings to the holy fire at my hermitage, but I will return and visit you again."

Then Vibhandaka returned from gathering bitter fruit and fallen nuts and dry, gnarled roots. He strode grandly up to his home, with his tawny-yellow eyes flashing. His body was covered all over with fine blond hair, right down to the tips of his nails, and he moved like a lion, strong and graceful. Vibhandaka threw his wild vegetables into the hut and stood over Rishyasringa, who sat staring vacantly into space, and said, "Why aren't you cutting firewood?"

Rishyasringa didn't hear him.

A little louder, Vibhandaka asked, "Did you polish the ladles and spoons?"

No answer.

Vibhandaka shouted, *"What happened today? Have you lost your mind?"*

Rishyasringa sighed, rolled his eyes up, and looked at his father. He sighed again and said, "The world is empty, wherever I look, because my friend is gone."

"What friend?"

"Father, a religious student came by today, as shining and gracious as a god. He was very beautiful, and he wore his dark hair very long, and it was fragrant and tied with golden strings. His smooth skin was fair as fine warm gold, and on his chest were two soft, round pillows. His clothes were

149

She taught him the hidden dharma of playing catch with a rubber ball

wonderful, not at all like mine, and in his hair he wore a flower I have never seen, and round his neck a sparkling ornament. His waist was slender, and he had musical rosaries on his wrists and ankles. His voice was happy and clear, like a bird's song in the morning, and over his eyes were beautiful black curves. He carries the large round fruit that falls to the ground only to leap up again into the sky, and he held me, and caught my hair to pull down my mouth, and covered my mouth with his, and made a little murmuring sound. He gave me sweet fruit, without any skin, or any stone inside, and flavored holy water that made me very happy, and made the Earth seem to move under my feet. Then, with eager devotion, he left to return to his hermitage, and now my heart is sad and my soul longs to see his noble figure again. I would like to be his companion and friend always. Father, what is the name of those vows he practices?"

Vibhandaka frowned and said, *"Well let me tell you, that was a Rakshasa!* Even so do they appear in daylight. That Rakshasa discovered that he could not overcome you, and so he tried to weaken you with frilly food and poisoned water, so he could return at night and tear you apart with his bloody fangs and crunch you to death and eat you up! That is a grim and fearful being you have seen. Were his eyes red from drinking blood?"

"No."

"He was in disguise! But have no fear, he will not succeed in obstructing our life. Tomorrow I'll hunt him down and kill him! And my prayers will protect our home.

But do not ever look at one of those gruesome demon monsters again!"

"I promise to avoid Rakshasas forever," said Rishyasringa.

✿

Now, Rishyasringa was simple, but not that simple. So when he saw Santa the next day, walking towards him through the trees, Rishyasringa ran to her and said breathlessly, "Let's go to your hermitage right now before my father comes back!"

Santa led him to the floating house and diverted him with all the things he had never seen before, so he never noticed how they floated down the river until they met the Ganges near Champa. Then the king's navy stopped them, and Lomapada came aboard and said, "Ask for rain."

Rishyasringa opened his mouth to reply, but a thunderbolt shook the sky before he said a word, and the rain poured down, shredding the river water around them and striking the dusty Earth like iron bolts. The king ran outside and stood in the downpour under the black skies and spitting lightning. In an instant he was soaking wet, and standing in the doorway of that floating house, laughing and crying all at once, Lompada shouted, "I marry you! Meet me at home!" And he was gone.

✿

As the rain fell, day after day, and the crops began to grow, Lomapada gave Rishyasringa half the palace for his own, and there Santa and her husband lived until the rains were over and the roads of the kingdom were passable again, no longer rivers of mud. Rishyasringa told the king, "My father will come glaring down the hills, stalking the goblin who carried me away."

Lomapada smiled at his new son, and replied, "I have forseen this. His curse, like a king's anger, would be devastating—but he will speak no curse against us. Prepare to introduce your wife to him, and think no more about it."

Then down the road from the hills came Vibhandaka, peering in every forest, watching through every night for a sign of that lurking Rakshasa, and slowly drawing nearer and nearer to Champa. But no sooner was he clear of the foothills than he found himself welcomed as a long-lost friend by the Anga people along the road. When he was tired and hungry at night or at noon, there was someone to lead him to food and shelter, someone standing by the roadside tending a herd of cattle or watching a plowed field.

The first night this happened, Vibhandaka said to the farmer who welcomed him, "I will find that evil fiend and burst his head into thousands of pieces for eating my son!"

And the farmer answered, "Yes, holy one, but welcome in Rishyasringa's name!"

"What? Where is he?"

"Your Majesty," said the farmer, "holy one, Rishyasringa has saved us all from death and now lives in Champa in the king's palace, and all these fields and cattle are his, so I make you welcome in his name."

"Who was that Rakshasa?"

"My Lord, that was Santa, Excellency."

"Who is Santa?" asked Vebhandaka.

"The King's daughter, Your Grace," answered the farmer. "There was no rain, you know, Sir, until Santa brought your son to us, and without him we would all have died, Your Eminence."

"I did not know this."

"Venerable Sir, whatever . . . "

"Enough," said Vibhandaka. "In the morning, get me a horse."

And for the rest of his journey to Champa, Vibhandaka found that his son owned every cow and every field along the road, and every day there was a better horse for him to ride. The second night he learned of the floating house. The third night he discovered that his son had married Santa. And the next morning Lomapada came to meet him and cooked their breakfast with his own hands.

That evening, decked with golden champaka flowers, Vibhandaka and the king walked into the royal palace arm in arm, and Santa served them dinner, and Vibhandaka gave his best blessings to his son and his marriage. And as the golden lamplight danced on Rishyasringa's magnificent antlers, Vibhandaka told him, "When your child is born you must visit me in the forest, all of you."

"Yes, Father."

"Then you must go?" asked Lomapada.

"At dawn," said Vibhandaka.

"My swiftest boat will take you . . . "

"No," said Vibhandaka. "I must walk, lest comfort destroy all men."

✣

"And now *we* must go," said Yudhishthira.

"Where?" asked Sahadeva.

"To Kailasa Mountain in the Himalyas, where the Yakshas guard the castle of Vaishravana, the lord of all wealth and treasure."

The Pandavas and Draupadi began their journey, Bharata, and when the chariots could go no further they hid them, and began to climb into the hills on foot. They were near Kailasa when Yudhishthira said, "Now cast down your eyes and don't say a word, for we must pass close by Rishava's Peak. Rishava was an angry man who hated company and conversation, and he lived on that hill all by himself and told the mountain, 'If anyone comes here and looks at you, strike down his heart with sorrow so he will not climb up here; and if anyone speaks, stone him, and call up the high winds and storms to sweep away his noise.' And though Rishava is long dead, his mountain still obeys him."

Carefully the Pandavas walked on, watching their feet, but just as they were passing Rishava's mountain, making their way over rough ground with sand and stones of every size, Yudhishthira turned his ankle and said, "Damn!"

Instantly a howling, rattling wind blew volleys of stones through the air, and the sun was hidden by roaring clouds of dust that scoured the sky. Dry leaves whirled and snapped in the wind, trees were split and broken, and it was dark as midnight all around.

Sahadeva bent over the clay jar that held their fire and took shelter in a cave, while his brothers hid behind boulders or tall anthills hard as rock. Bhima carried Draupadi behind a stone and bent over her as the biting rain came down in torrents thick as chariot axles. Thunder blasted the hills. Quick-flashing lightning fused the Earth into glass. A foaming river, filled with spinning sticks and mud and rolling stones, began to flow underfoot. In every direction there was nothing but water. All heaven and Earth had disappeared.

Suddenly it was over. The sun was shining. The water shrank away to a sparkling rivulet and then was gone. Nakula wrung the water from his long black hair and helped Yudhishthira to his feet with a smile.

They went on, until a hundred great mountains had thoroughly hidden that ill-mannered hill from sight behind them and Kailasa rose before their eyes, dull silver against the sky.

That, Bharata, is the side of Kailasa that faces the world, but it was the far side that the Pandavas climbed, up to a high grassland where a giant tree spread wide its soft leaves and blossoms and sweet fruit. In the ancient and blessed retreat of Narayana the Pandavas rested against the stout trunk of Narayana's Tree, in the shade of its heavy limbs, high above the world. The tree was smooth and cool against their backs, and they were tired no more.

From the mountain's breast they saw waterfalls roaring below, falling into channels of coral and ruby, into a network of rivers that led into lakes red with lotus pollen where elephants bathed and flocks of swans and wild red geese rested. On the crests and ridges of Kailasa above them, on the peaks made of gold and gems and dyed through with mountain metals, there grew silver leaf trees, and trees the color of fire, and of molten gold, and of the sea where it is deep and clear. Rivers and streams of color ran through the mountain stones and cliffs, black and brown and yellow and white, and caves of red ore glowed like the setting sun changed into stone.

⚜

One day Draupadi was sitting in the morning air when the northeastern wind blew into her lap a white lotus with a thousand petals. She had never known a flower so fragrant and beautiful, and she carried it to Bhima and said, "Look what a wonderful flower! Oh Bhima, even when Arjuna is here, I turn to you for help . . . If only I had several of these flowers, I could make our home of branches and boughs so beautiful."

"Where did you get it?" asked Bhima.

"It blew down from the mountain."

Bhima picked up his bow and arrows. "I'll go look," he told her, "and if I find any more I'll bring them back for you."

Then Bhima left their home near the giant tree, and began to climb through the forests and meadows above, in search of the home of the thousand-petaled lotus. Peacocks danced on branches to the dancing bells of Apsarasas that they alone could hear; they danced as if it were about to rain and spread their tails like crowns for the trees. Black bees stuffed with honey were resting on flowers everywhere. As he went higher and higher in the forests and glens of Kailasa, deer gazed at Bhima with grass in their mouths, and, all unseen, the wives of Yakshas followed him with their eyes.

Bhima followed a narrow path into a thick grove of plane trees, and coming around a turn he found the way blocked by a monkey lying across it. The animal was copper colored, with broad shoulders and a short neck. He had red ears, his long tail was a little bent at the end, and he lay with his eyes closed and his head on his arms.

"Out of my way, monkey!" cried Bhima. "Get away!"

The monkey only opened his sleepy red eyes a little and shut them again.

"Go away and let me by!" said Bhima.

The monkey looked at him for awhile, licked his sharp white teeth with his coppery tongue, and said, "I am ill, and was resting peacefully. We animals are ignorant, but why have you no better manners? And what is a dunce like you doing here anyway?"

Bhima frowned and bit his lip. "Then who are you in the shape of a monkey?" he asked.

"Why you simpleton, I *am* a monkey! Can't you see well? Please, go on home and learn to be a gentleman."

"You're in my way," said Bhima, "so move."

"Ah, great hero," sighed the monkey, "I am too sick to get up. I haven't even the strength to crawl away. It takes all my energy just to breathe. The unearthly honor of talking to you will probably kill me."

"Then shut up. Go somewhere else."

"It wouldn't do any good. You can't go any farther than this anyhow, because this path leads to heaven and is used only by the gods. I am telling you from kindness, and if you go on the gods will pelt you with every kind of curse and destruction."

"I am not asking you about curses and destructions!"

"Well, if you want to get by so badly," said the monkey, "Just move my tail aside and go ahead, if you can't forget it."

Bhima caught the monkey's tail in his left hand to push it away, but it would not move. He grabbed it with both hands and pulled and strained and rolled his eyes till he was exhausted. But for his life Bhima could not move that monkey's tail even the width of a barley corn.

"Whew!" Bhima sat down, wiped the sweat from his brow, and looked carefully at the monkey. "What is this?"

The monkey yawned and clicked his tongue in his mouth, and said,

"Look! The Son of the Wind leaps into the air.
And flies through the clouds with a roar,
While the enemy waves on the green salt sea
Splash and foam below."

"Hanuman!" Bhima touched his hands to his forehead. "I am your brother Bhima."

Hanuman laughed and laughed, rolling in the dust and wiping the tears from his eyes with his paws. Then he scampered through the trees, swinging from limb to limb, hanging by his tail, spinning and tumbling and laughing and falling. Finally he calmed down a little, and sat in front of Bhima with mischief in his little red eyes.

"Bhima!" he said, slapping the ground with his tail. "Do you have a banana?"

"I didn't bring any food," answered Bhima.

"No food! Listen:
The monkey chief is perfect;
No one can equal his learning and strength.

But for his life Bhima could not move the monkey's tail

In Lanka he tears the trees and seizes the clouds,
And burns Ravana's city with his tail!
Now I'll go tie up Duryodhana and bring him here, and get a banana in Hastinapura."

"No you won't, thank you, Hanuman."

"Listen, you poor Pandava, no power on Earth can save Duryodhana if I set out after him. I'm like lightning— thundering and swift, bright and shining and hard to look at!"

"You took Rama's ring to Sita when she was a prisoner. Why did you not carry her back with you?"

"Alright!" Hanuman spun round and round on his haunches. "You want to do it yourself just like Rama." Suddenly he was still again, and touched Bhima's arm with his paw. "Are you sure you didn't bring anything to eat?"

"Nothing. There's food all over the place."

"A wise man does not grieve at defeat nor rejoice in victory," said Hanuman, "but I am only a monkey, and I am disappointed in you. You're not very thoughtful. I'm old enough to deserve a little respect, you know."

"You're a monkey, sitting here chattering like a human being and acting like you own the world!"

"It's a good thing to be," said Hanuman. "A monkey chases everything, but never catches it because he is instantly distracted by another thing. Always the joy of running and leaping, and never the awful clutter of possessions no longer desired. Don't tell anybody that I live here. I will live as long as the story of Rama is heard on Earth, and I don't want to be disturbed. But you can visit me any time."

"We won't be here long," said Bhima. "When Arjuna returns we must leave."

"Perhaps you might return someday." Hanuman made some vague gestures in the air with one hand. "If you go over, and across, and up, and then look down, you'll see the lotus lake."

Later in the afternoon Bhima stood on the brow of Kailasa, looking down on the lake that was a bed to the thousand-petaled lotus flowers, pure white and pale blue. Bhima stood resting his chin on his hands, leaning on his bow and smiling, when all the shadows from the sun disappeared and winked back instantly. There was a flash of light from near the summit above him, and from the corner of his eye Bhima saw a huge gate of jewels silently close.

That was the gate to the castle of Vaishravana the God of Wealth. Bhima saw the castle of gold and crystal; the huge high walls of jewels and watery pearls, thick as a road is wide near a great city; the soaring towers and turrets of silver and ivory, with clear windows of diamond sheets and sharp roofs of turquoise and lapis lazuli; the rows of shining silk flags and pennants waving in the wind on amber flagpoles; and the gardens of flowers and trees outside the wall, where uncut piles of gems slept in the shade. All wealth was there, Bharata—all that men count for wealth and worldly treasure was there, and is yet there, high, very high, in the thin air and white sunlight of the Himalyas, in the brilliant moonbeams that show by night the true colors of things.

A Yaksha with ears like pegs and perfectly round eyes had swung shut the main gate to Vaishravana's castle. He ran to

Manibhadra the Yaksha king and whispered to him, and Manibhadra clattered away in his armor through the endless palace halls. He finally found Vaishravana and said, "A mortal stands down the mountain."

"*What?*" thundered Vaishravana.

Manibhadra's lavender face was pale and his voice trembled. "A man, of golden skin and heavy arms, stands looking at this castle!"

"Harness the horses!" said Vaishravana. The Treasure Lord, who travels far in the World on the shoulders of men, waved his four pale white arms about and quickly picked up a diamond noose and a crystal sword, a supple bow of rhododendron wood, and a handful of iron and stone arrows. Manibhadra tied the golden war garland over Vaishravana's brow.

Then half the castle rose into the sky behind eighteen thousand horses, set in a giant chariot of dark clouds held together by bright rainbows tied in colored knots. Those horses flew so fast towards Bhima that they drew the sky forward with their feet and devoured the air with their lungs.

Bhima found himself standing in the shadow of half a city hanging in the air over his head. Vaishravana leaned out of a window and called down, "Who violates the Castle of the Dawn of the World?"

Bhima was still resting on his bow, smiling down on the lotus lake. He didn't look up and he didn't answer.

The Treasure Lord jumped out the window and came to rest sitting in the air an arm's length from Bhima. He bent nearer and whispered grimly, *"Who are you?"*

Bhima smiled at him.

"No matter. It's not important," said Vaishravana. "You'll just have to be killed anyway."

"See all those lotus flowers?" asked Bhima.

"What flowers?"

"The thousand-petaled ones. Down there in the lake," said Bhima in a gentle voice.

"Ah!—this is a great wonder! When the full moon comes out from behind a dark cloud at night, it is not more wonderful."

"Why?"

"You have not come here to rob me," answered Vaishravana.

"All the things you have are overlooked by the birds and dismissed by the animals," said Bhima. "I came for some flowers of fragrance."

Vaishravana licked his lips and said, "I'm sorry . . . but you've got to die. Because you've seen my castle."

"Oh."

"Won't you tell me your name? Before you die at the hands of my thirty-six million Yakshas?"

Bhima took a very deep breath and blew Vaishravana's armor right off. Then he whispered, "I am Bhima, the Son of the Wind. Take care, Treasure Lord."

When they saw this outrage, thousands of Yakshas flew from the aerial chariot and fell into formation behind Vaishravana. But the Treasure Lord waved them back and the weapons vanished from his hands.

"The mind is harder to tame than a monkey," said Bhima, "yet try to think of bringing me an armful of those flowers."

"Kaunteya, are you here with your brothers?" asked Vaishravana.

"We await Arjuna near the tree Visala, at the hermitage Badari."

"Bhima . . . it is an honor." Vaishravana looked up at his Yakshas. "Manibhadra! Bring some of those flowers in that lake—one armful, and be quick!"

The Yaksha King poured the lotuses into Bhima's arms, bowed low to him, and vanished. The Treasure Lord said, "Take these as my gift, and take also my protection; while you wander over the world I will guard all of you. Will you not be my guest awhile?"

"You are kind to invite us," said Bhima, "but . . . "

"I have no real friends in all the Worlds."

"We must meet Arjuna at Narayana's Tree—so says Yudhishthira. If we leave we may miss him."

"Then it is so, if Yudhishthira says this. But after?"

Bhima clenched his huge fist like a five-headed snake. "Then comes Duryodhana."

"And after?"

"Both a monkey and a god have now invited me to return," said Bhima. "Kailasa is a good home."

"Enjoy the good and bear the bad," said the Treasure Lord. He gave Bhima silk to weave the flowers together and returned to the chariot. The horses turned, and the castle flew away with a whirling sound, as of a thousand soft-winged birds flying into a tree to rest. Bhima was alone on the mountain. Vaishravana's home was no longer to be seen, and only Bhima's father, the Wind, moved through the valley below and up the mountainside, flashing through the trees, swaying the flowers on the lake.

Then the Universe is water; water
without end or beginning; without
Earth or sky; without space or light;
without sound or movement. Then
the dark waters lie still and silent
and waiting, touching nothing.
*What shape shall I take to rescue
the Earth from this flood?*

8: an IRON net

When Bhima returned with Draupadi's flowers the rain began to fall and all the Earth was peaceful. In the forests of Kailasa, while the rain fell day and night, the animals were talking—the yak and the deer, the monkeys and boars and bears, the elephants and oxen, lions and leopards, buffalo and tigers—and the frogs ran joyfully about, and the sparrows and cuckoos sang. Black clouds domed the sky, stainless lightning replaced the sun and moon, and water ran racing down the hills to flood the plains and give back again the lost energy stolen from the plants by the summer sun.

Then came autumn with new grass and cool nights. The stars and planets were nearer to the Earth at night, and in the day there was no dust. The air was as clear as the new necklace of rills and rivers worn by the mountain, and white birds flew past day after day on their way to the brimful lakes of the south.

❧

Matali drove Indra's chariot down through the air, and landed Arjuna in the grass beside Lord Narayana's tree. Like the sun wearing a garland of light, Arjuna stood before Yudhishthira with the heavenly diadem and all the shining weapons of heaven! Yudhishthira threw his arms around Arjuna.

Into Draupadi's hands Arjuna poured ornaments from heaven, and as the jewels fell, one bright as sunlight flashed and blinded them, and when they could see again the heavenly chariot had gone.

The Pandavas descended Kailasa, leaving behind the cliffs and crags, the cascades and plunging waterfalls, going down by narrow ways into the lowlands. When the Silver Mountain towered away behind them, Yudhishthira looked back and thought "May we all return to you again, Kailasa." And the wind blew and whispered to them: *"The World is wide! The World is wide!"*

❀

So began the twelfth year, when the Pandavas returned again to Dhritarashtra's kingdom and made their home in Kamyaka forest, near Dwaitavana lake, among the flowering oak trees and the golden quince. Sakuni told Duryodhana, "They have returned. What could be more pleasant than to see them living as peasants in the uncomfortable forest?"

Duryodhana told his father, "I am going out to count our cattle that roam the countryside," and left Hastinapura with Karna and Duhsasana and Sakuni, with eighty war chariots and thirty elephants. Near Dwaitavana lake Duryodhana's men set up his tents, and when Duryodhana had rested he called out, "Build us pleasure houses along the lakeshore, so we may enjoy ourselves."

While Duryodhana and Karna were laughing and talking together, several Kurus went towards the lake. But when they drew near they found their way blocked by two Gandharvas.

"Stand aside!" said the soldiers. "The Kuru king is coming here!"

But the Gandharvas smiled and answered softly, "The lake is closed by order of the Gandharva King and it is forbidden to enter. And so, before you die here for nothing, return and tell this to Duryodhana."

The soldiers returned, and Duryodhana himself with all his warriors marched on the lake. And at the same spot the unarmed Gandharvas again said, "Go back."

From the back of his elephant Duryodhana looked down at the two Gandharvas and said, "Dhritarashtra's son, the mighty King Duryodhana, will go where he chooses. Stand away!"

The Gandharvas laughed at him. "We have truly heard you are a fool," they said. "Are we your servants? Hurry—hurry up and go."

Duryodhana told his elephant to advance, and the Gandharvas fled away through the air. "Come on!" cried Duryodhana. "Follow me. We have frightened them away." His men cheered and rushed forward.

The Gandharvas flew like shooting stars to Chitraratha's side and spoke to him. The Gandharva King removed an

Apsaras from his lap, and with a smile he slowly put a flower behind his ear.

"Take them!"

⚜

Multiplying themselves by illusion, ten Gandharvas attacked every one of Duryodhana's men from every side at once. In an instant fear and panic had scattered everyone but Karna and Duryodhana. From his chariot Karna held off the Gandharvas with sheets of light in the sky and surrounded himself and Duryodhana with blinding shields. But Chitraratha clouded over the walls of light and sent them crashing down like flat stones on top of Karna. Duryodhana's elephant trumpeted in fear and ran blindly towards the lake, and Karna lay stunned under the wreckage of his chariot.

Chitraratha seized Duryodhana, so violently that the Kuru prince thought his life itself had been pulled out of him, and threw him into an iron net hanging in the sky. And after Duryodhana, the other Gandharvas threw Sakuni and Duhsasana and every Kuru they could catch into the net. But Karna they left lying where he had fallen, for Chitraratha knew that no Gandharva net could hold him.

A few of Duryodhana's men escaped and ran to the Pandavas for protection. Yudhishthira said, "I will protect you; be still. This is the natural result of yet another of Duryodhana's schemes, but we cannot let Gandharvas steal away the Kurus." He told Bhima and Arjuna, "Go and get them out."

Arjuna and Bhima found the Gandharvas near the net, toasting their victory with milk and honey. Arjuna called over to them, "Let down your captives, at the command of King Yudhishthira."

"Oh child," they answered, "we obey only Indra. No one else can command us."

Bhima said, "You have no right to imprison men. We peacefully ask you to free the pop-eyed little king you hold in your net like a fish."

"No! No!" they answered. "Never!" And they would have laughed longer, but from Arjuna's bow a thousand arrows flew at them.

The Gandharvas swarmed through the air. Arjuna built a cage of arrows around them, and when they would have flown out the top he laid on an arrow roof. They were all trapped within, and many lay dead upon the ground.

Then Arjuna heard the sound of a lute string plucked in the air, and when he turned to it a fireball was rushing at him. Bhima knocked it down with a slung spear and it lay quietly burning in the grass. Arjuna held his bow drawn back, scanning the sky. There was nothing visible. Then Chitraratha suddenly appeared sitting in the sky holding a lute.

Chitraratha bent his head with the five-crested golden crown and smiled. "Here am I, your dear friend Chitraratha, and you are fighting against me!"

Arjuna put down his bow. "Why have you built that cage around my people?" asked Chitraratha with an injured look.

"Let the Kurus go," said Arjuna.

"But Duryodhana came to mock you. So I came also."

Bhima said, "Let him spy or not, or be your prisoner forever."

"No," said Arjuna. "You will do me a kindness to let him go."

Chitraratha sighed, "I am your friend. I will do it. But he will *always* be planning some evil against you. I saw and had no patience. I have no business here. I came only for fighting Duryodhana."

"He will not forget you," said Bhima.

The cage of arrows began to sway in the wind. The arrows caught fire from friction and burned away to ashes, and the Gandharvas were free. Chitraratha struck his lute again and the slain Gandharvas were restored to life. The iron net came gently down. Then Chitraratha frowned and vanished in a bright vermillion flash of light.

Yudhishthira helped Duryodhana out of the net and said, "What else can we do for you?"

Duryodhana walked away and said nothing, while the others all thanked Yudhishthira for saving them.

Duryodhana reached his camp at nightfall, and when Karna returned sometime after midnight he found Duryodhana sitting on his bed.

"Well met!" said Karna. "By good fortune you have defeated the Gandharvas after my own weapons failed us. No one but you could have driven them off."

Duryodhana looked disgusted. "I have been shamed and disgraced," he said. "I was captured. They had us all in a net, and Yudhishthira saved us. Now that I have been made tribute to the Pandavas I shall stay here and take my life by starvation. In the morning, lead the others back to the city, and let Duhsasana take my place with you. My life has no value to me now. It would have been much better to have died today."

"That was no fair fight," said Karna. "Relent. The subjects of a king must always aid him; the Pandavas only did their duty. The Gandharva King is Arjuna's friend and would not harm the Pandavas. He let you go from friendship. Or did Arjuna defeat him in battle?"

"No, he did not."

"Then where is the shame in this? Do not melt away with grief like an unfired bowl full of water."

"Everyone will laugh at me," said Duryodhana, "and so I shall die."

"Then you are but a child without wisdom. Be pleased with the Pandavas, and return them their kingdom in thanks. Then you will be happy again."

"I will never change my mind, Karna."

"Then . . . you are a child and foolish—and I shall die with you." Karna walked to the door of Duryodhana's tent and out into the night.

Duryodhana, alone in the tent, slowly tore his robe into rags. He spread grass on the Earth and sat on it. Touching some water in a bowl, he resolved to die and took the vow of starvation. He withdrew his mind into itself and watched as his senses shut themselves off from the world. His eyes were cast down—open, but he saw nothing—he heard nothing, felt nothing. His self held the threads of that body called Duryodhana, held loyalty and sorrow, shame and ambition, love and energy and desire and friendship and all the others—the hundred thousand black and white and colored threads of life—and made ready to break them and be free.

Then Duryodhana felt the cold. He had never been to the snow mountains, nor known such a chill in all his life. He went back, just to see, but round his body there was only the warm night air of Kamyaka forest. Then Duryodhana stepped back behind his eyes and looked up.

He saw Kalee standing black and terrible before him, the Goddess dressed in slit-tongued serpents hanging from her waist dripping poison, and wearing a necklace of human heads running blood over her breasts. In ten arms she held weapons and fire and disease and fear; her eyes and hair were wild, and she danced to the sound of screams.

Duryodhana smiled. "I have nothing to do with you now," he said, and again cast down his eyes.

Kalee stood still and looked straight down into his soul. "Duryodhana, do not die," she said. "I myself made your body, the upper part of diamond that can be harmed by nothing, and the lower half from mountain flowers. Be patient, do not die."

Duryodhana looked up into her savage eyes. "That you made me—does this make me your servant?" he asked.

"You who are so hard to conquer: listen. Brave warriors will fight with you against the Pandavas. I will harden their hearts. Those who live by weapons I will destroy. I am going to kill the warriors who kill. Those who now love the Pandavas will exist only to defeat them; all the Kurus will stand with you in battle. Suyodhana, good warrior, you can never be defeated by any fair weapon."

Duryodhana blinked and Kalee was gone. He heard his

men talking in the camp, and saw the morning sunlight through his tent. He got to his feet and threw back the tent curtain. The fresh air had never been so fragrant; the morning sun streamed in at his feet with clean new colors.

Karna sat by the entrance, his face covered with dust and stained with tears, his ornaments scattered. Duryodhana knelt beside him and said, "Never mind all that now. Come and eat with me."

Duryodhana returned to Hastinapura just in time for the marriage of his sister Duhsala to the Sindhu king Jayadratha. Returning home with his bride, Jayadratha stopped at Dwaitavana lake, and while his servants watered the horses and elephants Jayadratha drove his chariot alone through the forest. Then in a clearing he saw the Pandavas' house, and saw Draupadi standing at the doorway, with one arm over the branch of a tree.

Jayadratha got down from his car and approached her. "Who are you, standing here alone in the forest wind?" he asked. "I am Jayadratha."

Draupadi let go of the tree and smoothed her robes. "I am Draupadi, and it is not for me to speak with strangers from the doorway," she said. "But my husbands are gone hunting. If you will wait, they will be glad to welcome you."

"Ah, Draupadi," said Jayadratha, "who has not heard tell of your beauty? And now that I meet you I see that the tales are less than true, for you have made my heart a prisoner. You must stay hidden in the forest no longer, but leave your husbands who have no kingdom and come grace my palace, where you may be seen and admired."

"Jayadratha, be on your guard," said Draupadi angrily. "Cover your foolishness and go!"

"Look—come for a ride with me in my chariot. Just over to the lake."

"No. Do not stay here. From one look at your face the Pandavas will knew everything and you will come to injury."

"But might you not also come to harm speaking to me this way? I am in no fear of Pandavas, Princess." Draupadi turned her back on him, but Jayadratha caught her and leapt with her into his car, and his horses broke into a run.

Deep in the forest the Pandavas saw animals run from the direction of the lake and heard the warning cries of the birds telling that many men had come to the forest. They left off hunting and drove back to their house.

Near the house they found a little deer girl weeping beside the trail. Yudhishthira stopped his chariot and sat beside her. "Why are you sad?" he asked, "Tell me what has happened."

The deer girl stopped crying and wiped the tears from her face. "Oh, alas, Bharata—a jackal has dared to enter the lions' cave."

"No fear. Tell me."

"Jayadratha has stolen Draupadi. I saw him carry her away. I love her because she is kind, and I play with her by the stream and watch her. And now, all the white milk will be poured onto ashes."

Yudhishthira put his long arm around the fawn. "We will certainly get her back. When was this?"

"Not long ago—and *that* is the way he went." The little girl stood up and smiled. "Bring her back, King Yudhishthira. I am timid and afraid."

"These words cut like darts," said Bhima. "There are the broken branches from Jayadratha's car!"

When the Pandavas broke free of the forest they saw Jayadratha far ahead on the road to the west. The Sindhu King saw them coming and stopped. He told Draupadi, "Too soon! Even you are not worth my life, and I wish you no harm. Alone in this chariot I can easily outdistance them."

He helped her down. "Farewell, Princess."

Draupadi sighed. "Hurry and get out of here, Jayadratha!"

Jayadratha flicked the reins over the backs of his horses and his chariot flew away. Draupadi watched him go, then turned and watched the Pandavas racing up to her. In an instant they were upon her. Bhima and Arjuna thundered by without stopping, but Yudhishthira and the twins halted.

Sahadeva ran to her and held her in his arms. "Are you all right?"

"Yes," answered Draupadi. "Will Bhima and Arjuna catch him?"

"Yes, I think so! We'll take you back home and wait."

Draupadi looked at Yudhishthira. "Will you follow and see what happens?"

"Yes," he said. "Shall he die?"

"He . . . did me no harm."

"If we kill him," said Yudhishthira, "that is an excuse for Duryodhana. Jayadratha is now his brother. Later, we will have our kingdom again. With your permission I shall postpone his death."

Draupadi looked to the west. "Yes, do so."

Nakula and Sahadeva turned back with Draupadi, and Yudhishthira drove swiftly after Bhima and Arjuna, who were far ahead, chasing Jayadratha as fast as they could, side by side in their chariots. But they could see that he was rapidly drawing away from them.

"He will soon be only a dust cloud!" shouted Bhima. "And then he will be gone!"

Arjuna did not answer, but standing in his swaying chariot he put an arrow on his bow and sent it flying after Jayadratha. It broke the axle; the car fell over on its side, and the Sindhu king was rolling head over heels along the road.

Jayadratha picked himself up and stood holding his sword. Bhima and Arjuna reined in their horses near him, and Bhima said, "Choose which of us you will fight."

"Light in my hand is the sword," said Jayadratha. "Either of you, or both—or all three."

Yudhishthira had joined his brothers. They spoke quietly together for a moment, then Yudhishthira called out, "Jayadratha!"

"Yes?"

"Go where you will. We will not harm you."

"I insist that you fight me!"

"With Draupadi's permission I will not. Be patient, the time will come."

"Forgive me, Pandavas, I have acted against dharma, I did not first challenge you for her."

"We are to let him . . . just walk away?" asked Bhima.

"Yes," said Yudhishthira.

"I have always obeyed you," said Bhima, "and . . . I obey again! She was not hurt?"

"No," said Yudhishthira. "Come away."

❖

It was growing dark when Yudhishthira, Arjuna and Bhima returned to their forest home. Draupadi and the twins were sitting round a fire, and they joined them there and told them what had happened with Jayadratha. Then there was a movement at the edge of the firelight, and an old man, shaggy and dark, walked noiselessly up to them and sat down.

"Welcome, Vyasa," said Yudhishthira. "It has been many years. Will you have dinner with us? We've had nothing to eat since morning."

Vyasa smiled and Draupadi went inside to her kitchen. She lit the cooking fire from the tiny flame that burned for the household gods. Then she realized that they had no food.

She frowned, and thought, "Oh, Krishna! What will I do?"

Krishna stood smiling and leaning back against the wall. Draupadi jumped and put her hand to her breast. "Oh! You scared me."

Krishna said, "Princess, you got me out of bed and I'm hungry. Give me a little something to eat."

179

"That's just it. There's nothing."

"Can't your husbands catch anything?"

"Only king Jayadratha."

Krishna looked around the kitchen. "Nothing at all? I don't believe it. Just let me take a look," and he began to go through the pots and pans.

Draupadi watched him. "Why were you in bed so early?"

"Don't you know I have sixteen thousand wives?"

"You do really? I heard that but I never believed it."

"Well, why should I deny it? But look." Krishna took a rice grain and a tiny shred of vegetable from the rim of an iron pot. "Now sit down facing me, close your eyes, and be quiet. This is hard to do."

Krishna sat down on the kitchen floor, holding the bit of leaf and the grain of rice in his fingers. The sounds of the forest night fell away, and the fire flickered and died. Krishna began to speak softly in the silence.

"Now listen . . . so have I heard—

The moonlight is your smile. Earth and sky are your illusion.

At the end of Time, first comes the drought, then the seven suns that bring fire and leave Earth hushed in death and deep in ashes, overhung by burning colored clouds.

Then the lightning breaks and the water falls. Drowned are the sun and moon, and the Earth and stars. You swallow the winds and float sleeping on the dark waters, resting on Sesha the thousand-hooded serpent white as pearls.

Then you awake, and like a winking firefly at night

180

during the rains, you dart over the water, seeking
Earth. You dive and bring her back as before, and place
her on Sesha as before, and create all beings as before.

And after Time has begun again, when Sesha yawns,
quaking the Earth, do you not go to him and say:

"Just a little longer?"

*Narayana—if I have said well, take this food for all
the world."*

Krishna swallowed the bit of vegetable and the grain of
rice. The fires danced into life, and Draupadi heard the
Pandavas talking outside with Vyasa.

"Princess, open your eyes. It is done."

Draupadi looked at him. "I was hungry before, but
now . . ."

"Now no one in all the world is hungry," said Krishna.
"Everyone is full of food right up to his throat." He
shivered. "But it is very hard to do."

⁂

Krishna returned to his home far away, and Draupadi joined
the Pandavas outside. The night was cool and still, and in
the forest the partridge who feeds on the nectar of
moonbeams gazed with bright eyes on the full moon as it
rose from the trees.

Draupadi said, "We have no food for dinner."

Arjuna's eyes smiled at her, "Never mind," he said.
"Vyasa promised to tell us a story."

"But aren't you hungry? Aren't you, Vyasa?"

A gentle smile wrinkled Vyasa's face. "No, no, Princess.
What kind of story shall I tell?"

"One of love," answered Draupadi.

Vyasa looked at their faces in the firelight. "Then I shall tell you how love won over Death himself."

❖

Listen—

Savitri, the daughter of the Madra king Aswapati, was young and very beautiful. Many men came to her father's court to marry her, but she desired none of them, for they were every one graceless and idle and vain, and puffed up with pride, and stiff with empty conceit. Then Savitri told her father, "I will myself go out in my golden war chariot, and I will not return until I have found my husband."

She went to the towns and villages, but they were afraid of her, so she turned into the forests to find her mate. Her chariot broke its way through the trees, and the birds flew away in fear, while of the animals, some stood their ground and watched her, while others ran behind rocks, or into caves, or dug into the Earth, and still others hid themselves in the trees and closed their eyes.

Savitri went to the forest retreats of Brahmanas and Kshatriyas who had retired from the world, and sometime later she returned to Aswapati and said: *I have found him.*

"Who?" asked the king.

"He is Satyavan," answered Savitri. "Because Time took away King Dyumatsena's sight, so that he became blind, an enemy drove him from the throne of Salwa, and Dyumatsena went to live in the forest with his wife and their only son, Satyavan."

"Ah, I am content," said the king. "I will make

arrangements; we will go to him together." When Savitri left him, Aswapati called his minister and asked, "What of Satyavan?"

"Majesty," replied the minister, "he was born in his father's city, but as a babe in arms he was taken into the forest and has lived there ever since. He is loyal and kind, and is handsome as the moon, and has the power and energy of the sun. He is generous and brave and patient as the Earth. He has only one defect and no other—a year from this day Satyavan will die."

Aswapati told Savitri what he had heard and he said, "Change your mind. Do not marry into unhappiness."

Savitri replied, "Twice I will not choose. Whether his life be short or long, I have taken him as my husband in my heart."

Aswapati saw that her heart did not falter. "It will be as you say. Tomorrow we will go to Dyumatsena in the forest."

Then on foot the king took Savitri to Dyumatsena's hermitage, where he sat beside the blind king on grass mats under a tree, and asked him to accept Savitri for his daughter.

"How will she bear living in the forest?" asked Dyumatsena.

Aswapati said, "She and I both know that happiness and sorrow come and go their ways wherever we may be. I bow to you in friendship. Do not disregard me; do not destroy my hope."

"You are welcome," said Dyumatsena. "Blessed be you both."

❀

*And drew forth his soul, a person
no larger than a thumb*

The two kings made the marriage between Savitri and
Satyavan, and Aswapati returned to his city. With love and a
happy marriage the year of Satyavan's life passed quickly
by, and Savitri counted off the days till but one remained.
The night before he was to die she watched Satyavan asleep
by her side until the dawn. She cooked for him but did not
eat, expecting the hour and the moment, and thinking:
"Today is that day."

When the sun was two hands high, Satyavan set his axe
on his shoulder and went into the forest with Savitri to
gather firewood. Softly she followed him in seeming smiles,
watching all his moods.

Soon they came to a fallen tree. Satyavan started to cut
away its branches, but he was trembling and wet with
perspiration. When he stopped to dry himself his head
began to ache, and the light hurt his eyes. He put down the
axe and lay down with his head on Savitri's lap to rest.

When he shut his eyes his face was for a moment pale and

184

drawn. Then the color returned, and he was asleep on her thigh, peacefully. Savitri ran her fingers through his wet hair. But she felt someone watching her, and looked up.

A large man was looking at Satyavan with dark, quiet eyes. His skin was dark green, and he wore red robes and a red flower in his loose black hair. He stood but a bow's length from Satyavan, holding a small noose of silver thread in his left hand, gazing steadily at Savitri's husband with a look of great patience and kindness.

Savitri gently placed Satyavan's head on the Earth. The god looked at her, turning his head, but never his dark eyes, and she said, "Lord Yama, I am Savitri."

Yama spoke softly. "The days of Satyavan's life are full, and I have come for him."

The Death Lord reached into Satyavan's breast, on the left side, somewhere near the heart, and drew forth his soul, a person no larger than a thumb, and bound the soul in his noose. And when the soul was taken and held, Satyavan's body no longer breathed and was cold.

Yama withdrew into the forest, but Savitri followed and walked beside him. He stopped and said, "Return, and make his funeral."

Savitri said, "I have heard that you were the first man to die, to make your way to the home that cannot be taken away."

"It is so," said Yama. "Now go back. You cannot follow any farther. You are free of every tie to Satyavan, and every trust."

"All who are born must one day follow you. Let me only go a little farther, as your friend."

185

Yama stopped, and slowly turned and looked at Savitri. "It is true. You have no fear of me. I take you for my friend, and do you take in return a gift from me, whatever I can give. But I cannot give his life again to Satyavan." "

"Friendship may come after only seven steps taken together," said Savitri. "Let Dyumatsena's blindness fall away from him."

"It falls. Now return, for you are tired."

"But I am not," said Savitri. "I am with Satyavan for the last time. Give me leave to walk on awhile."

"I give. Always I take away, and again take away. It is good to be giving. Follow then if you will, and take another gift from me, except only as before."

"Let Dyumatsena regain his kingdom," said Savitri.

"He will," said Yama. He and Savitri walked on, to the south, and the branches and hanging vines parted for them to pass and closed behind. They came to a stream, and the Death Lord held water in his hands for Savitri to drink.

"It is not hard to give," said Yama, "for when life is finished, and all must be given up, it is not difficult. There is pain in life, but none in death. What is very hard is to find one worthy of giving anything to. No one escapes me. I have seen them all." He looked at Savitri. "Yet . . . this water is not clearer than your heart. You seek what you want, you choose and it is done, you do not wish to be anyone else. For long I have not seen this. Ask another gift, anything but the life of Satyavan."

"Let my father have one hundred sons."

"He shall have them," said Yama. "But ask of me something more, for yourself, anything but Satyavan's life."

Savitri answered, "Then may I too have one hundred sons by my husband."

Yama sat down on the riverbank and watched the water flow by like a silver serpent. "With no thought you answered me. You told the truth. How can you have sons if Satyavan is dead? But you did not think of that."

"No."

"I know you didn't. But he has no more life. It is all gone."

"That is why I asked nothing for myself, for I am one half dead, and I do not wish even for heaven."

Yama sighed. "I am forever equal towards every man, and I more than anyone—I know what are truth and justice. I know that all the past and all the future are held fast by truth. Danger flees from it. How much is your life worth without Satyavan?"

"Nothing, Lord."

"Will you give me half your days on Earth?"

"Yes, you may have them," said Savitri.

Again Yama's unblinking, unmoving eyes rested long on Savitri. At last he said, "It is done. I have taken your days and given them to your husband as his own. Shall I tell you the number of those days?"

"No. Will we go back now?"

The Death Lord held up his silver noose, and it was empty. "His soul rests with you. You will carry it back yourself."

Yama stood up and walked on alone, to the Land of the Dead, with an empty noose. As Savitri turned back, a lightning bolt fell striking a tree near her home.

It was night when Savitri returned, and Satyavan's corpse lay chill in the moonlight. She sat beside him, with his head in her lap, and felt his skin grow warm against her body.

Satyavan looked up at her, as one returned from a long journey will look at his home when he sees it again. Then he sat up and said, "I have slept all day. I had a dream, of being carried away."

"That one has gone," said Savitri.

"It was not a dream?"

"It's late. There burns a tree to guide us back." She helped Satyavan to his feet, and steadied him, with his arm over her shoulder and her arm round his waist. "I will carry the axe, she said, "and we will talk when we are at home."

In the hermitage, Dyumatsena was feeding wood to the fire and telling his wife stories of the kings of time gone past. He looked at Savitri and Satyavan when they arrived, and said, "There are stars in your hair to my new eyes, and gold from the firelight on your skin. Today I have recovered my sight."

They sat down and Savitri said, "Yama came to carry off your son, but he left without him. And from kindness he gave your sight, and soon your kingdom, and also sons for Aswapati and for us. Now stay, and I shall make our supper."

But Dyumatsena put his hand on her shoulder and would not let her rise, but brought the food to her himself. When they had finished, a messenger came from Salwa, and Dyumatsena said, "If it be no secret, tell us why you have come."

"There is no secret to keep," said the man. "I come from the king's minister, who says: *Majesty, with a new knife I have taken away the life of the unlawful king, and his friends have fled the city and dare not look at me. I hold the kingdom for you in those same hands. Now do what is best.*"

"That is all my story, Princess," said Vyasa. "Savitri made misfortune into happiness, and here you do the same for your husbands, for though they are banished and in exile, they do not lose heart with you to love."

Kausika the brahmana, who is now
roasting in Hell, set his heart on
Virtue, and in all his life never told
a lie, even in jest.

Once having seen their helpless
victim run past him and hide,
Kausika sitting where the rivers
meet answered the thieves: *"That
way."*

So be as the swan, who drinks
from milk and water mixed
together, whichever one he choose,
leaving the other behind.

9: VIRata

Majesty, a month had passed since Vyasa's visit, when the Pandavas, hunting in the forest, saw a magnificent deer watching them from among the trees. They stalked him on foot, and when they were very near each one sent an arrow flying at him. But they did not hit him, and the deer bounded away and stopped again to watch them at a distance. The Pandavas followed, and he led them deeper and deeper into the forest, until finally he vanished without a trace.

Tired and thirsty, the Pandavas rested under a tree. Nakula said, "We should have hit him, we had enough chances."

"Well, we didn't," said Yudhishthira. "Climb this tree and see if there is any water nearby."

From above, Nakula saw water-loving trees growing not far from them and heard the call of cranes. Yudhishthira sent him to bring water in his empty quiver.

But Nakula did not return. Yudhishthira sent Sahadeva after his brother, with arrows and a bow, and waited a long time for him. But he didn't come back either.

Then Arjuna followed their footprints. Yudhishthira thought, "Nothing can stop Arjuna." But Arjuna did not return.

Yudhishthira told Bhima, "Go, and I will follow after a hundred heartbeats. If you meet anything at all, cry out to me."

When Yudhishthira started to follow him, Bhima was out of sight, moving noiselessly through the forest. Yudhishthira carefully crept along, an arrow fitted on his bow, but he heard no sign of danger and saw no menace. The forest ended at the edge of a crystal lake, and Yudhishthira moved out under the open sky. He could not believe what he saw there.

Like fallen rainbows, his four brothers lay motionless on the lakeshore. He bent over them. They were dead, without a mark on them, without a sign of life.

They looked like the Guardian Gods of the four quarters of the world struck down at the end of Time. Yudhishthira sat near the water and whispered, "Arjuna, you lie dead, Gandiva bow beside you, your arrows spilled over the sand. And my hopes are dead with you. Bhima . . . all is now fruitless. How have you died, with no footprint here but your own? Who could do this? Each one of you was powerful as a thundering waterfall, and the color on your faces has not yet faded. It is even so—but first, I will drink . . . "

"Do not!"

Yudhishthira looked up, but there was no one. Then again the invisible voice spoke.

"This is my lake. I am a crane, living on tiny fish. And I

have slain your brothers, for they would not answer my questions."

"Who are you to have done this?" asked Yudhishthira. "A bird could not do so."

"I am what I am," said the voice. "Good fortune to you! Your brothers drank of my lake without answering me, and they are dead. First came Nakula with an empty quiver. I told him: *First answer my questions, then take as much water as you will.* But he drank anyway, and died.

"Then Sahadeva came, and it was the same; his rashness cost him his life. When I spoke to Arjuna he challenged me to show myself. He sent iron arrows flying in every direction. But I asked what need he had of such trouble, when he had only to answer me and then drink. But he scorned me, thinking me small and helpless, and drank as he wished, and died.

"Bhima came and I spoke to him. He heard me, but did not look up, and because he thought he would have to fight against me, he first killed his thirst, and also himself. Now you have come, and I tell you the same: *First answer my questions, then drink however much you will.*"

Yudhishthira thought he was under a spell, but he listened to the deer and the bear among the trees, and to the birds singing, and the rushes and canes swaying in the wind, and he knew he was not.

"Ask."

"Who then is the friend given by the gods?" said the invisible voice.

"It is the wife who is that friend and safe refuge," answered Yudhishthira.

"What is heavier than the Earth?"

"A mother."

"What is higher than heaven?"

"A father."

"What is swifter than the wind?"

"The mind is swifter than the wind."

"What is more numerous than the blades of grass in a meadow?"

"Our thoughts number more than that."

"What does not move after its birth into the world?"

"An egg does not move."

"What has no heart?"

"A stone."

"What is the support of man?"

"The clouds."

"Who is the friend of the sick?"

"The physician."

"And the friend of the dying man?"

"That friend is charity."

"Who is the guest that all life is host to?"

"Fire."

"What is all the universe?"

"It is but thin air and empty space."

"What forever travels alone?"

"The sun."

"What is reborn after its birth?"

"The moon."

"What is the best of all things that are praised?"

"Skill."

"What is the most valuable possession?"

"Knowledge."

"What is not thought of until it departs?"

"Health."

"What is the best happiness?"

"Contentment."

"What makes one wealthy if it is cast away?"

"Greed."

"And what is greed?"

"It is poison."

"What covers all the world?"

"Darkness."

"What keeps a thing from discovering itself?"

"That is also darkness."

"What enemy cannot be overcome?"

"That is anger."

"What is honesty?"

"That is to look, and to see every living creature as yourself, bearing your own will to live, and your own fear of death."

"How may peace be false?"

"When it is tyranny."

"What is an incurable disease?"

"A false friend."

"Why are friends forsaken?"

"For avarice."

"What is envy?"

"Grief of the heart."

"And what is grief?"

"It is ignorance."

"What causes desire for possessions?"

"Nothing else than the possessions themselves."

"Who is in Hell, though he lives on Earth?"

"The wealthy man who neither enjoys himself nor gives to others."

"What is it that men call good fortune?"

"That is the result of what they have done honestly."

"Who is dishonest?"

"The unmerciful."

"What is hypocrisy?"

"The setting up of religious standards for others is hypocrisy."

"Kindness, profit, and desire are each hostile to the others. How may they be brought together?"

"When a wife is kind, then all the three are in one."

"Who is truly happy?"

"The man without any debts."

"What is the greatest wonder of all?"

"Every day Death takes lives beyond counting, yet those who live think: *Death can never come this day to me.*"

"What is the rarest thing?"

"To know when to stop."

"What is true wealth?"

"Love and kindness are better than gold; honor is more valuable than rooms full of jewels. I don't know what you think of all this."

"You answer well," said the invisible voice. "I am your father Dharma. I came to test your merit, and I have found it true, and I return your brothers to life."

Yudhishthira wet his upper garment with water and wrung it out over his brothers, so that they came to life. He

198

told them, "Because you would not obey Dharma, he made poison of the water and you were dead until I answered him."

Arjuna picked up his bow and scattered arrows. "I feel better than before I died. When we reach our chariots, I will shoot a deer for each of us."

"One deer will do," said Sahadeva.

"Why only one?"

"Because at midnight tomorrow, the thirteenth year begins."

❖❖❖

The next day, having hidden their chariots by illusion, the five Pandavas and Draupadi easily slipped out of Kamyaka forest past Duryodhana's spies, crossed the Yamuna river unseen, and entered the Matsya country ruled by the aged king Virata. By the road near Matsya city was a cemetery strewn over with charred corpses, and there grew a giant Sami tree, the kind whose twigs and branches are made into firesticks.

Yudhishthira said, "Our bows and swords must be hidden or we will be known. No one will come near this tree except to burn the dead, and it will not be cut down, for it is the sacred mother of fire."

Nakula took all their bows and swords and arrows, wrapped them in leather, and carried them up the tree. He hid them where rain could not go, nor anyone see them from below. When he had come down, they saw shepherds approaching driving their sheep to the city, and Arjuna and Bhima chose a corpse and hung it from a limb.

Yudhishthira told the shepherds, "We are hunters from the hills, and that is our mother, who has died at the age of one hundred and eighty years. We are hanging her here by the custom of our ancestors."

The Matsya men wished them peace, and hurried by.

The Pandavas walked a little farther towards the city; at sunset they made their camp in a field by the roadside and talked over how they would live disguised in Matsya.

⚜

In the morning Yudhishthira went to Virata's court. Virata saw him by the palace door and told one of his men, "There stands a fair man, very tall and slender, with a wide face and a bent nose, holding something tied in blue cloth. Bring him here."

Yudhishthira came, and the king asked, "Who are you? I have never seen you before in Matsya."

Yudhishthira replied, "I am Kanka the brahmana. Having wandered for many years seeking knowledge, and having in the forest learned the science of dice, I now desire to live in Matsya."

"And what will you do?"

"If you will support me in your household I will teach you dice, and also how to move the four-colored ivory chessmen." Yudhishthira untied his blue cloth and showed Virata his golden dice, set with turquoise dots. "With these or with others, of one color or red against black, I can teach you to play so that you will never lose. But if I stay with you, let it be said that I shall not be involved in any dispute because of dice."

"Kanka, you are welcome," said Virata. "It will be as you

say, and I will answer for you. To you all my doors are open, and if anyone pressed down by misfortune, or seeking work, comes to you, then come straight to me, at any hour, and on your word I shall see him."

That afternoon Kanka and Virata were playing dice when the king glanced out a window and saw a tall, heavy man, dressed in black, passing by below. He was fair, his eyes were large and dark as a bull's, there were three creases in his thick neck, his shoulders were broad and his arms long and graceful. He walked like an elephant, he was proud and sensitive, and he wore his hair bound in a cloth and carried a large brass ladle.

"Look," said Virata, "there passes another stranger."

Kanka said, "I met him on the road. His name is Vallabha. He was King Yudhishthira's cook, and he made many meals for me."

"Were they good?"

"Better than here in your palace, Majesty."

"Call him in and let me talk to him."

Bhima came in, and told Virata, "I served Yudhishthira but now he has vanished and I have no work. I have come to Matsya from the Kuru kingdom."

Virata said, "Vallabha, you served an unfortunate king, and you are unemployed through no fault of your own. If your master had only had my friend Kanka with him, he would never have lost Indraprastha at dice. Where has the Pandava king gone?"

Vallabha looked sad and hopeless. "No one knows, Majesty. But I think that he and his brothers have finally died of shame. Their exile weighed heavily upon them, and though I made my best dishes for them, they would not eat, but slowly wasted away from grief. Not only their bodies, but their minds as well failed them, and one day, having entered the deep forest with Draupadi, they did not return. Even she could not cheer them. Tigers or bears may have eaten them, for they had no strength. I waited many days. But then there was no more food, and I am no hunter, so I had to leave the forest and wander away."

"When the spirit wishes to leave the body, it will not long remain," said Virata. "Duryodhana had not courage enough to kill them himself, yet he has succeeded after all. Now go to my kitchen and make our dinner, and if you are as good as Kanka says I will put you over all my cooks."

⚜

In the evening Draupadi went to the women's gate of Virata's palace, dressed as a serving maid. Her fine black hair, soft as the touch of a breeze, was bound with silk into a single braid that fell forward over her shoulder. She wore a scarf over her head, and was dressed in a single piece of expensive silk that was soiled and worn. A maidservant came from the palace to light the lamps in the courtyard, and when Draupadi asked, she opened the gate and led her to Sudeshna, Virata's Queen.

"I seek work in your majesty's service," Draupadi told the Queen.

Sudeshna was surprised at Draupadi's beauty, but she thought, "She must really be a servant, for no other woman would injure her reputation doing this work."

Sudeshna asked, "Who are you?"

202

Draupadi replied, "Majesty, Satyabhama, the wife of Krishna, called me Malini, the garland weaver, but truly I have no name but Sairindhri, the serving maid. I am a sairindhri, very skilled in dressing hair, in making perfumes, and in tying together garlands of jasmine and ginger, lotus and blue lily petals. I left Dwaravati to see the world, but only with Satyabhama's permission. Now I have come very far. Let me work for you, and earn good food and fine clothes."

"I cannot believe you are a sairindhri," said Sudeshna. "Your dark blue skin sets off your black eyes like the setting of a jewel. Your eyelashes are long and curved, and your voice is sweet as love. You could be the mistress of however many servants you desired, all by a glance, or the Queen of all Earth's kingdoms. You are a goddess, sent to test me. Are you Lakshmi? Which goddess are you?"

"No goddess," smiled Sairindhri, "but only a maidservant out of work."

"But the king has seen me often," said Sudeshna, "and you not at all. You will burn us with your beauty. Though you do nothing, the women will envy you and no man will be able to resist you."

"Queen, your own name means good-looking, and you do not belie it. No one needs to see me but yourself. Also, I have five Gandharva husbands, the sons of Chitraratha, who watch over me. I desire no man of Matsya."

"But why serve others then?"

"Majesty, those Gandharvas wait for me always. But once I go to them in heaven I can never return. And they tire of heavenly women. Let me serve you, but I will not wash anyone's feet, nor eat leftover food."

"Alright," said Sudeshna. "You will serve only me, to make me more beautiful."

❦

King Virata, very comfortably full, sat smiling to himself after dinner when Kanka joined him. "Vallabha has become my personal chef," said the king. "After such a meal, I am ready for anything."

"Come outside with me a moment then," said Kanka. "Since you spoke before everyone that I am your agent, I think that many who hesitated to approach you are now coming to me. There is a cowherd outside who predicts that tonight the round silver moon will be swallowed up."

"Forever?" asked the king anxiously.

"No. Rahu the demon will swallow the Lord of the Lotus, but because Rahu has only a head and no body . . . "

"Ah! Of course, I remember," said the king. "The moon will come out his neck—I know. I am well educated. I studied all the natural sciences as a boy. When Rahu stole a sip of amrita, the sun and the moon told Narayana, who sliced off his head with the discus before he could swallow. But that head is immortal, and whenever he gets the chance . . . but who told you this?"

"Tantripala, a stranger like myself, by birth a cowherd, and unemployed."

Virata called for a lamp. Kanka led him behind the palace to the cow barns. There a bearded man dressed in deerskin met them and spoke in the tongue of the cowherds,

"Majesty, I am Tantripala. I know instantly the past and future of all cattle I see. When I care for them, they are never ill, and they multiply under my hand. And I have some lesser skill in reading the stars."

Virata craned his neck and peered up at the sky. "What then? Can you see Rahu?"

"No," answered Sahadeva. "The Meteor King is dark as smoke and cannot be seen. But I have made calculations with numbers, and from that I believe he will overtake the moon tonight. And if my prediction comes true, that will prove my skill and perhaps I might find work with you, Majesty."

"As an astronomer?"

"No," said Tantripala. "This is an exhibition to catch your attention. I am better skilled at caring for cattle."

As he spoke the moonlight dimmed, and Virata looked up into heaven's depth. The moon became a ghost of himself, then a sliver of light growing, then again the full moon.

Virata was relieved. "Ah, the King of Stars is free!"

"This one speaks truth," said Kanka. "I would hire him."

"Don't you want to be my astronomer?" asked Virata.

Tantripala smiled. "But wait till you see your cattle increase. You will be more wealthy than ever. Each cow will give more milk, and the wild ones will gentle."

"Can you talk to them?"

"Majesty, they say nothing of interest. But someone who understands them ought to be with them to put the right ideas into their minds, so that they may know when they are happy."

"I hire you," said Virata. "Care for all my hundred thousand cattle, and Kanka will give you a room in the palace."

⚜

During that night, Arjuna sat in the fields under the stars gathering his power deep within him. When the moon disappeared he said, "Now I call down Urvasi's curse—may my manliness be gone for one year."

When the moon hung low in the west he said, "May my hair be long as my shadow."

When the sun rose he said, "May golden ornaments grace me."

Wide gold bracelets hid the white scars of the bowstring on both his arms, and his long hair fell to his knees, set off by earrings and ornaments, when Arjuna entered Virata's court the next morning. Virata saw him, dressed in women's robes, of slight frame and dark, with square shoulders high as a lion's, long wavy hair and large red eyes.

The king summoned him and asked, "Who are you? You dress as a woman, but you were not so born."

Arjuna replied, "I am Vrihannala, a son or a daughter, without a father or mother."

"How could this happen to one like you?"

"Majesty, what good would it be for you to hear a story that can only give me pain to tell? But I am an expert in singing and dancing, and in playing on the lute. All this I can teach to your daughter Uttarah, that she may have talents to enrich her beauty."

Once Virata heard Vrihannala play the heavenly music learned from Chitraratha, he ordered his servants to make

The moon became a ghost of himself

certain that Vrihannala was no longer a man, and then led him to the women's part of the palace. There in the inner apartments Vrihannala began to teach music and dancing to the princess, and there he lived with the women in an impenetrable disguise.

Another stranger approached Virata when the king went to look at his horses. The man was dark and handsome, with a broad chest, and arms hard as iron. His pale eyes were burned by the wind; his hair was bleached nearly white by the sun.

Nakula said, "Jaya, Virata Raja. I am Granthika, a horseman from Sindh. Put your horses in my care, and they shall never be lame. They will be faster, they will live longer, they will never fall or bite. I will feed them carefully and make iron plates for their feet."

"Did you work for the Sindhu king Jayadratha?" asked Virata.

"He almost consulted me once," replied Granthika, "but two of my brothers solved the king's problem for him, doing just what I would have done. But Sindh is a desolate land, will you not hire me, Majesty?"

"Yes, you are welcome," said Virata.

In this way, the Pandavas and Draupadi lived unknown in Matsya for nearly a year, as well hidden as though they were once more in their mother's womb. Yudhishthira and Nakula shared with the others the gold they won at dice and horse racing; Bhima and Sahadeva shared food from the royal kitchens and milk and butter from the cows; and Arjuna sold old clothes from the inner apartments, dividing what he received with Draupadi and his brothers.

Now during this thirteenth year, Bharata, in heaven Indra resolved to beg from Karna his armor and earrings. But the Sun Lord Surya discovered is intent, and spoke to Karna in a dream, as he slept in Champa.

The Eye of all the World told his son, "To save Arjuna, Indra will come to you in the guise of a brahmana to take your natural armor and ornaments. With these you can never be defeated. Never give them up, or you will shorten your life. Refuse him, and make him take something else, for he cannot insist on taking part of your own body."

But in his dream Karna answered, "If he comes I will give him what he asks. Whatever is asked of me, I give it, for honor's sake. And this, by itself, lengthens life in this world and supports it in the next. I will not save my life by any meanness, for honor nourishes as a mother, and I shall protect her, even by offering up my body in the sacrifice of battle."

The Sun Lord said, "Do not anything harmful to yourself. Honor loves nothing better than taking life, yet when you are dead you will care no more for her than for the garland of flowers around the neck of your corpse as it burns. If you wish to defeat Arjuna, trust to my words."

Karna said, "Lord of the Day, you are more dear to me than my own self, but I can withstand Arjuna with armor or without it. You have come and told me this, thinking: *Karna knows no other god in heaven*. And for this, I will not surrender my armor without receiving something in exchange from Indra. For the rest, you must forgive me."

Surya said, "You seek fame as well, and you will have it," and vanished from Karna's dream.

The next day, as he sat outside in the morning, Karna told all his dream to the Sun, and Surya said smiling, "It is even so!"

Then at noon came a kindly old brahmana. His clothes, though worn thin, were spotless and clean; his white hair was neatly brushed; his eyes were clear. He looked at Karna and said, "Anga King, give me."

"You are welcome," said Karna, kneeling in the sunlight. "Villages with cattle, a necklace of gold, beautiful virgins—which will you have?"

"Majesty, give such things to those who ask for them," said the brahmana. "But for me, cut off your armor and your earrings, Maharaja."

"Take rather a homestead, and many fields."

"But I don't want them."

"I can't give you what you ask," said Karna. "Take instead the entire kingdom of all the Earth."

"No."

"You want nothing else?"

"Nothing."

Karna laughed. "But it is you, Indra, who ought to be giving gifts to me! Aren't you ashamed to pretend to be poor and beg for things?"

The Thunder Lord smiled. "I do it to increase your fame!"

"At least give me something of yours in exchange, or you can go away just as you came."

"There is nothing the sun cannot see," said Indra. "Tell me what you would have."

"Lord of the Gods, it is said that you have an infallible dart that cannot leave your hand without killing the one at whom it is thrown. Is this true? Is the dart truly so?"

"It is true, every word, just as you say."

"I will cut away my armor for that dart."

Indra thought of that weapon and it appeared in his hand. It was taller than a man, fitted with radiant wings, and sharper than words. "When I throw this," said Indra, "it returns to my hand. After you throw it, it will return to me with the blood of your enemy on it. But if you throw this dart when your life is not in great peril, it will fall upon you."

So Karna with his sword cut off his armor and earrings, and gave them, wet with blood, to Indra in exchange for Indra's Dart, and on Karna's body no scar remained from those wounds.

Than the strong,
There is always one stronger.

10: the invasion

After the Pandavas had passed nearly a year in Matsya, Virata's general, Kichaka, came one day to the inner rooms to visit his sister Sudeshna. There he saw Sairindhri, and he no sooner saw her than he desired her.

Kichaka told the Queen, "She should not be a servant. Let me have her."

Sudeshna said, "First you must win her. I will let her go only if she wants to. But go to your home, and I will send her over for some reason."

Kichka went home and had a fine meal prepared for two. In the palace, Sudeshna gave Sairindhri a bottle of old wine, and told her, "Take this to Kichaka."

"Majesty, send another," said Sairindhri.

"He will do you no harm," said the Queen, and fearful of drawing attention to herself by refusing, Sairindhri obeyed.

She found Kichaka sitting on his bed, with a banquet laid out before him on a low table. He was strongly built and handsome, dressed in the finest silks, wearing golden earrings and bracelets. He had black hair and olive skin, and he stroked his moustache and smiled happily at Sairindhri and rose as she entered the room.

"Dear one," he said in a winning voice, "stay here and live with me as my wife. Do not continue to be a servant. Here you will find the happiness you deserve, and your beauty will not be wasted. I will throw away all my other wives. I will share my wealth. I will do anything you wish, if you will favor me with your love."

"May you always have good fortune," replied Sairindhri. "I do not deserve this honor, and also I am already married to five Gandharvas."

"No, Sairindhri," said Kichaka. "I don't believe in Gandharvas. I am myself the real lord of Matsya. Virata is old and depends on me to protect the kingdom. I am the best man in all the world whom you could possibly choose for your husband."

"Kichaka, you are like a child trying to catch the moon. Do not seek for what you cannot have."

"Will you not sit down and drink with me?" asked Kichaka. "I have robes and ornaments ready for you to put on."

"No. Take this wine, then I must go."

Kichaka caught hold of Sairindhri's arm. "The Queen has many servants. Surely you can spend the day here with me."

Sairindhri broke free and fled, with Kichaka running after her. She ran to the palace and fell weeping at Virata's feet. Kichaka followed and caught her by the hair, smiling at the king and at Kanka the brahmana, who watched him with narrow copper-colored eyes.

"What is this?" asked Virata.

216

Kichaka said, "A timid doe, Majesty. But one worth chasing."

"No," said the king. "Let her go." He asked Sairindhri, "Who are you who seek my protection?"

"I am Sairindhri, the Queen's servant," she said. "Do not allow this one such freedom with those who work for you. I am already married. Surely my husbands will kill him for this. They are heavenly Gandharvas, very jealous, and it is a wonder that he is still alive."

"Not knowing what has happened," said Virata, "how can I say anything?"

"He tried to force me to stay in his home."

"Is that true, Kichaka?"

"Yes. What I want, I take!"

Virata asked Sairindhri, "Did the Queen give you to him?"

"No, she only sent me to take him some wine."

"Then return to her, for you have done her bidding. Kichaka, you may speak with me later of this, but you may not steal her."

Kichaka said, "Yes, Majesty. Sudeshna will not refuse her to me!" And he left the palace smiling to himself.

Sairindhri said, "If my husbands harm him, that will harm your kingdom."

Kanka the brahmana looked at her. "Your husbands have done nothing. I do not believe they will harm Kichaka if he leaves you alone. So do not interrupt our dice game by lying on the floor and weeping like an actress."

"You will be safe," said Virata. "I cannot rebuke Kichaka in front of you, but I will settle this alone with him. Tell the

Queen that I order her to keep you by her side. We cannot be too careful when dealing with Gandharvas, and their forbearance is our good fortune. Think no more about it."

"My husbands are extremely kind," said Sairindhri, and went her way to the Queen. But as she walked through the palace, Kichaka stepped out from a doorway and pulled her into an empty room.

"Sairindhri, let our union take place."

She cast down her eyes and whispered, "I was overcome by your concern for me. We must find a secret place. In the palace garden is the dancing hall used by Vrihannala. Meet me there at midnight, when it is empty and deserted."

Kichaka was delighted over his conquest. He tilted back Sairindhri's head and looked into her eyes. "Now you will know a man worthy of you at last. I will meet you there." Draupadi smiled sweetly, and turned away.

When Sairindhri returned, the Queen saw that her eyes were red with anger and asked, "What is wrong? Did he hurt you?"

"He tried."

"Then he is shameless after all. If you like, I will have him slain. I put my trust in him to behave well."

"But Virata protects him."

"Sudeshna laughed. "That is nothing. I have only to say a word, and. . ."

"You need not," said Sairindhri. "Others will slay him. Now I'm going to take a bath!"

⚜

Bhima was resting in his room off the kitchen. As soon as he saw Draupadi's face he closed his door and asked, "What?"

She held him closely. "Oh, Bhima, are you still alive? The others are dead. . . I do not know them. . . they are servants to Duryodhana. . . and I have no protection. Do not be lost to me!" She began to cry silently, hiding her face in his breast. Bhima pressed her soft hand to his cheek, and himself wept for a moment. Then he held Draupadi till she stopped crying, and wiped away her tears.

"Now tell me," he said.

"It is Kichaka. He will not leave me alone. And I am only Sairindhri."

"Where?" asked Bhima in a flat voice.

"Midnight, in the dancing hall."

"Do not go, Draupadi." Three heavy lines furrowed Bhima's brow. Smoke shot from his eyes, and his eyelashes stood on end. He licked the corners of his mouth and said, "Do not be fooled by disguises. Sahadeva knows what is true. Nakula finds out everything by friendliness. Yudhishthira is unwavering, and Arjuna is generous. But—I am the Wind, from beyond the ends of the world!"

❦

A bed was at one end of the dancing hall, and there Bhima lay covered up when Kichaka entered the dark room at midnight. Virata's general looked very handsome, carrying a lamp, and walking to the bed as a moth flies to a flame.

"I have already set aside an apartment and servants for you," said Kichaka, putting his lamp on a table. "And since you have accepted me, all the women have said that there is not another man in all the world so handsome as I."

Bharata, Bhima had been burning with anger, but when he heard this he had to laugh. He jumped out of bed and made a courtly bow to Kichaka, and said, "Oh, it is good that you are such a treat for women! And how well you praise yourself! There will be, Kichaka, no one in the world like you."

"So she ran to the cook!" Kichaka drew his sword.

A hateful look fell over Bhima's face. Kichaka rushed at him with the sword. Bhima dodged away, but Kichaka kicked him while he was off balance, and he fell to his knees, gasping for breath. Kichaka carefully aimed his sword to strike off his head, and swiftly the blade flashed through the air.

Then a dark and wild wind seized that building and shook it like a leaf. The sword cut into the floor and Bhima was on his feet. He crushed Kichaka in his arms, cracking his bones with the snap of bamboo splitting in a fire. Roaring like a tiger, Bhima rolled his enemy up into a shapeless ball of flesh and jumped out the window as Virata's guards ran up with torches.

They were Kichaka tribesmen, and they stared at their general in dismay and asked, "Where are his arms and legs? Where is his neck? Surely, no human could do this?"

❦

The Kichakas decided that Sairindhri's Gandharva husbands had killed him, and in the morning, when they took the body to be burned, some of them captured Sairindhri and carried her away to be thrown on the burning pyre.

They hustled Draupadi to the head of the procession, then at the cemetery they set a man to guard her while they built the pyre. He held Draupadi's arm with one hand, and a mace with the other.

Softly, a gold coin fell at the guard's feet, as though from heaven. He let go of her and bent over to pick it up and was kicked head over heels into the half-built pyre. A voice whispered in Draupadi's ear: *"Do not look!"*

Vaishravana the Treasure Lord was in the air over Draupadi's head, his face a nightmare mask of terror, laughing flames out of his mouth. He roared like a volcano, and grimaced with rage, and flashed his eyes, and waved all his arms about, and when the Kichakas could gather their wits they ran away to the city. The Treasure Lord pitched a few trees after them and roasted Kichaka's corpse to a cinder.

Then he was invisible, and gently holding Draupadi in his arms, he flew through the walls of Virata's palace to her room. There he let her down and flew away.

Virata was at his palace gate when the Kichakas ran up. They cried out to him, "Sairindhri is indeed protected by Gandharvas. Majesty, she is too attractive. If she remains here, we are all in danger."

"Be quiet!" said the king. "You have *dared* steal her to burn! You have dared too much! I am patient enough, and I am old, *but I am no serving maid!* Go hide somewhere before I get mad."

Sudeshna found Sairindhri in her room and wept over her, that she was safe. Together they went into the room where Vrihannala was giving dancing lessons, and when they saw her, the women all ran to Sairindhri, saying, "You are safe. You have returned to us."

"Sairindhri, from what danger have you escaped?" asked Vrihannala.

Draupadi replied, "Blessed Vrihannala, with your shell

bracelets, you who always live here so happily—what concern is Sairindhri's fate to you?"

Vrihannala smiled and brushed her long hair back over her shoulder and said, "Why, I have lived here with you, and naturally I care for you. But no one can read another's heart, so you cannot know mine."

❖

In Hastinapura, the last of Duryodhana's spies returned, and said, "They are gone without a trace. They have either died unknown or run away in fear. But also, Kichaka of the Matsya kingdom has died, and the old king Virata is without a general."

When he heard this, Duryodhana put the Pandavas out of his mind and sent a message to his friend Susarman, the Trigarta king, saying: *"Let us steal Virata's cattle while he is helpless."*

The King of the Three Castles gathered his men from the northern mountains and marched to Hastinapura. Duryodhana told him, "Go first, and draw Virata away from his city. Then return here and we will divide the cattle between us."

Then Susarman set out for Matsya, and the next day Duryodhana and the Kurus followed in his path.

When the Trigartas crossed over the twin river into Matsya and drove before them a few of Virata's cattle, the cowherds quickly told the king. Virata, and Kanka the brahmana, and Vallabha the cook, and the cowherd Tantripala, and Granthika, came out of Matsya in war

222

chariots, chasing Susarman. Then came the elephants like moving hills; then followed the horsemen like thunder.

By nightfall they could see the fires of the Trigarta camp. But when they came the next day to where the fires had been, they found the stolen cattle abandoned there, and in the distance they saw Susarman's army split in a hundred ways, impossible to overtake.

That same day Duryodhana and the Kurus took all the rest of the Matsya cattle. Again the alarm reached the city. But every warrior had gone with Virata, and in the palace there was only Virata's son, Uttara, ruling the kingdom for his father.

The young prince said, "I would drive them away, but there is no charioteer left in Matsya!"

Arjuna heard, and told Draupadi, "Tell the prince, that Vrihannala, once long ago, was a charioteer and will drive for him today."

Draupadi told Uttara, "Come to the women's rooms. Vrihannala once held the reins of Arjuna's chariot, when Khandava forest burned."

Uttara began to throw on his armor. "Send my sister," he said. "Have him come here right now!"

Uttarah ran to the dark-skinned Vrihannala like lightning racing to meet a thundercloud. Wearing only her heavy golden necklace and a zone of pearls round her hips below her slender waist; shining with excitement she held him in her arms fragrant with sandalwood. "My brother. They are taking our cattle. Come on!"

She led him to Uttara's lion-bannered chariot. There

Arjuna told the prince, "If it is singing or dancing, I know what to do, but I. . ."

"Singer or dancer or whatever," said Uttara, "just hold the reins and take me to the Kurus!"

And while all the women of the palace watched and laughed at him, Arjuna first tried to step into his armor as if it were a dress. He seemed not to know where anything went, and Uttara himself had to tie on his mail. Finally they were both in the chariot, with many bows and countless arrows brought by the princess, and Uttara told his sister, "Have no fear. The Kurus would never have come had they known we would be here to fight them!"

Uttarah and her maidens called out to Vrihannala, "Try to be brave. And bring us back some cloth for our dolls from the fine war clothes of the Kurus."

❧

The chariot sped away from the city. Soon Uttara saw the invaders; he saw Karna and Bhishma, Duryodhana and Kripa, Drona and Aswatthaman, and the down on his body stood up in fear.

"Stop, Vrihannala!"

Vrihannala said, "Be calm. We are not even close to them yet. You told me: *Take me to those Kurus*—so we must go there."

"Let them alone. Let people laugh at me. Still I don't have to meet them!" Uttara dropped his bow and jumped from the chariot, running back to the city. Vrihannala ran after him, his long hair flowing, and his woman's robes waving from under his armor.

He caught Uttara and dragged him back to the chariot. "Vrihannala, good Vrihannala of handsome waist, set me free," pleaded the prince. "A long life is best. I have no one with me. I cannot face those warriors tall as trees."

Arjuna laughed and set Uttara in the driver's box. "Then drive the car for me. Back to the city, to the cemetery tree."

"Oh, let the city perish into a desert, there is no need for a battle."

"Be still. Drive to the Sami tree." When they were at the tree, Arjuna said, "Climb it and bring down the package wrapped in deerskin."

"But a corpse hangs there!" said Uttara.

"Oh, fear the living and not the dead."

Uttara climbed and brought down the package and cut it open. In it were five bows and five swords, that shone like planets rising, and five conchshell trumpets, and the lightning crown, and arrows.

"Whose are these, Vrihannala?"

"That long bow," said Arjuna, "with a hundred golden bosses, with no knot or strain in it, is Gandiva, the bow of Arjuna. The one with golden elephants is Bhima's. The bow with sixty golden scarabs on the back belongs to Yudhishthira. The one with three suns is Nakula's, and this last, set with diamonds and gems, is Sahadeva's."

"But the Pandavas. . ."

"Please be still. Now the thousand arrows in two quivers—those are Arjuna's, and this is his sword with a frog on the hilt. The iron arrows are Bhima's, and the sword in tigerskin with bells is his. The quiver with five tigers on it and the dark blue sword in goatskin are Nakula's. Sahadeva's arrows are all painted with colors, and the thick ones with triple heads are Yudhishthira's. The curving scimitar is Sahadeva's, and the flexible sword of flashing Nishada steel is Yudhishthira's."

"But. . ."

"Be still. Have you alone not heard how the Pandavas must spend one year hidden in a city? I am Arjuna. Kanka the brahmana is Yudhishthira, Vallabha is Bhima, Tantripala is Sahadeva, Granthika is Nakula, and Sairindhri is Draupadi."

"Oh, welcome, Arjuna! But—how could you have lost your manhood?"

"That was my disguise, and now it is finished." Arjuna removed his bracelets and put on his archer's gloves of lizard skin. He tied up his hair, put on his sword and diadem, and set his bow and arrows in the chariot. He took his shell and said, "Put the rest back in the tree, and let's go."

While Uttara climbed the Sami tree, Arjuna sat facing the east and called to mind all his heavenly weapons with their binding spells. The weapons came, and joined their hands to him, and said, "We are here, Bharata. We are your servants."

He answered them silently, "Dwell in my memory."

Uttara knelt before him. "Command me. Into which part of the Kauravas shall we penetrate?"

Arjuna motioned him to get in the chariot, and blew the conchshell Devadatta. The horses fell down to their knees, and Uttara sat down with a bump in the driver's box. Agni the Fire Lord heard it, and down from the sky he threw Arjuna's flag that showed Hanuman the monkey chief. The flagstaff crashed into the pole socket, and it was not just a picture of Hanuman, but this time it was the monkey himself, yelling and screaming enough to make the blood run backwards. Even the lion on Uttara's banner began to roar and frisk his tail.

"Now press your feet on the floor and don't be afraid as if you were an ordinary person!" shouted Arjuna. He jumped into the chariot. "Just hold on, and I'll try Devadatta again!"

He put the shell to his lips and blew a second blast from it, and the birds fell stunned out of all the trees.

Uttara laughed. "Considering who you are, how can I say that this is wonderful?" He said something quietly to the four horses, and they knew they had a master driver behind them, and the chariot moved off with a shattering noise. Then Arjuna swiftly strung his bow. He drew it and let go and the bowstring rang in the air.

Duryodhana rode his bull elephant over to Bhishma's chariot.

"That can be no one but Arjuna," he said. "We have discovered him, and he must return to the forest for twelve more years!"

Bhishma smiled. "Duryodhana, now be on your guard, and choose between war and peace, for the thirteenth year was full when first you heard the cry of Devadatta and the twang of Gandiva bow."

⚜

Drona came over in his chariot. "Look, a jackal runs through our army—and he escapes unstruck. Stars spill from the sky though it is day, and the cows are lowing, gazing at the pale sun. Our fires die, our weapons will not shine, our flowers fade, and the dust darkens in the air."

"I will not give back the Pandava kingdom," said Duryodhana.

"Then take half the army," said Bhishma, "and set out for Hastinapura with the cattle. We will fight Ajuna with the rest."

Drona drew his chariot away and watched Arjuna. From Gandiva bow two arrows fell together at Drona's feet. Two others passed his head, and their feathers touched his ears.

Drona strung his bow. "Arjuna salutes me, and whispers in my ears. Who will win this day?"

❦

Arjuna said, "Listen and remember. In front is Karna, with a white flag showing an elephant rope. And in back, as usual, is Duryodhana on an elephant, with a gold flag showing an elephant. Kripa is in front wearing a tigerskin; his car is drawn by red horses; his flag is blue, and on it is an altar of gold. And there is Drona, with a gold flag showing a hermit's water-bowl and a bow. Beside him is Aswatthaman, whose flag is black and shows a lion's tail. There is Bhishma, with the banner of blue that has a palm tree and five stars, all in silver, wearing a white helmet and silver armor, with a white umbrella. Now drive around the army and take me to Duryodhana."

Uttara drove the chariot in bewildering mazes and circles

so no one could hit them. He cut off the cattle and sent them running back to Matsya, shaking their heads and calling to each other. Arjuna called out, "Run away, Duryodhana, and be quick!"

Duryodhana turned back, and the two were surrounded. But no one could hit them. They kept trying until their eyes blurred, and they never thought of warding off Arjuna's mantras.

So while thousands of arrows fell all around him and Uttara, Ajuna shot one arrow up into the sky and called down the weapon of sleep. All the Kurus fell asleep except Bhishma. Arjuna and Uttara stayed away from him and drove among the others, cutting pieces from the white garments of Drona and Kripa, the rich yellow ones of Karna, and the blue ones of Duryodhana and Aswatthaman.

Bhishma sent a few arrows after them, but they were weak and fell short. Uttara drove back to Matsya, and Duryodhana awoke in time to see them leave.

"Bhishma, stop him," he cried. "Where is my bow?"

"It is on the ground," said Bhishma, "as you might expect when you fall asleep in the middle of a battle."

Duryodhana rubbed his eyes and ground his teeth. "He will never again trick me like this. I could have warded it off, if I had only thought of it!"

❖

Uttara drove wildly into the palace courtyard, where Uttarah and her maidens ran out to meet him. But when the Princess saw that her brother was driving, and that an unknown warrior stood grimly in the car, with a flag that

229

chattered and fumed, she caught her breath and stopped short in wonder.

Arjuna jumped down and bowed to her. "Here as I promised are fine clothes for all of you."

Uttarah looked at her brother, and her eyes asked him, "Who is this man?"

Uttara leaned over and whispered in her ear. She turned red, and stole a glance at Arjuna. "To think that you taught me dancing," she said, and ran away into the palace.

Arjuna smiled up at the prince. "Put away the horses. Put the flag in the ground. Put my weapons away, and lead me unseen to a private room. Then bring your sister and the king and my brothers when they return."

When Virata came back in the afternoon and heard of the victory over Duryodhana, he had Matsya decorated with flags and flowers, and sent a bellman on an elephant to proclaim the event where four roads met. Uttara approached the Pandavas one by one and led them to Arjuna, and his sister found Draupadi and brought her with her father.

Virata faced the Pandavas. "Blessed be you, King Yudhishthira, and Bhima, and Arjuna, and Nakula, and Sahadeva! Blessings to you, Draupadi! It is good just to speak your names!" The old king embraced them all, smelling their heads, saying again and again, "It is good fortune. You have been here all the while, safe in my kingdom."

Then Virata sat down and said, "Take this land for your own. Let Arjuna take Uttarah for his wife."

Yudhishthira replied, "We do not want Matsya, Majesty. But let Arjuna answer for the other."

"Do not hesitate," said Virata. "Take her, Arjuna."

"Yes."

"Good," said the king. Uttarah stopped holding her breath and took Arjuna's hand.

⚜

Arjuna and Virata sent wedding invitations to all their friends. Drupada came, and Dhrishtadyumna, and his brother Sikhandin. Krishna came from Dwaravati, with his kinsmen Satyaki and Kritavarman, and brought from Kamyaka forest the Pandavas' hidden chariots. His brother Balarama and his sister Subhadra were there; and Sudeshna the Queen of Maysya; and most beautiful of all, Draupadi the fire-born.

Wine and venison, stories and music, the flashing of jewels and handsome eyes! Virata gave away his daughter, and with her seven hundred thousand horses, two hundred elephants, and a million jars of red gold. Virata gave gifts to all, poured butter on fires everywhere, and fed all his city for a week.

Cars, beds, food, drink, land, women—all were given, all regiven again and again and again in Matsya. "Cows, horses, robes, ornaments, gold and silver," said the king. "Free and with best wishes!"

And after the banquets and magicians and dancers and parades and acrobats and speeches, there were dancing bells for Draupadi, and Krishna with his flute, and a double drum for Arjuna, and King Virata sleepy on his throne, nodding his head to the most wonderful music in all the world.

Lord Indra sang to Kuru long ago:

Even the dust of Kurukshetra,
Carried away by the calling wind,
Once touching a warrior,
Death will bring him to my heaven.

11: δo not tell

Majesty, after the wedding Sanjaya the charioteer came from Hastinapura and said, "Yudhishthira, life is passing and unstable. Time is an endless ocean, and where is there an island in it? May the Pandavas prefer peace. Even with the entire world, you would never be free from pleasure and pain."

Yudhishthira replied, "Welcome to you, Sanjaya. We were given a kingdom by Dhritarashtra when we were young. Now let him return my own Indraprastha, or let him even give us five villages for our own. May the Kurus be cheerful and once more all meet together as friends."

"I will tell him," said Sanjaya, and went to another room of Virata's palace to see Arjuna and Krishna. They were drinking wine on a golden couch when Sanjaya entered, and Arjuna made room for him to sit beside them. But Sanjaya only touched the couch with his hand, and sat down on the floor at their feet.

Krishna handed him a cup of wine and smiled, but there

were tears in his eyes. "It is sad to me, Sanjaya, that the lives of the Kurus are nearly ended."

❧

Kripa and Karna and Vidura and Bhishma and Duryodhana were waiting with the blind king in the assembly hall of the Kurus when Sanjaya returned to Hastinapura. He said. "Dhritarashtra, I am Sanjaya. Yudhishthira waits, looking up into your face, to know what you will do."

"We are a forest," said Vidura, "and they are lions, because of whom no man dares to cut the trees. Their home is with us."

"We must give back Indraprastha," said Dhritarashtra.

"No!" cried Duryodhana. "I wouldn't give them the land they could pick up on a needle-point. I dare them to set foot in my kingdom again."

Karna told Duryodhana, "Without any help, I will overturn them myself if they attack us, who wish only for peace. But all they can do is talk us to death."

"Karna," said Bhishma, "Indra's Dart will avail you nothing against one protected by Narayana."

Karna whirled around to face Bhishma. "You must be ninety years old, but you haven't the wits of an infant. You've lived your whole life like a woman. Will you fight for Duryodhana or will you not?"

"Yes," answered Bhishma, "I will defend him. But there is truth where Krishna is, and there is victory where truth is."

Karna's eyes were blazing with anger. "No doubt! No doubt Krishna is even so! But I have heard enough. Now I put aside my weapons, and I will not touch them again while Bhishma bears arms. Duryodhana—once he is quiet I will win for you."

Karna and Duryodhana left the room, and Dhritarashtra said, "I take no part in this. Kripa, will you also aid my son?"

Kripa said, "Of all things, war is the most wrong and sinful. I will be loyal to him."

Then Sanjaya was alone with the king. Dhritarashtra asked him, "What will happen, Sanjaya?"

"Majesty, I have just seen Krishna. Covering himself with illusion he lives as a man, and no one knows him. He is like a worker in a field; we ride by, and see him, and forget him. But he is the soul of all creatures, and though the eye be open, it will not see without him."

"Sanjaya, how do you know all this, that others cannot see?"

"Blessed be you, Majesty, I have no regard for illusion. A truce to all crafty speech, Bharata. I tell you the truth:

Arjuna and Krishna hold every life in their hands.
They know how the birds fly through the skies,
The path of the far-going wind,
And to them there is nothing small,
And nothing large.

So have I heard. Now Krishna wants to withdraw the lives of your sons back into himself, and we can in no way stop him."

And when the king was alone, in the inner palace Karna fell at his feet and said, "I am Karna. Do not discuss this war to come with Vidura or Kripa. They will make you stop

Duryodhana, and if you do, he will surely die, and I will follow."

Dhritarashtra said, "I have been told how sometimes the seed is sown as always, and cared for as always, with the same rain falling, yet nothing rises from the Earth. When we have done all we can, what else can guide the result but Destiny? By Fate we receive wealth or poverty, we find victory or defeat. And if wealth has somehow come to us, we must guard it well, so it be not stolen or lost away little by little. I bow low to the gods who have clouded your mind."

Arjuna from Matsya and Duryodhana from Hastinapura arrived in Dwaravati to speak with Krishna on the same day. Duryodhana came first, and finding Krishna asleep, he sat down to wait by the head of his bed. Then Arjuna entered and stood near Krishna's feet.

Krishna awoke and said, "What have you come for?"

"There will be a war," said Duryodhana. "Be on my side."

"I will bear no weapons for either side. But you both may choose between myself unarmed, and ten thousand Yadava warriors who have heard of this battle and have asked me which side to fight on. Choose then, Arjuna."

"But I was here first," said Duryodhana.

"When I awoke, I first saw Arjuna. Come, Bharata, say what you want. I will give it! Say quickly!"

"You," said Arjuna.

"Ah," smiled Duryodhana, "then I may have the army!"

"Yes, take them, and you are welcome."

"I thank you, Krishna," said Duryodhana. "That is what I wanted."

Duryodhana went away and Krishna sat up. "Why did you choose me, Arjuna?"

"To drive my chariot. And will you go to Hastinapura as our envoy? Will you try to make peace?"

"I will do all this."

"But Duryodhana still fears you. He may try to harm you. Like a wild deer driven into a village, a liar mistrusts everyone, thinking that they are all like himself."

"I will go with Satyaki and Kritavarman and meet you again in Matsya."

⚜

In the time of year after the rains, in the season of dew, when the sunlight is mild and the air is clear, Krishna set out for Hastinapura. When he arrived there he drove to Vidura's house, while girls at the street corners threw flowers at him and ladies watched from carved stone windows and rooftops and balconies.

Vidura welcomed Krishna and Satyaki and Kritavarman, and Kunti brought them food and water. "What is the use of telling you how pleased I am to see you," said Vidura, "but your coming will do no good. Stay here with me, but don't court danger by trying to talk to Duryodhana. And if you have to do something useful, go rather to where the wide Ganges runs swiftly by, and there take handsful of sand from the bank and make a way for men to walk across, for now they have difficulty."

"My sons might as well be dead," said Kunti. "They were

born from my blood and the seed of the gods, yet now they live dependent on others. A king's wife does not bear sons for this. What does Draupadi say? She would not let frail morality interfere with a kingdom."

Krishna stood up and looked at Vidura. "I must go to the palace. It is time."

Alone, Krishna entered Dhritarashtra's court and said, "I am Krishna. I have come from King Yudhishthira seeking peace."

"Speak with my son," said Dhritarashtra. "I have nothing to do with this."

Duryodhana said, "Welcome. Take as my gift a palace to live in, and many cows."

Krishna answered, "No."

"We have no quarrel with you," said Duryodhana. "Why refuse our gifts? What's the matter with us? Aren't we good enough for you?"

"Prince, I have no other business here than to speak with you. I am only a messenger."

Karna laughed. "What words have been put into your mouth then, messenger?"

Like a sapphire mounted in gold, Krishna in his yellow robes stood before Karna and said, "My sandals upon your head, Karna. Though you are made of straw, shall I bow down to you?"

"I think you had better tell me quickly what you have to say," said Duryodhana.

Krishna turned to Duryodhana. "Be content with half the kingdom as before. Do not harden your heart against the Pandavas. They have fulfilled the conditions from the throw

241

"You," said Arjuna

of dice, and they are your brothers. Peace is not difficult; it depends only on you and me. They would not threaten you, and in no other way could you get such friends. Hastinapura will be more secure. Your own kingdom will be strengthened. Return their city and you will be far richer than if you try to keep all Kurujangala for yourself."

"As long as I live I will give them nothing," said Duryodhana. "When I was a child, Dhritarashtra gave away half my kingdom, but it shall not be given again. I would rather not live on the same Earth with them. Tell them to leave me alone and not pretend to have any claim on my land."

"But consider . . . "

"Krishna, what need of many words? Have you never heard the Kshatriya Dharma: *Stand straight and never bow down, for this alone is manliness. Rather break at the knots than bend!*"

Duryodhana and Karna went out, and Dhritarashtra said, "Krishna, who knows if we shall ever meet again? Stay as my guest for a few days."

"Bharata, I cannot," answered Krishna.

"Sanjaya has told me . . . . but who can know the future? No man has ever defeated Duryodhana."

"A clay pot cannot be twice broken. You have the strength to make peace, but not the will, so I am helpless. Farewell, Dhritarashtra."

Krishna turned to go, when Satyaki came in and whispered in his ear. "Tell the king," said Krishna.

"Dhritarashtra, I am Satyaki, kinsman to Krishna. I am able to read the heart from changes of expression in the

242

face. When Krishna leaves this room, Duryodhana and his brother intend to take him prisoner."

Dhritarashtra said, "It has passed from my hands. I do not know if my protection will stand or not."

"That's all right, sir," said Satyaki. "He's safe enough. But you ought to guard your son." Duryodhana entered with Duhsasana. Satyaki pointed at them with his left hand. "There they are—the little dogs barking at the sleeping lion."

"Silence, Yadava," said Duryodhana. "Such insolence spoken to a king is very dangerous."

"Why, I'm surprised," smiled Satyaki. "I knew you were sort of a bonehead, but I never dreamed you were a king. Why I . . ."

"Ah—Satyaki," said Krishna, looking at the floor.

"Yes, Krishna."

"Wait outside with Kritavarman and the chariot."

The broad-shouldered Satyaki shrugged and walked away. Dhritarashtra said, "Do not harm a king's messenger. Krishna cannot fall victim to you. He is the wind you seek to hold in a net.'

Duryodhana hung back, but Duhsasana drew his sword. "Father, we do not need your permission," he said. "Krishna has heard so often that he is something special that now he believes it himself. But he has gone too far above his rank this time. He is no warrior, but only a village lout who grew up with cows and shameless herdgirls."

"Duhsasana, you are very brave," said Krishna. "Here you see me alone and unarmed, and you are ready to speak to me of shame."

"In the king's name I arrest you!" shouted Duhsasana. "Follow us or be cut down."

Suddenly Krishna looked straight into Duhsasana. His black eyes were happy, and he said, "From the time you would have dishonored Draupadi until now—that is all the time of your life." Duhsasana saw too late the deadly chakra spinning on Krishna's hand, its nave hard as thunder, its razor edge flashing. The lion's roar of war was still in his throat, he had not taken his first step towards Krishna, when the discus was caught again on its iron pole, and Duhsasana's head rolled away and stopped between Duryodhana's feet.

From Duhsasana's body, loosened in death, came a bright stream of energy that bowed and entered through the center of Krishna's chest. The discus vanished from the dark hand, and while Duryodhana stood speechless, Krishna left the Kuru palace. Outside he met his companions, and arm in arm with Satyaki and Kritavarman he walked to their chariot without a glance to either side.

❦

Krishna made a sign to Karna when they passed his house, saying—*"Come"*—and Karna leapt lightly onto the moving chariot.

As Satyaki drove slowly out of Hastinapura, Karna spoke softly in a gentle voice, "One lies like a fallen tree, Lord Narayana, but they do not know. Even now, they know nothing. Only Sanjaya—but can a spoon taste soup?"

Krishna said, "Karna, who hates the Pandavas hates me, because we have only one heart between us. They are your brothers. Kunti is your mother."

"And I have been long abandoned by her, Krishna.

244

Adhiratha is my father, and his wife is my mother. From love for me, her breasts filled with milk the day she found me by the river's bank."

"You are the eldest brother. The Pandavas would all obey you."

"Yudhishthira would give to me his fancied kingdom?"

"Yes."

"And I would give it to Duryodhana. Without me, Duryodhana would not provoke this war. He made me a king. No one knows more about me than that I was a cast-off baby who somehow was not drowned. Even my wife knows nothing more."

"If Yudhishthira knew who you were," said Krishna, "he would not fight against you."

"Lord Narayana, do not tell. Bhishma set rolling the Wheel of Dharma—rolling over the land, over the years. Kshatriya Dharma! Duryodhana has swallowed a barbed hook baited with Yudhishthira's wealth. The Wheel has turned nearly once around. Let the Gate of Kings be open to the other world. *Lord, tie the knot of destiny.*"

Krishna was silent a moment. Then he said, "With Arjuna, you would be . . ."

"No. I am forever his enemy. How is the sun brightened by a garden of virtues? Arjuna and I are born warriors. We approach battle as other men approach their wives in bed. Do not let the Kshatriyas perish miserably of disgraceful diseases or of old age. Let them take oath to their king, and their king to them, as always we have done! When is there a day or a night that death may not come? Or are there any who have become immortal by not fighting?"

"I will say nothing. Now there is sweet water and fruit

245

everywhere, and the heat is gone. Tell Duryodhana: *On Kurukshetra plain, in seven days."*

Karna said quickly, "If we live I will come to you. Otherwise I will meet you in heaven. I do not think we will ever meet again as friends on Earth." Then he jumped out of the chariot and stood in the dust, in the sunlight, his head bowed low and his eyes closed. In a moment he was ready to walk back to Hastinapura alone.

*It is better to blaze up, even for
a moment, than to smolder forever with desire.*

12: SANJAYA RETURNS

At dawn six days later, while the warriors in their tent cities on Kurukshetra were waking to the sound of music, Vyasa entered Hastinapura and found Dhritarashtra awake in his palace with Sanjaya.

"Dhritarashtra, I am Vyasa. I come to you from Kuru's Plain."

What did you see?"

"Two great cities of silken tents face each other across the empty plain—every-colored houses for the kings and soldiers and animals, for the women and musicians and mechanics and physicians. Yesterday the tents were steaming in the morning air, and the flags were flying, and the armor and weapons that lay everywhere shone in the sun like white fire."

"What else?"

"From behind the fine tents black crows called to me: *Go!* Pale towers of mist, with high walls and deep trenches, rose everchanging from the river near Duryodhana's camp. Around the plain the trees are filled with kites and vultures vomiting blood, each having but one dismal eye, and one black wing, and one red leg. Though the sun is bright, a black circle surrounds it, and it is struck by meteors, and at night the eight points of the horizon blaze, and all the stars are hostile."

"What else?"

The ocean is rising, and all the rivers flow backwards. Cows are giving birth to asses, and when milked give only blood. In the temples the statues of the gods sometimes laugh and sometimes tremble. Children fight in the streets with wooden clubs. The holy fires are blue, and they bend to the sinister left, while the knaves and murderers of the city laugh and dance and sing. Every season's crops now appear on Earth, with one hundred heads of grain on each stalk. Sacred trees worshipped in the villages are fallen, struck by lightning or blown down by the wind. War flags are smoking, and lighted torches will no longer dispel night's gloom. Outside Hastinapura the wells are empty, roaring like bulls, but in the city they overflow and flood the streets. All your horses are weeping, and their tears are falling fast. When I entered here my left eye winked of itself. The Himalyas are exploding and tumbling down. This is fear and evil piled on evil. . .Will you do nothing?"

Dhritarashtra said, "My knowledge of life and death is equal to yours. But in what concerns my own interest I am deprived of judgement. Know me for an ordinary man, whose sons will not obey him. We cannot dispose our future; we are but wooden dolls, moved by strings. And now it is too late."

"Then do not fall into grief over what will happen to

those who live in those beautiful tents. It will be. . .but the changes of Time, and nothing more."

"I will hear of that soon enough," said the king. "Father, they who have tens of thousands live, and they who have but little also live."

Vyasa said, "I will give heavenly sight to Sanjaya. If he will go to Kurukshetra he will meet no harm, and he will know everything that happens, by day or by night, hidden or open, even what is only thought of within the mind."

"Go then, Sanjaya," said Dhritarashtra. "Stay in our camp, and return to me when it is finished. Then tell me."

"I must leave now, Bharata," said Sanjaya. He and Vyasa left the king and went through the palace halls, past the door to the throne room, rich and hollow and echoing and empty, where hung the great bronze gong that announced the king's visitors.

They stopped. "I am going home to the forest," said Vyasa. "We will meet again."

Vyasa took the heavy padded gong hammer from the wall and swung it in his dark hands. With all his strength he struck the gong, hard as a woodsman axes a tree. The glaring bronze rocked from the blow, but there was no sound, not a whisper, and from the gong a shower of fine black ash fell down on the polished stone floor.

The soot fell, and Sanjaya thought: *The words of Vyasa are always true*—and the last illusion left his quiet eyes.

That evening, the eve of the new moon, Bhishma in his tent on Kurukshetra said to Duryodhana, "All the rice and grain, all the land and women and wealth on this Earth cannot satisfy even one person. And to follow the Kshatriya Dharma is to follow a rule fit for butchers."

Duryodhana answered, "Grandfather. . .command my army tomorrow."

"If I do, Karna will not fight for you."

"Take it. Lead us, as only you can do."

"I will," said Bhishma. "I will do my best for you, you who are so hard to conquer. But I will not slay a woman, or one who resembles a woman, or one who was a woman born. So if the Panchala prince Sikhandin, Dhrishtadyumna's brother, comes against me, I will not even look at him."

"How is this?" asked Duryodhana.

Bhishma said, "Bharata, hear from me the story of Sikhandin."

Listen—

When I stole the three daughters of Banaras for Vichitravirya, Amba told my mother Satyavati, "*I belong to Salwa*", and we sent her to that king, whom she would have chosen at her swayamvara. But Salwa refused her, saying, "*I will have none of Bhishma's capture.*" And though she had never desired another husband, he told her, "*Go. Go.*" Amba was turned away weeping and broken-hearted, and she made her way, all alone, into the entangled forests of the west.

Tired and hungry after many days, Amba stumbled into the retreat of the hermit Akritavrana. He gave her food and milk, and made her a place to rest. But she ate only a little, then hid her face in her hands and wept.

"Tell me," said Akritavrana. For a long time she could not speak, while Akritavrana sat patiently beside her and wondered, "What will she say?"

At last she told him, and he said, "You fell into this ocean of misery because of Bhishma, and he is to blame for it. But forgive what is past. Together we will make a new life for you."

Amba turned on Akritavrana with fiery eyes, and cried, "No! I hate him. I want Bhishma to die and I will never forgive. What can a hermit and a woman do against Bhishma? I have nowhere to stay and nowhere to go. I have no protection in all the worlds, and for that I would like to destroy those three worlds!"

"Kill your anger instead," said Akritavrana. "I can send a message to Salwa, and he will obey."

"Holy one, my anger will burn me up if I hide it inside me. I am now a wanderer with an empty heart. Can you not help me? Not at all?"

Akritavrana sighed. "Yes, I can. Take that bow and this knife. Go one day farther into this forest, and with the knife make an arrow from a water-reed."

"Then?"

"You will know, when you have finished the arrow."

Taking curds and fruit and dried meat, Amba left Akritavrana, and stood the next day in a small meadow. By a river she cut and notched a straight cane. Under a tree she found feathers; with one stone she chipped another into an arrowhead; with thin vines she tied the shaft together. Sitting in the grass, she made the last knot and bit off the ends.

Clad in a sable deerskin, with a green serpent hanging across his chest, a tall white man with a silver crescent in his coiled hair stood watching her. He had four arms and a blue throat. The forest was still. Amba looked up and smiled.

Shiva did not smile, but held out a narrow length of patterned silk. "If you choose revenge, tie this round the arrow and shoot it into the sun. When again you find that arrow, you will remember."

The arrow flew, and Amba fell dead in the grass at the feet of Shiva the Destroyer. The last of her life then was the wind of her fall in her ears, and the hundred thousand tiny bells ringing and ringing—that none may hear and live.

☙

In Panchala, long before he lit the fire that gave him Draupadi, King Drupada asked Shiva for a child; and in a dream Shiva replied, "Your Queen now carries your son within her."

Drupada put his faith in those words, thinking, "It will not be otherwise. What is destined must take place." But when the child was born it was the girl Sikhandini, favored with such beauty that it seemed she had been made from grains of loveliness gathered from everything beautiful in the world. Yet remembering his dream, Drupada told everyone that a son had been born, and treated his daughter as a boy in every way, and no one knew what she was except Drupada and his Queen.

When it was time, Drupada chose the daughter of Hiranyavarman, king of the Dasarnas, as a wife for the princess Sikhandini. They were married in Kampilya and given rooms in Drupada's palace. But very soon the Dasarna princess discovered that her husband was a woman like herself, and told her servants that had come with her, and these sent messages in anger to Hiranyavarman.

Hiranyavarman was first sad, then wrathful, then wildly furious. He marched with his army towards Kampilya, and told Drupada by messenger, *"Idiot! You have humiliated and deceived me. Now I will slay you with all your city. Wait a little!"*

And Hiranyavarman answered, *"I will slay you; be calm."*

Sikhandini was in dispair to have caused a war against her father, and as the Dasarna army drew near Kampilya, she left the city one evening and wandered away into the forests. While she was aimlessly going here and there, Sthuna the Yaksha, sitting in a tree, saw her pass below and called down, "Wait. Tell my why you are here, and whatever you want, I shall give it."

Sikhandini looked up at him and said, "You cannot make my wish true."

"Yes I can," said Sthuna. "I will give you even what cannot be given, for those who give may one day have to ask in their turn."

"Yaksha—let me become a man."

"Why, there's nothing easier. But make a promise to me to return again after you have saved your father, and take back your sex. Now I will exchange with you."

Cheerfully Sikhandin gave his word to return to the

Yakshini and went back to Kampilya. Drupada told Hiranyavarman, "My child is a man. Believe' the truth, or send someone to bear witness."

Hiranyavarman was near without the walls of Kampilya with his army, and he quickly dispatched several young women of great beauty, who found Sikhandin in truth a man. Hiranyavarman was well pleased at the good news, and leaving his army camped peacefully in the country, he spent some days as Drupada's guest, scolding his daughter a little, and leaving generous gifts for Sikhandin.

And when he was gone, Sikhandin went back into the forest, and found Sthuni in the same tree. But she had a long face, and told the prince, "While you were gone, the Treasure Lord and Manibhadra came here to make sure that everything was all right, and when they heard what I had done, Vaishravana called out *"Stop the car!"* and summoned me before him. When he saw me he said, "Since, for some reason, you have given your manhood away to Drupada's daughter, I curse you to remain forever as you are. Oh, worst of Yakshas, you have done what has never been done by anyone—an unnatural, abnormal, simpleminded, underhanded act that deserves all the punishment I can think up, so no one else will ever do it."

"I was proud to hear this, but I threw myself on his mercy. The Lord of Wealth has small pity, but he did say that I will regain my true sex upon your death. Until then, you must remain a man and I a woman, though I do not see what is in this to make it such a curse. I cannot change back with you." Sthuni laughed. "He called me a wicked-souled wretch. . .but did I fulfill your wish, or did I not?"

256

"You did," said Sikhandin, bowing low with touching palms to the Yakshini. "You are all kindness and charity and friendship to me. I am pleased to be a man. Thank you."

"Don't mention it," said Sthuni. "I mean it. Don't tell anybody. I'll enjoy my life differently for a change, until I am again a stout and fearful Yaksha. Goodbye, prince."

"Farewell," said Sikhandin, and he started back to the city. But he mistook his way in the forest and came to an abandoned temple overgrown by trees and vines, half-hidden in the wood. Round it ran a ruined stone wall. Where the gate had been, stuck in one of the wooden gateposts, was an arrow, gray with age, made of cane, wrapped with a faded cloth of many colors.

"He remembers all that was between us," said Bhishma, "but to me he is still that same Sikhandini that he was born."

"We'll keep her away from you," said Duryodhana. "He is not one to be feared."

Sanjaya stayed at Kurukshetra for five days and five nights, and after sunrise on the sixth day rode to Hastinapura, quick as thought, quick as desire, and ran to Dhritarashtra. The king was in a dark, windowless room, sitting on a bed. Sanjaya brought in a lamp with him, and said, "I am Sanjaya. It is finished, and I have returned to you."

"Sit down," said Dhritarashtra, "and tell me. I have spoken to no one since you left, I have heard nothing."

"I cannot tell it all," said Sanjaya. "I have not the heart, and my words sound strange, and far away."

⚜

Listen—

As the two armies came together on the first morning, your son's was much larger and drew first onto the field of Kurukshetra. There were Duryodhana and his ninety-eight brothers, and your son Yuyutsu, and Bhishma leading them all, and Kripa and Drona, and Jayadratha, and Aswatthaman, and Sakuni, and Susarman, and Salya the king of the Madras, and Kritavarman, who fought for your son though he was kinsman to Krishna.

I pushed through the crowd of merchants and prostitutes and spies who had come out from the two camps and stood unarmed on the edge of the plain; we heard the drums that hung from Yudhishthira's chariot and saw the Pandavas' army approach ours. As with us, each king had an army, and I saw Dhrishtadyumna leading them, with the Pandavas and Drupada, and Krishna driving Arjuna's car, and Satyaki, and Sikhandin, and Virata, and his son Uttara.

A great cry rose from both sides when Yudhishthira's army appeared, facing the morning sun, all the metal shields and armor shining, and those of bent cane and thorns and leather dully gleaming, and the flags of war proudly flying. They came like a river across the plain, with the elephants like dark clouds swaying, and drew up in a row facing Duryodhana's men.

Bhima was the center of their line, and right across from him was Bhishma, dressed all in white on his silver car. Bhishma put his conchshell trumpet to his lips and blew the call for battle; and from both sides the other warriors joined in, sounding their conchshells and horns of brass, their drums and gongs and cymbals. But just as the two armies were about to meet, Arjuna leaned over in his chariot and spoke to Krishna.

"Drive out from the ranks," he said, "and stop somewhere in the center, between these armies."

Then Krishna drove that bowman, who will never be equalled on Earth again, out into the open in that rainbow chariot decked with a hundred silver bells and drawn by white horses. Arjuna stood between the two walls of warriors and looked long at Duryodhana's army.

Then Arjuna threw down his bow on the floor of his car and leaned against his flagstaff, gazing at the Kauravas. "There they are," he said, "Bhishma and Kripa and Drona, all ready to fight against me. The arrows peer out from my quiver, seeking to fly, and the long bow yawns untouched. But my heart is not steel, beaten into that shape. What happiness will it bring to kill them for the sake of a kingdom? They come here without a second thought—but this is not worthy of us, Krishna. We know better, we must act better."

Krishna turned round on the driver's seat and said, "You are my dear friend, Arjuna. If you wish, we shall drive away from here without once looking backwards. But unless he surrenders, Yudhishthira will die. Karna will kill Bhima, he will kill Nakula, he will kill Sahadeva, he will kill Yudhishthira, he will kill every man of the army; you cannot stop this war." Then Krishna sang a song—*My beloved, why yield, why give way?*—the Song of the Lord.

Arjuna picked up his bow. "Drive back, Narayana—and I will fight."

Krishna turned back, but as they passed Yudhishthira, they saw him throw off his armor which crashed to the Earth. And then, without armor or weapons, Yudhishthira jumped down from his chariot and went on foot into the Kuru army, where they made way for him without a sound.

Yudhishthira walked through the forest of darts and arrows to Bhishma's car, and bowing to his grandfather he said, "May we have your permission to fight against you."

"I give," said Bhishma.

"How shall we be able to defeat you?" asked Yudhishthira. "Is it possible?"

Bhishma replied, "Bharata, it is good of you to ask. Had you not come to me, I would have cursed you. Death cannot approach me without my permission. And I do not see the man who can even draw very close to me in battle."

Yudhishthira bowed his head and walked through the wondering Kurus to Drona's golden car. "Preceptor, give us permission to fight against you."

"I give," said Drona.

"Tell me, how can we overcome you in battle?"

"Yudhishthira," answered Drona, "so long as I hold a weapon in my hand, no one can defeat me."

Then Yudhishthira went to Kripa and said, "I bow to you, and ask your leave to do battle and war against you."

"Yes, I will let you," said Kripa.

"Alas, preceptor," said Yudhishthira. "I ask. . ." But he could not say the words.

And Kripa answered, "I understand. I cannot be slain."

Yudhishthira bowed and joined his hands to Kripa, then went back through the Kurus till he stood facing them all, and called out, "We will take for a friend whoever will come over to us now."

There was a movement within the Kaurava army, and your son Yuyutsu, born of a maidservant, slowly drove out towards Yudhishthira, and the Kurus made way for him to pass, and he crossed over into the ranks behind Bhima and Dhrishtadyumna.

Yudhishthira again put on his golden armor. As he finished tying it on and reached for his bow, on each side the sea-born conchshells white as milk began to blare, and already the bards and minstrels sitting alongside Kurukshetra were composing their songs of the great war of the Bharatas.

Earth is strewn over with bright
weapons and red with blood. She
resembles a dark dancing girl
dressed in crimson, fallen, confused
with wine, her golden bells and
silver ornaments all deranged . . .
But it is illusion. It is done in
play.
Who has been slain?
Who has done murder here?

13: TREES OF GOLD

Kshatriya Dharma is cruel, Dhritarashtra, for in the blink of an eye those two armies had rushed together in hopeless confusion. While I watched fearfully under the protection of Vyasa, the derangement of war was all around me: dust that dimmed the sunlight, the noise of crashing chariots and splintering wood, elephants and horses calling, bones and metal breaking, and the shouts and cries of warriors, telling their names and families, guided by costume and banner and secret words and signs.

There was Bhishma, in white robes and armor, first calling the names of those whom he killed, his white bow drawn in a circle, burning like smokeless fire. I could not look at him, and when I looked away, at the Pandavas, I saw men driven into the smiling wide mouth of Death.

Majesty, as the eye is drawn to the beautiful, so Bhishma's arrows flew, drawn to their marks. The Pandava elephants broke and ran, their chariots were stopped, their horsemen fled, and the blue flag with the fan palm and five star-flowers of silver cut through Yudhishthira's army and left it covered with arrows and blood like a red-blossomed tree with sharp branches and flowers of scarlet.

Yudhishthira saw, and he raced to Arjuna and said, "See Bhishma! From my ignorance he is my enemy. Now I shall return to the forest and end this battle, for life is valuable."

"Be still," said Arjuna. "Do not look up at Bhishma like a weak man. Hold your men back and wait."

Krishna drove away towards Bhishma, and Virata fell in beside Arjuna to guard his wheel. Yudhishthira's army ran past them to the rear, no two men going the same way. Then those two chariots were past Drona and Kripa, and Arjuna's car colored like a rainbow rushed at us like a flight of brilliant birds, or a fleeting Gandharva city made all of colored clouds in the sky.

One moment I saw the two chariots nearing Bhishma; the next, they had disappeared under a hail of arrows. Bhishma had seen them, and though Arjuna could protect himself, the Matsya king was dead, and Virata's driver turned away and left the field.

Krishna said to Arjuna, "Go on—shoot him down!"

But Arjuna looked askance at him and said, "When I was a child, I would climb on Bhishma and get dirt on his clothes, and when I called him Father, he told me that he was not, but was my grandfather. And he had such love, to play with that dark boy with curly hair."

Krishna jumped down from the chariot, the discus Sudarshana spun wildly on his hand, and he ran at Bhishma.

Arjuna caught his breath and bit his lip. He vaulted over the chariot-rail and tackled Krishna from behind. They both

266

fell down hard on the Earth, and Bhishma watched smiling, leaning on his bow.

"Oh, come," said Bhishma, "come to me. Adorable Krishna, I bow to you. You do me honor. If you kill me it will bring my greatest happiness."

Arjuna and Krishna lay in the dust looking up. Krishna turned and glared at Arjuna. "Let me go!"

"No." Arjuna's face was all innocence. "Be peaceful, or I will never let you go."

"All right. I won't fight."

"The chakra."

"All right!" The discus vanished. Arjuna let him up, and Krishna went back to the chariot, his eyes shining under their dusty lashes.

Then the sun set, and the warriors withdrew to their tents for the night, leaving Kurukshetra covered with lances and arrows and flags, with whips and bows and armor, with bright axes and burnt-out flame-cloths and the shattered earthenware jars that had been filled with snakes of lethal poison. And as the Pandavas walked through the twilight to their tents, whenever they blinked their eyes they still saw before them the proud figure of Bhishma; white, white, white on his silver car.

❧

That evening the warriors relaxed with women and music, not speaking of battle, forgetting war, so that it was again good to look at them. The streets of our camp were lighted by golden lamps burning fragrant oils, and through these streets Duryodhana rode on horseback, handsome with victory. His friends greeted him in many tongues, and he answered them like a king. At that moment your son had no anger, no impatience, no malice, no fear, no love of argument, no care for gain—and I saw victory walking by his side. That was no illusion, but I thought, "How long will she stay?"

Duryodhana stopped at Bhishma's tent, and there he entered, bowing to his grandfather, and said, "Our army is the shoreless sea, irresistible, crested with waves in a terrible storm. Do not spare the Pandavas from kindness."

Bishma answered, "Be silent, Duryodhana. Man may be the slave of wealth but wealth is no man's slave. So I am fighting for you. But I will never slay the innocent, or those without weapons, or chariot drivers, or women, or those who run away or surrender or are fighting with others.

"Forgive me, grandfather, I meant no unkindness, I know we will win. The very night air is bright and sparkling. Only—I have heard, when one is about to die, then he sees that all the trees are made of gold."

On the second morning Bhishma again scattered the Pandavas while our men laughed and cheered, and I could not believe my eyes when I saw the ape banner of Hanuman, which had stood fast in their fleeing army like a rapids rock in a river, itself turn back in retreat. But, as the Pandava army poured off the field or plunged into the river Ganga, Krishna stopped near a blue lotus flag on silver that I had not noticed before, and Sikhandin leapt from his own car onto Arjuna's chariot, and they turned back, towards Bhishma.

Arrows washed in oil sped at Bhishma from the bows of Sikhandin and Arjuna, but Bhishma would not look at them. Like winter's cold those arrows pierced him by the hundreds till there was not space on his body for another arrow to strike. And as the gods above folded their hands, Bhishma fell headlong from his chariot, so covered with arrows that he did not touch the Earth.

Krishna stopped the chariot. Arjuna and Sikhandin set down their bows. All over Kurukshetra the fighting stopped, and down from the webbed fingers of the gods fell a soft and silent rain of flowers. From both sides the warriors gathered round Bhishma, assembled together as in days of old.

Then Bhishma spoke. "I am alive. Bring pillows, for my head hangs down." Many kings brought fine pillows covered with rare and costly silk, but Bhishma refused them and said, "Arjuna, give me a proper pillow for my head."

Arjuna drew three arrows from his quiver, and drove the points into the Earth so that the feathered ends held up Bhishma's head. Arjuna knelt and whispered, "It is done."

Bishma said, "These arrows that burn are not Sikhandin's. Bring me water." Again many kings brought water before Arjuna could rise, but Bhishma once more refused them, saying, "I am not now in the world of men and this water is not for me. Arjuna, give me water to drink."

"I will." In the silence Arjuna took Gandiva bow and walked once around Bhishma. He put an arrow to the bowstring and sent it sharp and ringing into the Earth. There, where it hit, water rose from the ground. I gave Arjuna a cup, and in it he gave the water to Bhishma.

Duryodhana knelt beside Bhishma and said, "The physicians have come, grandfather."

"Thank them for coming," said Bhishma, "and tell them to go away. I will not die before the winter solstice. I will lie here awhile on these arrows. You have seen, Duryodhana. The deeds. . .the deeds of Arjuna that are beyond knowing!"

The son of the beautiful ocean-going Ganga fell silent and closed his eyes. Through the tears in my own eyes I saw the brave Kurus and Pandavas leave for their tents, while men from each army made a trench far and wide around Bhishma, set guards to protect him, and set his flag flying to mark the place where he lay.

In the evening Karna came to Bhishma and told him in the fluttering darkness beneath that war-flag, "I am Karna, at whom you looked with hatred while I stood before your eyes."

Bishma saw him. "I do not hate you, Bharata. But you wished for war while I tried to find peace. That is why I spoke harshly to you. But the wheel will not stop turning. Yet listen to what you have heard from me before: live with your brothers in peace. You are the best warrior in all the world, but let war end with me. You have the courage and the kindness, more than anyone else, to do this for me."

Karna answered, "Even against them I will fight. I have come here that you may give me your permission, and your pardon for my past unkindness to you, done in anger."

"I give both," said Bhishma, "and I have failed again. You who think you are as good a warrior as I. . .I tell you, you are much better."

271

"I will lie here awhile on these arrows"

When Karna had gone, Krishna walked unseen beside Bhishma, and in a dream loosened the chains of hope that tie life: *I am the Lord; This I have; This I will get; This one I have slain; That one I will slay tomorrow; I am rich, and noble and happy; Who else is like me!*—so that all the pain vanished and was gone, and the thirst, and hunger, and Bhishma slept on in peace, on the points of the thousand arrows.

✤

Karna put on his sword. It was in Duryodhana's tent, later in the evening, and your son asked him, "Who will lead the Kurus?"

"Let it be Drona," answered Karna. Then Duryodhana went to Drona and made him commander of his army, pouring water from the Ganges over Drona's silver hair, tying the silver thread around his wrist.

"What shall I do for you?" asked Drona.

"Capture Yudhishthira alive," said Duryodhana. "Without him, their army cannot have the will to resist us, or the passion to avenge his death. Can you do it?"

"Only if Arjuna be drawn from his side, Bharata."

Karna will do that."

"No," said Drona. "If Karna challenges Arjuna the armies will stop fighting to watch. I need the entanglement of full battle to succeed. But I know a way."

Drona went to Susarman, the King of the Three Castles, who agreed to lead the Trigartas against Arjuna in the morning. Before the holy fire they took a vow to defeat Arjuna or die. Over their armor they put on grass robes tied with bowstrings. Then each one rolled three balls of rice flour and followed Susarman to the river to perform his own funeral.

The new moon had set when Susarman kindled a pyre by the Ganges' banks. In the flickering light and shadow one rice-ball was thrown by each warrior into the fire, for his soul to eat when he was dead; one into the river, to please the moon who gives to the dead their heavenly bodies; and the third they gave to their wives, that their families might not die away on Earth.

Then the Trigartas returned no more to where other men were, because their word had not yet been made good. They slept outdoors, away from Duryodhana's tents, and the starlight fell upon Susarman, asleep on his elephant, his head between the globes of his animal's head, as though he lay between the deep breasts of his Queen.

❖

On the third morning the sun rose shining brilliant as a woman's smile, shining like a golden lion leaving his cave in the hills, chasing darkness away like a herd of black elephants. And it is true that Death waits for his hour, since all those warriors were not slain at once in the battle that followed, amid their cries that filled the air: *Seize! Here! Cut! Strike! Wait! Look! Where?*

The challenge came to Arjuna from the Trigartas, and Dhrishtadyumna told him, "Go to them. I have found out all their plans from my spies, and never while I command his army will Yudhishthira be captured by Drona."

As the two armies met like two oceans surging together, Arjuna sent his arrows at the Trigartas, who swarmed about his chariot and blocked its path. When he saw his men fall by tens and hundreds, Susarman on his elephant remembered a spell. Darkness fell over Arjuna and Krishna, filled with harsh voices rebuking them, and hungry animals rushed at them—tigers and lions, leopards and wolves, iron-billed falcons and snakes with fiery tongues.

A high mountain appeared in the sky, crowded with cliffs and trees, a mountain whose fountains and springs poured down a rain of spears and lances and showers of blood and bones and fire, all partly hidden in dark-blue clouds and rainbows. And through all this Arjuna sometimes saw Susarman mangled and slain; sometimes saw him on a hundred sides at once; now visible and now invisible; sometimes small, soaring into the sky and diving through the Earth to rise again somewhere else; and now again on his elephant, rushing at the chariot to crush it.

But it is foolishness to fight Arjuna with illusion. An arrow bearing the Naga mantra left Gandiva bow and entered the Earth. Thousands of serpents rose and bound the Trigartas so they could not move. They covered Susarman's elephant like vines on a stone wall, and held the king fast bound on his back.

Another arrow with its mantra sped up into the air, and the Trigartas yawned, so that their memories came out their mouths, and the Nagas vanished. Susarman looked around him in surprise and amazement. He came down from his elephant and fell at Krishna's feet and said, "Lord, what is this war? Let me be blessed, I will go home."

❧

"Drona is too close!" cried Dhrishtadyumna. "We must

escape. Someone must break into the Kauravas, but who has the skill?"

The blue-eyed prince Uttara answered, "I can drive in, but I don't know how to get out of their army again."

"We will all follow," said Dhrishtadyumna. "Drona may expect us to fall back, but not to advance."

Uttara took the reins from his driver and drove his car past Drona in winding coils and networks of confusion. He entered our formation, but there he was swallowed up and lost. Jayadratha swept down behind him, and there was no longer a path through our army. The Pandavas saw no way to enter, saw only the silver boar on Jayadratha's flag before them. Uttara was alone, and there he was killed by Salya and Sakuni fighting together against him.

Arjuna and Krishna were returning from the Trigartas when they heard the Dhartarashtras cheering, and heard Yuyutsu call out to them, "Having slain only a child, do not rejoice!" Then your son Yuyutsu cast down his weapons in anger and went into his tent.

Arjuna asked Yudhishthira, "Where is Uttara?"

"How shall I face you?" answered Yudhishthira. "He went alone into Duryodhana's army and was slain. We were to follow, but Jayadratha cut us off; he stopped Bhima and Satyaki and Dhrishtadyumna and myself."

None but Krishna and Yudhishthira could bear to look at Arjuna. His face bathed in tears, Arjuna cast his glances at us like a madman with fever, breathing deeply and trembling. He squeezed his arms and said, "Your weapons and armor are only ornaments on you. But it is my fault, for knowing you all to be weak I went away."

Krishna said, "Bharata, tears burn the dead like liquid fire. Do not weep."

"But he must have thought: *Arjuna will surely rescue me,*" whispered Arjuna to Krishna. And having himself said these words to his own self, Arjuna pointed with his bow at Jayadratha. His chariot began to move toward us—straight, without wavering, as though we were none of us in his path at all.

"Listen," said Krishna, "when we get near him do as I say and no otherwise, or your life will be forfeit."

"Yes, see—Drona has fallen back. He is meeting with Jayadratha. He has seen us return and knows what we intend."

⚜

Drona sent Jayadratha to the back of your army, but before he could send anyone with him Arjuna called out, "Preceptor, let me enter your army today."

"Fight against me first," answered Drona.

Arjuna sent a few arrows at Drona and then drove quickly behind him. "Where are you going?" asked Drona. "Do you not always fight until your foe is defeated?"

Arjuna said, "You are not my enemy but my teacher, and also there is no one who can overcome you."

On his lotus-colored elephant with its golden throne and net armor of steel, Duryodhana asked Drona, "Why did you let him get by?"

"Now that he is gone," said Drona, "I can capture Yudhishthira. You can head off Arjuna. Our men will let you pass while they delay him. Get in my car a minute."

Drona tied your son's armor with secret knots. "It is tied

with Gandharva strings; it will repel all weapons for you," said Drona.

When Arjuna came out behind your army he found Duryodhana awaiting him. "The king is dead," cried the Kurus, but Duryodhana laughed at them and struck Arjuna in the shoulder with an arrow, so that the Pandava dropped his bow and fell weakly to his knees.

Arjuna struggled to his feet, and Krishna said, "There he is, on that elephant like a blazing mountain, under his white umbrella with its golden chain."

"Welcome, Krishna," said Duryodhana, covering the rainbow chariot with thirsty arrows.

All Arjuna's arrows fell away from their mark, and Duryodhana said, "Bharata, are these your famous arrows?"

"What's wrong?" asked Krishna.

"Gandharva knots!" said Arjuna. "But he is careless—so!" Before Duryodhana could release another arrow, Arjuna broke his bow and knocked down the royal umbrella over his head. From within the smothering cloth Duryodhana called to his elephant: *Attack!*— but the animal refused to obey him, like a poor man's wife her husband. By the time Duryodhana could see again, Arjuna and Krishna were nearing Jayadratha.

"Now be careful," said Krishna. "When Jayadratha was born, his father Vriddhakshatra learned that his son would one day be beheaded on a battlefield and set his curse upon the murderer. So whoever causes Jayadratha's head to fall lifeless on the Earth, his own head will be instantly shattered to bits. Vriddhakshatra lives near here in the forest where he retired in his old age."

"I understand." With a razor arrow Arjuna struck off Jayadratha's head, and with other arrows he pushed the head through the air and let it gently fall into the forests round Kurukshetra, into the lap of Vriddhakshatra, who sat on the Earth outside his forest home in prayer. Vriddhakshatra had withdrawn his mind from the world and noticed nothing. After a few moments he returned from his meditation and stood up without once glancing down into his lap. And as Jayadratha's head fell to the ground, Vriddhakshatra's head burst into a hundred thousand pieces.

⁂

Hissing like a black cobra in his golden car, Drona kept his eye on Yudhishthira as a hawk watches a sparrow in the sky. His eyes were copper red; his arrows winged with feathers and gold all bore his name. From the corner of his eye he saw Drupada take aim at him and at once threw a fatal dart of gold and lapis lazuli at the Pandhala king. Drupada fell, a cliff of stone shattered and tumbled down by the lightning of Drona's glance.

But Drona had looked away. Under his red banner, Dhrishtadyumna came at Drona like his own death; he jumped from his chariot onto the backs of Drona's horses, holding his dark shield decked with a hundred moons of silver, and a curved sword blue as the sky.

I saw Bhima's flag approach, a blue-eyed silver lion, and heard Bhima cry: *"Aswatthaman is slain!"*

The short arrows for close fighting, known only to Drona, fell from his hand. Gray with grief, Drona freed the heavenly weapons in his service and sat down in his car on a grass mat without any weapon. The sky flashed everywhere with equal light, and the sun was lost, and when I looked back I saw Dhrishtadyumna covered with blood, holding Drona's head in his left hand.

"Do not leave us without a gift," cried Dhrishtadyumna, and with a horrible cry he threw the head into the midst of the Kurus, who ran away from him in fear. Your soldiers all called to each other: *"Wait, do not run"*—but none who said this stayed on Kurukshetra themselves.

Arjuna came back and asked Bhima, "Is Aswatthaman dead?"

"There is an elephant of that name," answered Bhima. "I killed him."

"Why did Dhrishtadyumna strike him when he was unarmed?"

Dhrishtadyumna answered, "Yes, I have killed your friend Drona! Yes, thinking of the truth we told him a lie!"

Arjuna answered, "I cannot see who will protect you from Aswatthaman." Arjuna and Krishna drove off alone. Shaking his head, wiping away the tears from his eyes, Arjuna looked back at Dhrishtadyumna, and though he said nothing, yet he thought: *"Shame to you, who do not know what warriors are."*

So was Drona slain, Dhritarashtra. So did he die, dark-skinned and covered with arrows; eighty-five years old, his white hair falling to his shoulders; struck down with a lie when he had no weapons; dead in his chariot while Bhima embraced Dhrishtadyumna.

Aswatthaman asked Duryodhana what had happened. Your son could not speak, pale and shaken he made a sign to Kripa: *"Blessed be you, tell him."*

Kripa said, "Our men run from where Drona has died."

"How is it so?" wept Aswatthaman. From his eyes fell tears of fire, like drops of pitch from a torch. "How could anyone do this?"

"He had put down his weapons," said Duryodhana. "They told him you were dead. Now without him we are the sky without stars; a woman without a man, a river without water. Our men will not stop running until they reach their homes, however far."

"A man wishes only for his son to surpass him," said Aswatthaman. "That is why Drona taught only to me the weapon that no man can call twice and live." Aswatthaman looked at the Pandava army. "The weight of such men overburdens the Earth. I will free her."

He held an arrow on his bowstring.

"You are silence among secret things;
Upon you all this world like a row of pearls is strung.
—Now go!"

First touching water with his hand, Aswatthaman sent a deadly arrow of gold flaring into the sky.

Down upon the Pandava army fell ten thousand arrows with fiery mouths and ten thousand gleaming darts; one hundred thousand swords and maces and axes; a million razor-edged wheels spinning; and heavy iron balls roaring and tumbling.

"The weapon of Narayana!" Krishna pulled Arjuna down from his chariot. "Everybody, tell them not to run, on the Earth, quickly! No weapons!" Krishna and Arjuna ran in opposite ways, all along the Pandava lines, knocking down the swords and bows, pulling the men down from their horses and cars and elephants, so that each one stood on the Earth unarmed, telling them, "Do not think of war. If you even fight against this in your mind, you will die." Bhima would not leave his chariot. He was afire as all the weapons fell on him alone. But Satyaki knocked him down with a long pole.

Up and down Kurukshetra the Pandavas stood unarmed, their hearts at peace, their faces turned away from us. It was the hour between day and night when Aswatthaman's weapon failed, when the pale red sun took away the splendor of our armor and bright shields, and hid all the light in his own fire till the Earth and sky were the same color.

Aswatthaman set down his bow and slowly walked away into the night, and said *"Oh, is everything untrue?"*

KALEE, you like war; you are white and your eyes are smoke-colored; you are black and your eyes are many; your eyes are yellow gold. You live hidden in fearful places, and for victory I bow down to you as your child.

The man who will speak to the Goddess at dawn can have no enemies; and snakes and all animals that have fangs and teeth, from them he has no fear, as also from kings. If bound, he is freed. Victory and wealth are certain for him. He is sure to overcome all difficulties. With health and strength he lives for one hundred years.

14: the enchanteð lake

Majesty, that evening, when the new moon hung low in the
sky, full-arched and radiant as Kama's bow, when the
Pandavas were pulling our arrows from their bodies and
bathing, when their physicians were giving them drugs and
speaking mantras over their wounds, Karna walked into
Arjuna's tent and Krishna said, "It is a sin not to slay those
who deserve it!"

"No sentry came with you?" asked Arjuna.

"But they did not see me," answered Karna.

Krishna said, "Why have you come here wearing your
armor and armed with your sword?"

"You forget that I know you," answered Karna. "Knowing
everything, why do you yet seek to beguile me?" He
touched the hilt of his sword and said to Arjuna: *"If you are
not afraid, meet me tomorrow on Kurukshetra plain, and
fight with me."*

And Arjuna, touching his own sword, replied: *"Gentle
warrior, be patient; I will be happy to kill you.*

❧

Seated like the gods on jeweled beds of tigerskins, the Kurus were meeting in Duryodhana's tent when Karna returned and said, "This dark night is like a hundred years, like the death-night of the world, and on the field the headless dead stand on the stumps of their legs, groping blindly for their murderers."

Aswatthaman told your son, "Bharata, you saw my weapon fail. We can never win. Shame to war, Duryodhana. Let me speak to Arjuna. Share Kurujangala with them. I do not see anywhere the end of our sorrows, like a drowning man unable to see the ocean's shore."

"My ninety-eight brothers, with their red silk banners and red robes, were killed today by Bhima, by iron arrows polished on stone," said Duryodhana. "Vast was my army— in the beginning. Where have they gone, and how has this battle come upon us? Where are the Kurus now? Aswatthaman—*Who?*"

"Then let it be Karna!" said Drona's son.

"They killed Bhishma by deceit and Drona by a lie," said Karna. "For this Kunti's sons are all alive, but the Pandavas are stained forever, like the moon. But come to me for your refuge. Let the fever of your heart vanish—tomorrow I will fight Arjuna at last, and if I live I will slay them all."

All our hearts turned to Karna, and Duryodhana thought Arjuna already slain, and felt as though reborn after death. I alone knew that Karna thought to himself, "I am already dead; Arjuna is only the means of it."

Water fragrant with mantras and herbs and flowers was poured over Karna's head from brimful vessels of gold and earthen jars, from elephant tusks and the horns of bulls, to install him as our general. Brahmanas told him, "They cannot look at your flying arrows, any more than owls can look at the sun. Vanquish the Pandavas with Krishna and all their followers." And for victory your son gave Karna gold, and a silver necklace with a breast ornament, and ten thousand cows.

Fair and handsome, his curly hair soft and dark and wet from the holy water, Karna said, "Duryodhana, for you I will give my breath and my body that are so hard given. May I see your kingdom like a flower free from thorns. Who else has any chance to save you but I? I have no fear of battle for I have seen how the world is always changing and impermanent. Yet now with Drona dead and Bhishma dying, who can believe even that the sun will rise again? We are abandoned. Now is the time to mourn for all of you, and for the Kurus, and for the Earth."

"My friend, I have chosen these enemies," said Duryodhana. "Do not hold affection for them in your heart as did Drona, who for all that received only treason."

"That is not so, Majesty," answered Karna. "He fought his best for you, and there was never the slightest fault in him."

"But he let Arjuna pierce our army; he did not seize Yudhishthira."

"Where is the wonder in that? Seeing how destiny defeats us whatever we do, how many have not died or left us? Where is our youth, when we could do anything we desired? Where is the spring of this year that is now near winter? I think it is true that Time is awake when the world sleeps, intent on his own ends."

"Yes," said Duryodhana, "there are those whom the gods

love, who are always sure of success and happiness. They
have no more intelligence than other men, they are not
better in any way, yet they will win where others fail. Good
fortune follows them when they walk or run and lies beside
them like their shadow when they sleep."

Your son was silent awhile. Then urged on by Death,
caught in the net of the past, he said, "They were not born
so. Our fate may change at any moment. Why should there
be restraint on anyone? Why should one not be free to do
just as he will? Now tell me—what is necessary for us, and
what is still more necessary?"

When the immortal Dawn had pervaded the wide spaces,
the depths, and the high places with her brilliance on the
fourth morning, I saw the sky over Kurukshetra so crowded
with the gods who had come to watch us that their heavenly
chariots could hardly squeeze by one another. With his
hands marked with thunder-wheels Karna strung the bow
Vijaya that only he could bend. He strung flower garlands
of dead black iron over his chariot and made King Salya his
charioteer, to balance Krishna, and filled a second car with
long arrows winged with vulture feathers, to balance
Arjuna's unfailing quivers.

Karna's arms were red with sandal paste; blue and gold
champa flowers hung round his shoulders. He mounted his
chariot carrying Indra's winged dart that lay alone in sandal
dust in its long golden box, the fatal dart Karna had
worshipped for a year with lights and beads and food and
flowers and incense, and had long kept it for Arjuna's death.

288

Its wings were bright as sunlight; to hold it was sweet as childhood remembered; to face it was bitter as Time.

We looked at him as at a Wishing Tree. Karna terrified even me, but I could scarcely keep from calling out to him: *"Do not go!"* as we followed him onto the field in silence, without music, walking round the dead that lay on the Earth like bits of fire, still seeming to be alive. There Karna stopped, with sixty million arrows of iron and steel and wood and silver, bearing arrowheads pointed or barbed or cleft, or shaped like a calf's tooth, or a boar's ear, or a crescent, or the head of a snake or a frog.

Karna bent over and said to Salya, "Who will win and who will embrace the Earth he has died for, desiring her no longer? Even the storm-wind cannot move the mountains; even the sea-waves die on the shore. Go a little farther and wait there for him."

By his tent, Arjuna put flowers over his armor and drank deeply from a bowl of wine till his eyes shone bright as the arch diadem on his head. He touched a brazen mirror that gave him back his strength redoubled, and fastened on his arms the bracelets of good fortune, the flawless jewels and life-giving herbs sealed in golden capsules strung together on silver chains. Then Arjuna was in his car, and Krishna was driving the silver-white horses in their pearl harness over to Karna, while the rest of the Pandava army followed a little behind. At a sign from Dhrishtadyumna they stopped far from us, and all together we watched, with the forest ascetics who were sitting at the edge of the wood and the plain, and with the gods above.

Karna loudly slapped his armpit and Arjuna answered

him. The sky became overcast, hiding Arjuna in mist and fog; lightning clouds higher than mountains towered above; thunder rolled across heaven, and the rain and dew of Lord Indra fell gently down. Indra's rainbow hung over Arjuna, and the dark heavy clouds seemed to laugh as rows of white cranes flew through them. Arjuna strung his bow and whispered to Krishna, "Will you and I walk together any more?" And Krishna answered, "Ah, be still!"

Then Surya angrily burnt away the clouds and bathed Karna in sunlight that shone from his armor and earrings as dancing sparks of colored fire and burning streaks of liquid gold. Arjuna called out, "If I am a worthy guest, grant me the hospitality of battle."

"I am honored," cried Karna, "I could never turn you away!" Arjuna's horses were still walking slowly, when suddenly Karna's chariot raced at him, crashing over the plain, jarring the Earth under its wheels, and Karna gave that desirable guest a million arrows striking all at once to pierce his armor, like the charity of a perfect host who offers all his home to the wayfarer. Death himself would have felt pain from those arrows.

Arjuna danced on his car like Shiva dancing covered with blood in the burning ghats at night. He clapped his hands and there was darkness, but we could still see his bowstring flash as he drew it back to his ear. I thought, "Now arrows are the dice, and Gandiva bow the throwing box. Who else will forgive what Arjuna will? And whose anger is more unbearable?"

Down from the sky boulders flew at Karna, who crushed and shattered them with his arrows and ground them to sand that fell sparking and burning through the night sky. He surrounded Arjuna with crackling flames, and from that weapon the robes of the Pandava warriors caught fire, though they stood far away, and the Earth was scorched black. They were ready to run when Arjuna quickly spoke some mantra and the fire was gone, and we were in cold water up to our shoulders.

From Karna's bow a hot desert wind swept the plain to dry the water. The sun returned; the wind was gone swirling away; there was no sign from the fire, no fallen sand, and we stood again as before the beginning.

Arjuna's white arrows, their wings of peacock feathers blazing, pierced Karna like new-sluffed serpents with downbent heads entering the Earth. With an arrow sticking in his forehead, Karna cut Gandiva's bowstring with a snap that made my ears ring. Then for awhile those two archers filled the sky with death in perfect balance, with arrows long and thick and short, while the gods sometimes said: *"Excellent, Karna!"*—and sometimes: *"Excellent, Arjuna!"* Tired in the afternoon, they stopped to rest beneath the shadow of their arrows locked together in the sky, looking at one another while the Apsarasas of heaven fanned them with young palmyra leaves and sprinkled cool sprays of sandalwater over their bodies.

And after, Arjuna began the battle again. Before Karna could reply, Time invisibly told him: *"The Earth is devouring your wheel."* Karna's chariot tipped over to the left, and the wheel on that side was locked fast. When Karna jumped down and pulled at the axle hub with his feet on the ground, Earth that had swallowed his wheel rose four fingers' breadth, with her seven islands and her hills and waters and forests, but the wheel would not come free.

Then Karna saw Arjuna take aim at him, and wept with anger and said, "I am afoot and unarmed. Arjuna, wait for me now; be not a coward."

Yet Arjuna would not wait, so that Karna thought, "Now my life is in peril," and abandoning his war against the Earth he leapt onto his chariot and opened the long box.

Karna shook the dust from Naikartana dart; rumbling thunder shook again in the clear empty sky; and all creatures that were able fled away in fear. I ran, but still I saw the keen and polished dart with golden bells in Karna's hand, inspired with anger, able to destroy whatever it met. And before Arjuna could think, Karna threw the dart and cried: *"Arjuna, you are slain!"*

That shock brought the lattice of arrows crashing down. Indra's dart threw off flames from its wings; fire circled its head; and always it gained speed, blasting the air from its way, aimed true at Arjuna's breast.

Krishna pressed his foot down so that Arjuna's car sank into the Earth and the horses fell down. The awful dart struck to bits the diadem of lightnings atop Arjuna's head and flew flaming into a starry constellation in the sky of heaven. Arjuna's crown, a guardian and a fragrance to its wearer, lay broken on the Earth.

Wet with blood, Arjuna's long hair fell over his face and down his back. Flames show out from every pore of his body. *"Oh, may it kill him!"* wept Arjuna, and shot from Gandiva an arrow irresistible as a Rakshasa at night—an arrow with a flat crescent head, razor-sharp and broad as two hands held out hollowed.

As Karna fell beheaded, so fell our fame and happiness and pride and hope, and also our hearts. Karna's head was as unwilling to abandon his body as a treasure owner all his wealth, but Arjuna stood victorious. Karna never expected Indra's dart to fail, and so he took no guard to himself.

The wheel was free, and Salya drove the empty car away. It was evening, the deep metal drums of heaven roared untouched in the air, and Lord Surya, forever kind to his son, with his last ray touched Karna's body and sank crimson with grief behind Sunset Hill. The gods left the sky and victory left our side forever.

Duryodhana wept, "Oh, Karna. . .," and Arjuna bound his head with a white cloth. Yudhishthira drove over to Karna and wondered, "Who was he?"

Your army was a death-field. We were pale and ready to run again; our mouths were dry and emptiness was before our restless eyes. Not one man still wished to fight for you. The enemy made no move, but steadily looked at us in silence as the sunset died, and the wind sighed in my ears: "Alas."

From both armies we gathered round Karna by lamplight. He was still beautiful to us, still frightening to them, not very changed. For a moment the rivers stood still and every man felt pain in his heart. Duryodhana came, and then rode slowly away, often glancing backwards at Arjuna's car, and at Kurukshetra covered with iron tiger-claws held by severed hands, covered with hammers and bearded darts, with yokes and fans and chains, with broken spears and wheels, with swords and rings and blood-dyed arrows and bells and dead flowers and fallen heads with bright crystal earrings whose open mouths were filled with blood.

His head bent, Duryodhana told us, "Who can win always? The dart was baffled like the hope of an unfortunate man. But now rest for the night."

Yudhishthira told Arjuna, "I cannot believe that the strongest warrior in all the world is dead. Thirteen years I have not slept without thinking of Karna."

The gentle night wind smelled of the Earth and her green plants; the stillness of evening became the silence of night; and under the stars Karna's body stiffened and grew cold.

⚜

At a ford on the Ganges we met Duryodhana. Kripa, still on his chariot, told your son, "The blood-fed flowers are rising from the field. All is slaughter; what have we left to do? We tremble before the wind."

Duryodhana was on foot; he threw back his head and answered in a level voice, "Again and again and again I cannot endure that Karna is dead! Has some magician poured our kingdom on the fire?"

"Kaurava, a man may die for his family, or a village may burn for a kingdom—yet abandon the three worlds for your own self's sake! Do you know where you are? Break that self, and all is lost without a refuge."

"At the dice game, Draupadi was young and dark, her skin warm in winter and in summer cool; but I told her, 'Choose one of us and you will not need five husbands. Or like a sweating doe, you are free to weep or to thirst!' Kripa, were you there, do you remember that insult awful as conscience? Never will she forgive me."

Then Salya came as quickly as a god flying to eat the well-done smoke of a sacrifice and said, "In my rage I can split the Earth, scatter the mountains, and tear up the seas. Let me lead your army tomorrow, for I easily deserve this many times over. My life for you, Majesty. . .but forgive me, it is not right to praise or humble oneself before others."

Duryodhana said, "Long ago you told Bhishma, *You must not say—Give me your sister,* so he bought Madri for gold. Do you hate her sons now?"

"Not at all. But I am here, on a riverbank, held fast by desire, unable to change or break away."

Once the water was poured over Salya we took courage from him. Our lion-roars split the night; we laughed and sang. I thought, "Once more. . ." Duryodhana said, "No one will fight alone tomorrow. Let all who wish to go leave us now," but no one went, and in the Pandava camp Krishna told Yudhishthira, "Only you can stop Salya."

❖

Yesterday, on the fifth morning, Salya told us, "Meet the Pandavas with their friends, and quickly killing them, turn back from the fight!"

Sakuni came over to me on horseback, and said in Duryodhana's hearing, "We need every man; I will command you."

Duryodhana smiled. "Sanjaya is not in my army. He has no help for you now."

"Do it!" Sakuni shouted at me.

"What, Oh Lord, prepare your funeral?" I asked.

Duryodhana laughed happily. "Beloved gambler, now you must fight," he said. "There was no defeat in our gambling hall, but now it will be done. . .unless you are afraid without your dice."

Sakuni rode away, and Duryodhana embraced me. "Oh, very good, Sanjaya!" he said. "But death does not bow to brave men. For me, if you will, wear today one of my swords and a shield of armor, and stand carefully, facing the enemy." Still smiling to himself, Duryodhana climbed on his elephant and sat under his flag of gold hung with golden bell-bracelets, showing a gemstone elephant.

Majesty, I do not go to a war without arms, and I found my sword and armor while Dhrishtadyumna waited on the field, taking care of Yudhishthira's army. Your son Yuyutsu stood facing us with his plain gold banner; I saw Yudhishthira's flag, a golden moon and round it all the planets, and below on the flagstaff two drums and many soundstones. There were the golden-maned lion on white of Satyaki; the silver swan of Sahadeva; and the handsome Himalyan Sarabha with eight legs and four eyes, with its back made of gold, on Nakula's flag.

Salya's car carried his flag of a silver elephant and four golden peacocks crowing on his flagstaff tied round with heads of wheat. He drive out opposite Dhrishtadyumna; the chariot-fighters blew their moon-white shells; the bowmen cheered; and women were widowed as blood sealed the dust on the Earth.

Dhrishtadyumna's car raced forward, but at a glance from Yudhishthira his right wheel locked in fright and the car spun away to the side. Yudhishthira drove straight at Salya, the drums on his flagstaff beating like thunder. Yudhishthira, whom we always thought so harmless and soft, was sharp and savage, his eyes trembling wide in rage; he broke Salya's bow and cut off his car wheels. Salya picked up his sword and jumped to the ground, holding a dark blue shield with a thousand diamond stars that looked like a round piece of the night sky. He ran for Yudhishthira, but the Pandava king threw a spear of coral and steel shrilling with bells, whose very shadow was fatal to every life. Salya tried to catch it like a leaping flame, but the spear went through his shield, through his chest, and into the Earth as into water, vanishing disdainfully away. From her love for him, the Earth rose up slightly to meet Salya as he fell bathed in blood and lifeless, like a dear wife receiving her husband in her bed at night.

Sakuni with a long shining lance, on his mountain horse with a silver breastplate, cut round behind the Pandavas where no chariots could move through the wreckage on the field to stop him. Sahadeva and Nakula left their cars and mounted two horses whose manes and tails were blue as peacock down, one dark as night, one white as the day. Sahadeva, wearing one black glove on his swordhand, first reached Sakuni, and his twin an instant later. Though I shut my eyes I saw the gambler fall cut into three parts from their two swords.

Still with my eyes closed I saw darts run whistling through the sky; and the fork-tailed shrikes and black crows flew by us to our left. Heads and bodies fell with a soft noise like ripe fruit from a shaken tree. I saw again sparks cover Bhima, who pressed our men deep into the miry Earth, and who laughed softly and said, "What more can I do to you?" For every Kuru killed by Bhima, another fell dead from fear at seeing the first one die. Those who did not die fell down; their weapons fell from their hands; they cried weakly and watched with half-shut eyes; they ran away, crying: *"He is no human being!"*

I opened my eyes.

I looked, and one moment saw the warriors bleeding, paralysed; then in their place I saw tall Flame-of-the-forest trees bending red in heaven's groves. One moment there were elephants, their bright armor cut and falling; then the grey Himalyas without their clouds at winter's coming. Now a blood river ran; now arrows were sticking in someone's face—then I saw the red rain rivers of the hills, and bees ravishing a lotus for her sweetness.

Earth was a woman marked by her lover, the ground was covered with serene planets and stars cast down from heaven at the end of their merit. Now I heard screams of pain; then the delicate laughter of Apsarasas, the ring of their jewel collars on their breasts. In the air. I saw them welcome the dead into heaven; on Earth I saw the dying carried away unrecognizable, and their rescuers still return.

I smelled the Apsarasas' perfume and their flowers of desire, and I wept that I had no one before me to kill for them. I smelled blood so fresh that I looked for wounds on my own body, and for a way to run from Kurukshetra.

All this I sensed quicker than I can tell, Dhritarashtra. Quicker than the arrows flying so close that those behind touched the heron feathers of those ahead; faster than the chariots that when an arrow flew from them, after a league the arrow and car arrived together. Horror's fascination entranced me as the rules of war fell broken at my feet. Now drivers and animals were killed, nor did the warriors first call their names and give warning even to those unarmed. Now horses ran down foot soldiers and chariots were crushed by elephants, and the four divisions of the armies fought with anyone—but you know those rules, Bharata. Yet they were not written in blood by men driven to murder all about them, knowing nothing whether the victim were friend or enemy. And we had not the time to care for such a little thing.

Then our army became a river lost in the desert sands. The Kurus looked at one another and at Duryodhana, and thought, "The King should not fight alone, ignoring us—but. . .it is me Arjuna pursues; it is me he is chasing!" And Dhrishtadyumna killed with his arrows the small number left of our men, who had but swords or no weapons at all and stood afoot unable to reach your son.

I could only see Duryodhana, although very wounded, was still alive. He saw that all around him were only his enemies, but among them all he was then the only man. He felt no fear and no loss. He did not waver, and at whatever man of the Pandava army I looked, I saw him pierced by your son's arrows, or by the lances hurled by his elephant. Duryodhana had never to shoot a second arrow at his mark; none could approach him. He was alone their target, without one to stand by him.

When his bow was broken he cut down their arows with his sword, but the elephant died under him, and I saw him jump like a panther from a limb and stand on foot holding only his mace bound in hempcord, then disappear into the forest.

The Pandavas raced down the field to our camp. Dhrishtadyumna and Satyaki stopped near me in their chariots, and Dhrishtadyumna asked, "What is the use in keeping Sanjaya alive even for an instant?" He laughed and drew his sword.

I was very afraid and felt like a sinner in Hell, but I realized that facing me Dhrishtadyumna was weak as wet sand. Never had I seen this happen to him. He was numb and could not think. I took not a step back, but held my ivory-handled sword and smiling told him, "Come to me, Panchala!"

There was the thunder of another chariot coming close behind, and we turned to see Arjuna and Krishna.

"By no means kill Sanjaya," said Krishna. "Release him, for he stands here protected by Vyasa."

"I do not see Vyasa," answered Dhrishtadyumna, "and I do not need Sanjaya."

I looked at Narayana and thought, "Please, Lord! Let him try!"

But Satyaki stepped down from his car and joined his hands to me and said: *"Peace to you, Sanjaya, you may go. Give me your sword."*

"I command this army!" shouted Dhrishtadyumna.

With a sigh I gave Satyaki that sword I had never wet with blood and began to put off my armor. Satyaki did not look up at Dhrishtadyumna but answered him, "I obey only

Krishna of all men; or if you dislike my actions, fight with me."

Krishna looked hard at Dhrishtadyumna, then his eyes caught mine and he smiled. From Arjuna's car he took a spear, and holding it said, "Dhrishtadyumna, I put all God's anger against Sanjaya in this spear," and threw it up into the the sky. It rose and began to fall burning; fire flattened the air and Krishna bowed his head in his hands while the others turned and hid their faces. But I felt nothing, and as the spear fell onto me it vanished, and a garland of flowers instead circled my neck.

So I left them there and walked back through our camp and down the road to Hastinapura. Our sentries and old men, and our women, were running past me to your city, and the countryfolk had left their lands in fear of Bhima. Yuyutsu wept to see the flight and thought, "Lord, they fly on all sides. Duryodhana is dead and I am Dhritarashtra's only son."

He went to Yudhishthira and said, "I ask your permission, for I will guard them to the city."

Yudhishthira answered: *"Yes"*—and Yuyutsu's war-chariot sped away grinding the Earth. He asked me to go with him when he passed me, but I thought, "Dhritarashtra will wait for me and there is something missing," and kept on walking by myself. All around me women were crying, untying their braids, tearing themselves with their nails or with stones, striking their breasts; running and falling down or riding shocked and silent in mule carts. But soon they had gone by and I was alone.

❧

Now, Bharata, I had not gone far when I saw armor flash in the wood alongside the road, and I went in among the trees to see who it was. There I found Duryodhana standing alone holding his mace, badly wounded by many arrows. His eyes were so blinded by tears that he could not see me standing before him, and at first I could not speak for sorrow and only looked at him without his knowing. At last I said, "I am Sanjaya. I have been captured by Dhrishtad-yumna and again freed by Krishna. The Pandavas all wander searching for you, I know not where."

Duryodhana touched my hand. "I have heard no friend but you, charioteer. The rest must all be dead. Nearby is a lake covered with birds and flowers; lead me there and I shall rest within."

By his power of illusion Duryodhana charmed the water, making a place for himself; once he had entered he could not be seen, and the lake looked just as before.

Then three chariots came silently through the trees and I saw Kripa and Kritavarman and Drona's son. Aswatthaman embraced me. "By good fortune you still live, Sanjaya. Where is our king Duryodhana?" I pointed to the lake. "Alas," said Aswatthaman, "He knew not that we were alive, cut off from him in battle."

He raised his voice. "We three are here, Majesty. With you we can return and fight."

From within the lake Duryodhana replied, "I am tired, I will come out tomorrow."

"But they are also exhausted and mostly slain or wounded. We should not wait."

"I would expect no less than this of you," said

"I am tired, I will come out tomorrow"

Duryodhana, "but meet me here tomorrow. And Sanjaya, if they cannot come again, tell Dhritarashtra that his son has entered the depths of a lake."

But some hunters who every day gathered meat for Bhima were by accident passing through the forest, and at sight of Aswatthaman calling into an empty lake they whispered, "Hush! Why do we work day after day, shortening our lives?"

They went to Kurukshetra and, though forbidden by soldiers, approached and told Bhima: "*He is there*"—and received all their dreams of wealth while Arjuna said, "We have not lost him, and we can end this war."

When we heard the noise Aswatthaman said, "Joyfully the Pandavas come here. We will leave this place—let it be known to you," and your son answered, "So be it."

Kripa with one arm took me aboard his chariot. We hid far away, thinking, "Duryodhana lies stretched out on the bottom of the lake. The Pandavas have come. What will happen?"

It was late in the afternoon, and Yuyutsu had just entered Hastinapura. Vidura sat weeping and in a choked voice asked, "Why have you come back without Duryodhana?"

Yuyutsu answered him. "By Yudhishthira's permission I have protected the widows who fled in panic after Duryodhana ran to the east from Kuru's Plain."

Vidura stood up. "Good. Our honor now rests on your compassion. I see you again! Do not go to the king and do not return tonight to Yudhishthira. You are the only staff we have to walk by."

Then Yuyutsu went to his own house. Servants and

brahmanas met him with praising songs that cut him; that
night he did not sleep thinking of the certain and terrible
destruction of the Bharatas at one another's hands.

Wealth and power pass like a dream,
Beauty fades like a flower,
Long life is gone like a wave.

I am not a clown,
I am not a beautiful woman,
What have I to do in the palaces of kings?

15: the night

"Having crossed an ocean am I to drown in a roadside mudpuddle?" Bhima beat his eight-sided mace on the lake. The water was cool and transparent, but Duryodhana had made it solid by a most wonderful illusion. Bhima, nor even Krishna, could not enter.

Yudhishthira said, "Look how he has charmed the water! He can have no fear from any man."

Krishna answered, "He is the soul of illusion and an adept, and by magic you must destroy him. This is the truth. Take the help of acts and means."

Yudhishthira said, "Duryodhana, why have you done so to this water, and what sort of courage bids you hide from us now?"

"Because you are so surprised that fear should enter the heart, just break my spell," answered Duryodhana.

"Do not race with sorrow," said Yudhishthira. "Fight myself or one of my brothers and let Kurujangala be the stake."

"What do I want with this kingdom shorn and widowed

and destitute and reft of citadels? After I rest I will go to the forest. It is all yours, Bharata. But still I would like to defeat you before I leave."

"What king would give away his kingdom only because he was surrounded by his enemies?"

Duryodhana, who could not from pride endure the sun's own brightness, waved his arms and answered, "For all I've done to you, what have you ever been able to do to me? I made you into my servants, hiding from fear of me in your disguises. Like the year meeting the seasons, I will fight you one by one. Yudhishthira, judge the fight. One may not fight against many."

Yudhishthira said, "No, I am a Kshatriya, very cruel, without the least compassion; I have a narrow heart—to me there is no right or wrong; when I am in any difficulty I care nothing for the very gates of heaven. But choose a weapon."

"I have a mace with a sling," said Duryodhana from within the lake.

"Then take armor."

"Mine is of tempered gold, Bharata!" The solid waters shattered, then melted together. Waves went rolling to every side, and like an elephant rising from a lotus pond Duryodhana, drenched in water and blood, walked up onto the shore and stood before Yudhishthira. "Let whoever will fight with me on foot come forward."

The Pandavas and Panchalas seized each other's hands, and Yudhishthira said, "Bind your hair. Except your life, what else may we give you?"

Krishna said, "Yudhishthira, you are a fool! What rashness is this now? It is alone your fault that we are again in doubt and peril."

Bhima stood up, holding his mace with its golden moons and stars.

"See?" continued Krishna. "Bhima is strong enough, but Duryodhana has skill. We are in danger of losing everything; Duryodhana is in ease and comfort. Without doubt, surely Kunti's sons were born to spend their lives as beggars in the woods, and never meant to enjoy a kingdom."

Bhima looked at Krishna and spit on his hands. "Yes, Lord," he said, "what man in his right mind would challenge Duryodhana? He is defeated, he wanted to leave for the forest and give us what was not his, and having once run away and returned again, he is to be greatly feared. He has only one purpose: he fights for his life. And in his golden helmet he is as proud as though we had lost."

Duryodhana wrapped a new cloth of gold like a sheet of fire around his mace. "I'm glad it's you, wolf-belly. For thirteen years I have struck an iron statue of you with this mace, all for today! It would have been," sighed Duryodhana, "so much better had Kunti borne an abortion in your place."

Bhima spoke cheerlessly. "Krishna, sit down, do not hurt your eyes watching him die."

Krishna hesitated, and thought, "I will watch no more life-spilling. All by myself I can . . ."

"Then stand and face me brother."

"Balarama!"

311

Tall in his blue robes, with one stone ring in his ear, with wildflowers bowing round his neck, Balarama stood swinging a jar of wine, looking at Krishna with one eye, and said, "King Yudhishthira the Just, I would not fight for you, I would not fight against Krishna, but tell me—when you met with defeat, when your wife and brothers were driven from Hastinapura like cattle: *why didn't the Earth just curl up and die?*"

"You're drunk," said Krishna.

"Shh . . . since someone began this war, I have been bathing along the rivers in holy places . . . where the seven rivers disappear underground . . . bathing in the Clear river and the Bright, the Flood and the Delightful, the Wide and the Gold and Handsome . . . "

"Yes, have another drink," said Krishna.

Balarama answered, "But of course, and you. Have another wife." He emptied his winejar. "I heard how Duryodhana dove like a swan into a lake. Now King Yudhishthira, don't sit there shining like the full moon with a herd of stars around him. Come with me, this is no place to fight."

"We won't," thought Yudhishthira.

Balarama smiled. "Why yes you will," he said. "Bhima. Duryodhana. Follow me."

Balarama led them to Kurukshetra to the west, to the south side of the river where there was no sand. "Here."

Crack! We heard it from where we hid, we saw the flashing lights of burning sparks as they rose in a glistening whirlwind when those murderous maces met. Duryodhana

312

spun in the right mandala; Bhima turned always to his left; each charmed their magic circles to ward out pain and questions. Great fear entered those who watched, and Balarama smiled and fell asleep.

They circled or stood still, or jumped up or backwards, in and out, dodging and bending. Duryodhana struck Bhima once and again so quickly the air burnt. Bhima's armor fell from him broken, like a wind-tossed cloud in the sun. His eyes rolled and he shook his head, leaning on his mace.

Duryodhana gazed with wonder at the amazing patience of Bhima, who with tranquil soul lifted his weapon from the ground that the match might continue. Your son circled him slowly, trying to find an opening, but on no side was Bhima careless. As I would handle a light sword, so those two thrust and guarded with their dreadful irons.

Then Bhima drew your son off balance. He threw his mace. Duryodhana tried to avoid it by jumping up to let it pass beneath, but Bhima had aimed at his head and the mace broke Duryodhana's thighs. Duryodhana fell and dropped his mace, its jeweled bonds and knots all severed, and lay on the Earth like a poisonous snake broken and cast down to die. There was for a moment a silence that echoed through the forest, before any realized what had happened.

Then the Pandava soldiers cheered; the animals neighed and snorted; the men shuffled their feet. Cymbals and drums tore the air—but very many trembled, lakes turned to blood, and women seemed to look like men, and men like women, when your son fell.

Balarama awoke. "Bhima! I taught you . . . do not strike

below the waist." He stood up. "Sorrow and shame to you! Never has this been done! Or are you ignorant, that you may act as you like?"

Duryodhana said, "Let it be. Bhima has paid off his wrath and his mother by a fair or unfair act. I am fallen and your words will not raise me. Why did you lead us here?"

"To Kuru's Plain?"

"Yes."

"When hundreds of years ago Kuru plowed this field without leading in any watercourse or sowing one seed, curiosity led Indra to approach. He asked why Kuru walked through dust when he could as well spend his days in the cool honeysuckle houses of the palace garden in Hastina-pura.

"'Not as well,' answered Kuru. 'This is a dust bowl,' said Indra. 'No,' said Kuru, 'it is a future battlefield that will lead to heaven.'

"'It is a wilderness,' said Indra, 'Your Majesty's time is far too valuable for this.' But Kuru kept right on plowing until Indra returned and said, 'Murder is evil and war is a sin, or where is the field for the assassins of kings?'

"'Lord,' answered Kuru, 'I will stop every sacrifice and fire; I will lead the Kurus into the forest where there are no books.'

"That midnight," continued Balarama, "Indra stepped in through Kuru's third-story window. On his ankles were white-silver bells that made no sound, on his head was a fragrant diadem of light. 'You are sleepy,' said the Lord of the Gods. 'Here, I'll fix it.'

"Kuru motioned Indra to sit beside him, but Indra said,

314

'No, I have come only to sing you a song. And he sang, and after, bowed low and vanished."

"That dust-song is true?" asked Bhima.

"Yes." Balarama called for his chariot. "Why should one die elsewhere! Now I return to Dwaravati by the sea."

Balarama left them, and Krishna told Duryodhana, "I forgive you."

"You!" Duryodhana angrily tried to rise. Holding himself on his two arms, he said, "Slave and son of a slave! Only by crooked ways could you win."

"You followed your pleasure, now all have died," said Krishna.

"Oh, torn by grief, live on in this unhappy world! How will you look at the widows, Lord Narayana? How will you avoid their curses? How will you drag on your miserable life? But from heaven, I shall send you my fullest pity. I leave you now, though to your eyes I do not move."

Yudhishthira breathing quickly thought to himself, "Yes, I envy you. We are now the creatures of Hell, with grief our companion forever."

But Bhima bowed to his older brother and said, "The Earth once more comes to you who have no foes alive. I give—your breath of glory, your garland of fame."

And the twins took Yudhishthira's arms and smiled, "We see everything, Dharmaraja, we just don't say very much."

Krishna told Yudhishthira, "He called that fair-browed woman, faultless and amiable, *Wife of slaves, you have no husbands now! They are sterile seeds without life.*"

"You mean poor little butter-eyes?" asked Duryodhana.

"He will look no more on women," said Bhima. "This

Duryodhana is slain. He is now a piece of wood; do not spend more bitter breath on him. Let us leave this place."

But when Duryodhana fell silent, the eighty-eight thousand Siddhas who live between Earth and the sun said in one voice, "Praise to King Duryodhana." The evening sky was empty and blue; the Pandavas were sad and shamed.

Krishna told them, "Though he was tired, even the gods could not have won against Duryodhana without cleverness. Do not take it to heart. The gods have fought unfairly against a strong enemy, so we may do it too. We have victory and the evening; let us go to our tents." Hearing this lie from Krishna, the Pandavas were again cheerful and blew their conches.

Dhrishtadyumna took his army into our camp, which was the more graceful and elegant of the two, where they rested on the soft beds left in the abandoned tents, eating our fine food and wines. In front of Duryodhana's tent Krishna stopped Arjuna's chariot and told him, "Get out. Take down Gandiva bow and your arrows. I shall dismount after you—this is for your good."

Arjuna obeyed. "Stand back!" Krishna dropped the reins and jumped. Then and there the ape that topped the mantle of Arjuna's car disappeared; the upper parts of the car, then all the chariot and the four horses burnt to ash without a flame as they stood. There was only a heap of grey dust which the wind began to blow away.

The irresistible rainbow chariot was gone. Krishna said,

"Long since was your car destroyed by Drona because you would not fight against him. It has been ashes for two days, held together only by illusion. You guarded yourself but not your car, so I did it for you."

The Pandavas and Satyaki and Krishna rested awhile by themselves while Drishtadyumna brought the Panchala women and musicians from his camp to ours, and opened our treasure-chests.

Draupadi and the Pandava women were still in their own tents, and Krishna said, "As a beginning act of blessing we must remain in neither camp tonight." So they went to the riverside and fell asleep.

I told Kripa what had happened to your son, and we went to Duryodhana.

Weltering in agony, covered with dust, Duryodhana with difficulty was gathering up his flowing hair, frowning in anger, looking on all sides and suddenly sighing over and over. We ran and sat down beside him.

Aswatthaman wept. "Why do you lie here alone in the wilderness? Tell me truly. I do not see your brothers beside you, or Karna, or the hundreds of kings that were in your army. It is surely difficult to learn the ways of Yama. What is this? Duryodhana—where is your white umbrella, your yaktail fan, and all your army?"

Duryodhana wiped the blood from his eyes and said, "I will tell you the story of Death, and how no god has control over her."

Listen—

The books are all different; men argue and reach nothing; and Truth is hidden in caves. But I have heard this tale.

At the beginning of Time men lived in the clear air and moved at will without any effort. Then the Earth was honey, sweet and delicious, and, few by few, men dipped down from the sky to taste her. Then they took more than a taste, though they needed no food to live, and as they ate they became too heavy to fly and their wings dropped off from them, while Earth grew crusted and dry and made her seeds, and the rains began to fall.

Then the last man could fly no more. Then there appeared women—but we called them men, as we name ourselves, you and I. And those who once flew did not change. But they began to desire the men, and after, to bear their children. Unchanged they are today, and they are women to us.

Everyone was immortal. Earth could bear no more weight. Brahma heard her cries and began to think about the total destruction of his creatures. But he said, "I can find no way!" Ever there were more and more people living on Earth. And in his anger Brahma filled the heaven, the sky and the Earth all with fire.

"Ah!" thought Brahma. "This is the way."

But Shiva fell at Brahma's feet and said, "Be merciful, what you have made, do not destroy."

"I have no kindness," answered Lord Brahma. "I have no grace."

"Had you not I would never have come to you," said

318

Shiva. "Everything belonging to you is blasted with fire. Look on living things again another way."

"Earth came to me in pain," said Brahma. "I found no way to help her and became angry. I said, 'Beautiful One, I know already why you cry, but for this wish of yours—I have nothing!' And she turned from me, weighted down and bent."

"You will make her ashes," said Shiva.

Brahma said, "Lord of the night-wanderers, I withdraw my anger. Go. I have a great doubt, but I will hold my fire within myself."

Yet when he did so, from the doors of the six senses of Brahma came a woman of red eyes and dark-tanned skin, brilliant in her earrings and arm-bands, who smilingly looked at Brahma and Shiva and went her way to the south. Brahma called after her: *"Wait, Death. Kill all creatures, including idiots and priests."*

But she answered him, "No!" and ran away, and hid somewhere and cried.

Brahma found her, and said, "But no one will find fault with you, for you do my bidding. Death, only living creatures will die."

"No," she said. "It is cruel. Go away."

So Brahma left her and spoke to no one, smiling on the worlds without anger. Death wandered the Earth, taking no life, for one hundred trillion, two hundred seventy-seven billion and eight thousand years. Then Brahma came to her and said, "Death, I have not seen you for a moment. What are you doing?"

"Do not call me Death!" she replied. "I will never kill for you."

Brahma looked at that winsome girl. "I will make them equal. You will not have to take them, either men or gods or devils. I will make greed and anger and malice and shame and jealousy and passion. I will make them this way and that way. I will make disease and war from your tears. Those two only I will make that way. Do nothing—they will all come to you, soon or late. There is nothing to do, nothing to stop doing, for you or for them. But only greet them well in their hour. You have nothing else to say, they will kill themselves. And only the foolish will weep over what none can avoid."

Then Shiva began his dance, for till then, though he raised his foot, he could not put it down.

❖

"So don't be stupid," said Duryodhana. "This story can free people like you from sorrow and from the touch of love's tie. Every morning kings who desire their children to live long must hear this tale more dreadful than any Veda. It will destroy your enemies by hundreds; do you understand?"

"No," said Aswatthaman. The sun became his favorite form of fire and set behind the forest. "But though you were ever the favorite of women, you always told the truth. Yet do not pour on fuel to stop a fire, as you have poured out your life."

"If I had lived on," said Duryodhana, "I should only have grieved for those who died for me." He looked at me and struck his arms against the Earth, shaking his loose hair and gnashing his teeth. "Wonderful is the mind, Sanjaya. If it cannot have one thing, it will find it in the other; and so peace comes at last on her knees to me from a fatal war."

Aswatthaman said, "I see you surrounded by jackals and vultures who wait for you to die, as a king by relatives awaiting gifts and money."

"Prosperity did not abandon me before my death to wait upon another."

"Prosperity is frail as smoke," said Aswatthaman. Overwhelmed, he squeezed his hands and said hoarsely, "Not even Drona's death burns me so keenly as this."

"Why should Death not come to me before all your eyes?" asked Duryodhana. "I laid my commands on great kings. I have been killed in battle and not made into a slave. I see you all escaped alive from my war. Certainly I shall gain heaven, for I have learned all books, I can read and write, I have given gifts and ruled the Earth and stood over the heads of my enemies. I lived life like a god; whatever I wanted to enjoy was easily mine. What man in the world would not wish in his secret heart to be free from laws and rules, able to follow himself whatever the cost, able to do whatever he will? Krishna could not tempt me to peace."

"I have taken the measure of Krishna," said Aswatthaman. "He will not tell what he knows. Only give me permission, and in his presence and with his knowledge—I will kill them all."

"I have won him already," said Duryodhana. "I am going away with nothing, like a penniless wayfarer, leaving all my kingdom barren behind me. Sanjaya . . . you will live . . . remember, never trust the Pandavas, whatever they say. Tell my wife and my sister—provide for yourself against them."

"You say that you go now?" asked Aswatthaman.

"Soon."

"Then others still have time to follow you. We do not fight immortals."

"I'm glad I'm not a fool," said Duryodhana, "and that I see you again. End it now and go your ways, far from here where you will be safe."

"No! Make me your general!"

Duryodhana raised himself on his elbows and told Kripa, "Bring water." Kripa filled a jar brimful from the river. "Preceptor, blessed be you, if you wish me well install him as the commander of my army."

Kripa said: *"In the name of the Creator and the Destroyer—every time—and with reasons visible and invisible that are born of fate—every time—and at the king's command!"* He poured the water over Drona's son.

Duryodhana lay back. "Go away and leave me alone. I'll see you tomorrow."

The three made ready to go, but I said, "I will stay. Leave food and fire."

Aswatthaman, Kritavarman and Kripa drove away. Their war chariots fled with the light of day; then Night, the mother of the world, gently covered her child with darkness, as before, when she had not yet been first born.

⚜

They went far to the south before they secretly entered a forest dense and dark. There they camped beneath an ancient banyan tree of a hundred thousand branches and a thousand aerial roots falling to Earth like the columns of a living palace.

Aswatthaman could not sleep. To his eyes the starry sky was burning brocade, studded with the embers of war. There deep in the forest he lay awake, looking up into the banyan where a flock of black crows were asleep. And as he watched, a green-eyed tawny owl swept silently down, taking his victim so swiftly from a branch that the crows next on either side did not even stir.

Aswatthaman put the black lion's-tail flag on its ebony flagstaff. He covered his car, which was like a castle fort, with black bearskins; he harnessed his black horses; he put on his black armor and the helmet that hid his face in shadow. He shook Kripa awake. "All acts are touched with evil, like fire by smoke—therefore take your silver bow and come with me."

Kripa was instantly on his feet. "Such a thing . . . "

"It is unfair," said Aswatthaman. "It is against Dharma."

"No one could dissuade you," answered Kripa. "Put off your armor; take down your flag. You have not slept for many nights. We are masters of all weapons; what should we fear in the morning when we tell our names and crush the enemy? Go to sleep."

"One who lusts—how can he sleep?"

"He cannot," said Kripa.

"And an angry man?"

"No."

"One who has been defeated?"

"No."

"One who revolves in his heart many, many schemes to gain wealth?"

"Never," said Kripa, "but wait till light shall discover all things."

"I have no peace. *Find your tigerskin and your red horses.*"

"I would restrain my friend from sin," said Kripa. "As they chain a madman so would I speak him soothing words."

"For his own good!" Aswatthaman lowered his voice. "Let me tell you—you will not yourself murder a sleeping man. That is unnatural. But come with me . . . or we could go to Dhritarashtra and ask why we are here at all. Then we could guard him from night-hawks and gnats."

"Everyone believes his own ideas are wisdom itself. Do not mistrust me; do not bring me contempt. That man is not yet born in the world, who can break me from my friend who is a brahmana now, but will be born a worm in his next life. If he cares nothing, why should I?" Kripa awoke Kritavarman. "We two will go as your army."

"Follow me and wait." And Aswatthaman, whose father and mother were neither one born of woman, led them away. Through the murky night went the chariots, up to our camp buried in sleep, but there a pale giant guarded the gate. Round his waist was a tigerskin dripping blood; there were three eyes on his face; the very mountains would split to see him. The forest was still and quiet.

Aswatthaman threw his sword at him, and it was swallowed up. So were his arrows and darts and maces loaded with death. Drona's son got down from his car. He kicked up a long row of dirt into an altar and stood before it.

He thought, "My resolution hurries me on to its doing. If I do not avenge Drona, how will I open my mouth among men? If I do not, why would any father love his son? My armor makes no sound . . .

> *I have no fear of you;*
> *When can you not take me if you will?"*

Aswatthaman stepped up onto the altar and it turned to gold under his foot. He drew a small knife from his belt.

"You forbid what I sought. I take your protection; I am your sacrifice." But he could not move the hand that held his knife. The giant vanished. And Aswatthaman heard a voice, "Their lives are now full and their time is gone out."

There were no sentries; the tents were silent. While Kritavarman and Kripa waited outside, Aswatthaman built a bridge of arrows to cross the wall where there was no gate, knowing that those who wish others harm must enter a city by the wrong way, where there is no door.

By the blue light of his brow-jewel Aswatthaman kicked the women from Dhrishtadyumna's side, and with his hands shook him to death like an animal. He strangled Sikhandin. When the Panchala soldiers came against him, his sword became so bloody that it stuck to his hand. Silent was the camp when he entered; silent it was as he turned to leave it. Then the night-demons entered to drink the blood and crack the bones.

Kripa heard the Rakshasas saying: "This is sweet! This is monstrous! This is pure!"—and he called out his name. "I am Kripa, noble and quiet and mild-tempered!" Then he shot three fire-arrows hissing over the wall.

Aswatthaman strode through the burning camp as through the searing fires of Hell, tumbling the Rakshasas from his way till they cried out, "Mercy! We are yours!"

"Who lives yet?" asked Drona's son.

"No human but yourself," said a naked monster with five feet and backwards-pointing fingers. "You have killed them, or they have killed each other in confusion. They all sleep trustfully."

"You have found those who cling to Earth to save them?"

"All."

"Who can hide from you then?" asked Aswatthaman.

"There is no one," answered the Rakshasa.

It was nearly dawn. Aswatthaman rejoined the others, and under the sky like warm gold the three stood facing the light before sunrise with joined hands, to welcome the growing day. After the prayers of the twilight of dawn they drove to us by the lake. Kripa asked, "Majesty, have you strength to hear? Earth is no more overburdened."

"I have murdered Dhrishtadyumna and Sikhandin and all the Panchalas," said Aswatthaman. "The others were not there."

Duryodhana answered very faintly, "My quarrel was not with them. You have no more permission to fight for me. You have killed the innocent and left my enemies standing. No more . . . no more . . . now flee these ruins and save yourselves. I almost won . . . "

He fell silent, fixing his mind on the sun and his heart on the moon. I told him, "Where you go now, greet for me all those who have gone before."

Sanjaya said, "Only his body remained on Earth. He died in our arms as the sun rose this morning, and at the same moment, from grief I lost the heavenly sight of Vyasa, and on one of Aswatthaman's horses I rode here without stopping. So I have told you how all the Kurus and Bharatas are dead, how all the Panchalas and Gandharas and Matsyas and Madrakas are slain, how all the men and elephants and horses have fallen. Very few are left alive—only seven among the Pandavas and three of our army, and Yuyutsu. They survive, the rest are perished. The whole world has been destroyed by Time."

Dhritarashtra in his grief exhaled smoke and said, "My heart's core is diamond since it does not break. Shame to Kshatriya Dharma, shame to anger itself! Shame to man, who has such an end. Oh child, my son loved to fight; his advisors were fools; he had no wisdom, but was vain to think himself wise. He could not see things even when he looked at them."

"It is not his blame but your own," said Sanjaya. "Now do not start digging a well while your house burns. What Vidura and Vyasa told you has come exactly true, for it was nothing but the truth. Your palace has lost its beauty; comfort and happiness have deserted it. It is all empty and in disorder. I have been filled with sorrow since Duryodhana died, but this place increases it and breaks my heart. Now I can weep for them—for all of them."

"Have my sons no more love for me that they are dead?" asked Dhritarashtra. "Why will they never speak to me again, or clasp my neck and tell me: *Father, command us. This Earth is as much ours as it is Yudhishthira's.*"

"Pass it away," answered Sanjaya. "Majesty, one may be drowned by reflecting on bygone acts that no one remembers. Duryodhana fought the Pandavas as a man would fight his five senses, and so he lost."

"Though I never saw my sons," said Dhritarashtra, "still I loved them. I think of their ages; I was glad when they grew into men. How could they leave me now to blindness and old age? Why do I live on? What will become of an old childless couple? Having been a king and a king's father . . . you are well-skilled in narration, Sanjaya. Say no more."

❦

Whoever reads of this battle between the Kurus that is like a sacrifice with sugar grains and butter, and whoever hears of it ever without malice, the Fire Lord and the Wind will be pleased with him, and the Moon and the Sun forever. Vyasa has written this song that all men may have no sickness and have great wealth, and victory, and food, and every bliss in heaven, and to him no man is high and none is low. Again, all men are kings to him. God is eternal, and because it is God who is praised here, it is for this that such merit is gained by hearing of the olden time as equals that from the giving of cows, by day and by night for one year, with their calves, to those who deserve. The words of Vyasa can never be untrue.

328

part three:

in the end

OM!

Once having seen Narayana,
And Nara the best of men;
And having loved Saraswati,
I say:

JAYA!

16: the blade of grass

Vaisampayana said: "Majesty, when Dhritarashtra fell in a faint, Sanjaya carried him to his Queen. Vidura and Gandhari laid cold water on his face and fanned him, till he awoke with no hope of home or wife or wealth."

Janamejaya asked: "After Duryodhana died, where did his army of three men go? When did the Pandavas discover what had happened?"

Vaisampayana said: "Kritavarman returned to Dwaravati; Kripa first slept a long while well-hidden, then began to go the long way through the wood to Hastinapura. Aswatthaman broke his chariot and burnt it; he ground to dust his armor and weapons; and wearing only a grass cloth he walked alone down the far riverbank of Ganges."

Listen, Bharata—

Dhrishtadyumna's driver found the Pandavas after dawn, when the morning mists were clearing fast, and said,

"Everyone is dead. Aswatthaman was careless only once, so I escaped."

Yudhishthira wept, but Arjuna's eyes were dry. Arjuna asked the charioteer, "How?"

"I was hidden in a tree when Aswatthaman's lance struck the trunk, and the tree with every branch and leaf, and with myself, burnt fiercely into dead ashes. But later, taking up those ashes, Vyasa said: *Lord of the forest, revive!* First he fashioned a green sprout, then he gave it small leaves and little roots, then he made a trunk and branches, then the tall tree was grown as before with all its leaves. And I was still holding the same branch. Nothing lived in our camp that was human. I took iron shoes from a charred weapon-box, and when the Rakshasas would have stopped me I kicked them in the face—nor could they harm me, but fell to devouring those of their own that I had killed. After Drona's son I had no fear from anything else, but it was long before I found where you were."

Without waiting to hear more, Bhima backed his horses into their traces and drove away in his chariot. In Dhrishtadyumna's camp he picked his way through the hardened rivers of blood and fat, followed the chariot marks to the lake, and found Aswatthaman's path across the river.

Krishna told Satyaki, "Get your car!" He caught Arjuna's arm and spoke quickly, "Bhima rides to his death if we do not stop him. Once on the seashore at Dwaravati while you were in heaven and your brothers alone in the forest, Aswatthaman and I walked by ourselves on the lonely sands in the wind. He said, 'In exchange for the Brahma weapon that my father unwillingly gave me, give me your Chakra discus.' I said, 'Giving me nothing, take it.' I put it on the sand. He seized it but with all his strength he could not move it. I said, 'Arjuna never asked me such a thing, nor my sons, nor Balarama, nor any other. We hold you in respect. Let me ask—against whom would you have fought with that?'

"He answered, 'Against you! Now I leave you, for I may not have it, and for this you are without rival.' " Satyaki brought the chariot. "Now hurry," said Krishna. "Aswatthaman is restless. You alone also know this Brahma mantra."

As Krishna drove Arjuna through the river and after Bhima, Arjuna said, "When Drona taught us Brahmasira he said never to use it against men even in the greatest danger."

"He didn't want you to use it all," answered Krishna. They caught up with Bhima but could not stop him, till together the two chariots rounded a bend of the river and they saw Drona's son sitting at the edge of the water with Vyasa.

Bhima stopped and fitted an arrow to his bow. But when he released it, it did not fly off; it stuck there and hung swinging from the bowstring.

Aswatthaman laughed; the blue light gleamed between his eyes. Smiling at them he picked a grassblade in his left hand, looking from it to Bhima, then his eyes met those of Krishna.

"Do not say the mantra," said Krishna. "We will not harm you."

"I could not understand what Dhrishtadyumna was trying to tell me last night," said Aswatthaman, "but I have heard

never to trust you. Your word is a rainless cloud, and nothing more. The noise is meaningless. I bring you salvation, and release from bondage. I dissolve all bonds, and make you one with Lord Brahma. From the kindness of my heart you will not have to become hermits; in an instant all trace of your lies will vanish forever."

Aswatthaman's lips began to move silently. The Earth quaked as though to shake him off; all the trees and animals in the worlds trembled, and fear shook the sea. There was a harsh grating noise—Arjuna had strung Gandiva bow and stood on the Earth.

Bhima could not move. Aswatthaman turned the blade of grass in his hand and watched it carefully. It shriveled and grew straight again, glowing blue-white, casting Aswatthaman's shadow behind him in the yellow sunlight. With a great effort Krishna bent his head to Arjuna, and the Pandava put an arrow on his bow. He began to speak the same mantra.

At the same instant they finished that secret spell of death. Aswatthaman said: *"For the destruction of the Pandavas and of Krishna"*—and threw the blade up into the sky.

Arjuna released his arrow: *"For peace to all the world and myself."*

Two huge spheres of curling white fire were hanging like suns high in the air. Earth beneath began to crackle and burn; small pebbles and stones exploded, and the river steamed.

Vyasa told Krishna, "I am holding it. Aswatthaman, do you doubt my words too?"

337

Hanging like suns high in the air

"No," said Drona's son.

"I hold this one," said Krishna. "Arjuna—withdraw it."

"I will," said Arjuna. Majesty, it is harder by ten million times to call back that weapon once released, and at the slightest error Arjuna and all there would have died, and Earth become a desert with no life for seven thousand years. But he did it; then weak and sick he collapsed to his knees gasping for breath.

Vyasa sat before Aswatthaman and said, "Bring it down. You will not be harmed. I protect you."

Slowly Aswatthaman's fireball turned yellow, then orange. The flames flickered and smoked. Aswatthaman perspired and said, "I cannot."

"Your heart must be at peace and not burning," said Vyasa. "You are afraid of Bhima. He lied to your father. But he cannot move. You have my protection and Arjuna's weapon is gone."

"Alright." The fire was only half as large, and dim. "Because I trust Arjuna," said Aswatthaman, "I kill my fear. Because I trust you, I am not sad. Because Arjuna did not wish for my death, I let my anger go."

Like a torch in the daylight the pale flames were still there. "But I must have revenge."

Vyasa sighed. "Stop your sadness, kill revenge himself. Find that cunning ugly man who holds you tight as iron chains, aim true at him where he is hidden."

"I have no other purpose," said Aswatthaman. The fireball burst into bits in midair and was gone.

Aswatthaman walked over to Arjuna and bent over him. Vyasa waved Krishna back, but still he came on, to help

Arjuna. Then Vyasa for the thirtieth part of the day turned him to stone lest he be struck and slain.

Aswatthaman told Arjuna, "I wear this blue jewel on my forehead no longer; take it in return for my life." He pulled the gem from his brow and closed Arjuna's fingers over it, and whispered, "When you awake I am gone. This is more valuable than all Kurujangala. Only take care because it is not yours. Who knows if it may not bring you harm, when it was meant for me, since next to Vyasa I am best in knowing mysteries as you are. . .what you are, Lord."

⚘

Arjuna felt himself carried into a chariot; he felt a stone in his hand. He heard faintly some words and then awoke.

Krishna was driving through water. Arjuna stood up in the chariot and put his hand on Krishna's shoulder, saying, "It was always clear and sparkling with fire; now it is clouded and dull. Drive to Drona, You alone can find his head, which has been lost since Dhrishtadyumna threw it through the air."

"That gem destroys fear," said Krishna. "Keep it."

"He was afraid of Bhima." Arjuna held his hands to his head. "You have to find Drona for me because we have been friends for so long."

Krishna drove out onto Kurukshetra. Drona's body and his head were laid on a pyre. Krishna said, "Uttarah's son was also killed by a fragment of Aswatthaman's weapon. I brought him back to life in her womb. He will be the king Parikshita."

"Bring some fire," said Arjuna. "We must circle the dead, the eldest must lead. Who is older, you or I?"

"Go first."

Arjuna softly placed the blue jewel between Drona's eyes. The severed head was beautiful as a dark mountain with the moon above.

In the palace Vidura bent over Dhritarashtra and said, "Where there is nothing to gain and much to lose, the choice is not hard. Everything joined together must separate; everything living must die. We are all journeying together to Death, like a caravan, unable to turn aside or stop, that goes to a city unknown. What does it matter who gets there first?"

"The sorrows of life come only from life itself," said the king. "I will cast mine away."

"You cannot build out of such shadow," said Vidura. "Look for them, and every day you can find a hundred causes for fear and grief. The wild-honey tree is high, and the fall is long. Dwell on sadness and it will increase."

"I remember no evil that I have done which would bring me to this!"

"You are very indulgent. . .to yourself! Whose were Duryodhana and his brothers? Were they yours? Did you create them? Are you able to make a life?"

Dhritarashtra sat up. "Your words are nectar. Your words are the sharp sword of wisdom."

"Majesty, when I am dead, who can look at the corpse and tell what I was?"

"No stranger could," said Dhritarashtra.

340

"But you?"

"I know you."

"Then tell me—what am I?"

Dhritarashtra smiled. "I don't even know what I am."

"You are the king. A man comes and says: 'Majesty, I held a burning coal in my robes, and I was burnt, for it burst into flame against my skin.' "

"I ask how it happened."

"He tells you: *'I fanned it to put it out.'* "

Dhritarashtra answered, "Brother, I call him a fool."

"But he will not go. He implores you."

"I call my executioner to cut off his head."

"Now listen," said Vidura. "You have no one by you. He says he is your son, but now you have a sword."

"I ask his name!"

"Grief!"

"Oh Vidura, sword or no sword, I tell him—I have no son called Grief. I am strong, I pull him apart barehanded. Why do I need a sword? I am blind and cannot aim it, and the blood from ripping him apart I cannot see."

Sanjaya drove the old king to Kurukshetra. A short way from Hastinapura he saw a war chariot in the trees, covered with tigerskins, drawn by red horses, and he stopped the king's car.

"Majesty, I am Kripa, and I am tired. All our army fought fairly; none ever turned back. Aswatthaman has disappeared after giving his jewel to Arjuna; he could be anyone. With your permission I will go home to Hastinapura, or they will find me soon too, and I have no leave to fight longer. There behind you I see Vidura and Yuyutsu leading on foot the Kuru women from Hastinapura. There are Queen Gandhari and Kunti and my sister whose son is lost."

Dhritarashtra answered, "Go and live in my palace, but do not take a road where you must face those women now."

Sanjaya ran the horses to Kurukshetra. When he stopped on that corpseyard they could no longer hear the screaming and crying of the widows.

Sanjaya helped Dhritarashtra down and said, "Now is once you may bless blindness. Wait for me here. I must find the Pandavas, try to help them separate the dead before the others arrive. We could work for a year and this place would still. . .I leave you now."

"Who has joined us?" asked Dhritarashtra.

"Majesty, I am Vyasa. Sanjaya is gone. Alas, all the world is deceived."

"What is that splitting sound?"

"Arjuna unstrings Gandiva bow. The war is over." Vyasa continued, "Vidura will not be able to do any good when he arrives, for he has not seen this carnage but only heard of it. At first there is nothing. We exist in between. After, again there is nothing. As soon as one is born calamities rush at him like wild dogs. Sit down; I will tell you a story.

"Listen—A certain brahmana found himself in a forest that had no way out; it was filled with lions and tigers stalking him, each one always roaring. There was no one whose shelter he could take. He ran, but the animals kept pace. Round the forest was a net guarded by snakes so tall they touched heaven. Seeing this, the brahmana turned back. He ran over the mouth of a pit covered by hard vines and fell, but his heel caught and he hung there upside-down.

"There was a serpent in that invisible pit. A huge elephant, with six faces and twelve feet, walked menacingly round the chasm's edge. Black and white rats had nearly eaten through a tree that leaned far out over him. But many bees lived in the tree, and their combs dripped honey onto the brahmana. He swallowed it, but there was never enough, and he could in no way get free. But never at any time did he lose the hope of prolonging his life."

Dhritarashtra said, "How can we get him out?"

"Do you know this place?" asked Vyasa.

"Yes. The world is a wilderness. Such is its way, where we are each one limited to ourselves in an inaccessible part of it."

"Do you hear something?"

"Sanjaya is chopping wood with Krishna. Draupadi is weeping over her brother. And far down the road the Kuru women approach."

"We haven't much time," said Vyasa. "Understand me; do not only agree."

"I will."

"Life is a long way, Bharata. When we are tired we must rest again in the womb. The noble despise the lowly; the wealthy have contempt for the poor. We take leave of our senses and deceive each other. And watching this all is the witness, one's own self, so that he becomes our enemy who might be our best friend. This monotonous deceit wearies our soul. Without that, we would not have to rest so often."

Vyasa rose. "Bharata, I have much to do before evening. It is noon on Earth; I will have been to heaven and back before I meet you again tonight." The poet stepped to one side and vanished from the spot.

❀

The wailing and keening grew louder. Dhritarashtra heard nothing, but sat deep in thought. When the women caught sight of Kuru's Field, an awful silence fell. Then Dhritarashtra heard a voice: *"Majesty I am Yuyutsu with Queen Gandhari."*

Dhritarashtra stood there with his Queen. "My son, find silk to wrap the dead. Make pyres of the broken chariots and of fragrant wood soaked with butter. Return to Yudhishthira and ask him to come here with his brothers."

Soon the Pandavas approached, with Krishna and Draupadi walking behind. "Yudhishthira, what do you see?" asked the king.

Yudhishthira answered, "Majesty, women who would before have comforted each other for the slightest loss now dare not even look up from the ground before their feet."

Dhritarashtra embraced him. "You are now my sons. Where is the sadness in this? Are your brothers here?"

"Yes," answered Krishna. He held Bhima back, and set before the blind king the solid iron statue of Bhima that Duryodhana had used as a mace target. "Bhima is here, Majesty."

Dhritarashtra embraced the iron man, but wrath overcame him, and he crushed it against his chest until it cracked apart and fell in pieces. The king's broad chest was bruised and bleeding, and Sanjaya came to his side and said, "Do not act so."

"I have killed him," wept Dhritarashtra. "What have I done, Sanjaya?"

"Knowing what you felt, Krishna put an iron statue before you. Be calm. You meant no harm to Bhima." Sanjaya washed the blood from the king's chest, washed with water his eyes and face, and said, "Thank you, Krishna. Bhima, come now to the king and have no fear."

Dhritarashtra embraced Bhima and Arjuna and the twins, and gave them blessings. Yudhishthira knelt before Queen Gandhari. "I am Yudhishthira, Majesty. One sees others to be ignorant but seldom surveys himself; he scorns fault in others but never tries himself; there are none dear or hateful to Death and he ignores no one. Now do what should be done. If you have a curse against me, say the words."

While he spoke, Draupadi told Krishna, "Let *me* see her!" But Krishna held her back. "No, only wait."

Quick as the mind Gandhari turned away her head, but from within the cloth that covered her eyes her glance fell for an instant on the tip of Yudhishthira's toe and burnt it black. Arjuna quickly stepped behind Krishna; the others stirred uneasily, but nothing more happened.

"Go to Kunti now," Gandhari said, "but Draupadi, stay a moment with me." The Pandavas backed away, hardly able to withdraw their eyes from Dhritarashtra. The two Queens wept together. Krishna sat down by Sanjaya and the blind king, and with softly flowing words began to tell them, "one thousand six hundred sixty million and twenty thousand men have fallen in this battle. I will tell you their names. . ."

"A brahmani bears sons for austerities;
A mare, for running swiftly;
But a princess like your mother
Bears sons for being slaughtered.

Look, the dead all face those who killed them." Yuyutsu laid Duryodhana's body on his pyre, talking to him as though he were still alive. "See what has been done. Those who careered in battle now lie reluctantly like fires in fire while the five elements of their bodies burn and depart. Wives who would have bashfully embraced their husband only in private, now fit heads to the corpses, and limbs, saying, 'This is not his!' or, 'Here is that arm that used to loosen my robes and invade my breasts and touch my thighs, and protect friends and kill enemies.' Look, while trying to turn over corpses stuck to the ground with blood, or pluck out arrows, the women faint and must rest against other bodies. They cannot drive away the screaming vultures and crowing ravens that fan the dead kings with their wings. Some of the dead are yet in bright armor, holding their weapons sharp as glass, and because they regard them as still alive the animals have not eaten them. But elsewhere thousands of wolves drag away the silver chains and upper-arm bracelets, and there is no safety. Women still more afflicted try to comfort those in grief who weep, 'While sporting with the Apsarasas, remember me a little, for within your arms' clasp joy never left me for an instant!' You won Yudhishthira's kingdom at dice, but now Bhima has won your life."

Yuyutsu lit the pyre. "Now lie in the fire-chamber of your heart! You are in heaven. Do not cherish quarrels there as you did between our brothers who all trust in you."

Yuyutsu and Satyaki went over the field lighting pyres with their torches, freeing the dead. When they came to Karna, Yudhishthira looked at them and said, "He was our eldest brother. Kunti, covering her face, told us he was our brother. Light it."

Satyaki said, "But Yudhishthira, let go of the past now; what was Karna to you after all? The singers will praise his fame, but he is dead."

And so were burned the bodies of Jayadratha and Drona and Karna, of Duryodhana and his brothers, of Salya and Drupada and Sakuni, of Dhrishtadyumna and Sikhandin and Virata and Uttara, and of all the Kurus and Panchalas and Matsyas and Sindhus and Angas and Madras and Gandharas and many Trigartas.

After the burning, the women went to bathe in the Ganges, and there they saw Vyasa in the evening, sitting on a deerskin covered by grass and silk.

He said, "I am poison to grief. Like fire I burn his limbs and destroy his mind. Part of yourselves has died, but cease to bear them affection. At last you are free from them." Vyasa watched many of the women leave and waited till they were out of hearing. "But if you cannot leave them, listen. Stop crying. You will never meet the dead through sadness, nor will you die. Put out the lamps and torches.

Enter the water and cover yourselves completely. Then return again and stand along the bank beside me."

Then the women dressed in white, with no vermillion line through their hair, with no ornament and no flower among them, watched Vyasa walk into Ganga till she swirled round his knees. The murmur of the river became confused, and changed, and from within the water came the noise of horses and cars and elephants, of crashing chains and arrows rattling in quivers and creaking wheels, and of men calling to each other over the noise. Lights flickered underwater, reflecting from wavering armor and shimmering jewels.

An army rose by thousands from the river. All who had died in the war of Kurukshetra came, going round Vyasa in the center as a river round an island. Once on the land, women led the men away; wives their husbands, sisters their brothers, mothers their sons, daughters their fathers. And still they came Bharata; still like the gods from heaven they moved out from the parted river shining with light. There were both armies together without suspicion or reproach. They had lost all unfriendliness when they had put on their heavenly clothes and brilliant earrings; they had no jealousy, no unkindness.

The night was quickly past. Drona led the dead warriors back into the river just before dawn, and last of all went Karna, the sun-wheel again upon his breastplate, the sign of falling sunlight once more upon his back. Ganga closed over his chariot-wheels, she covered his flag, she ran over the tip of his flagstaff. They were gone.

Vyasa said, "Hasten into the water if you would go with

them, or they will leave without you if you take no faith
from my words."

It was a beautiful night. The air was fresh and clean, the
sky was weightless, the pyres glowed without smoke
through the fine river mist. While Vyasa summoned the
dead from heaven, Draupadi and Arjuna stood alone on the
battlefield all night.

In silence, resting in his embrace, Draupadi watched the
sky lighten and the stars dim. She broke off her cowrieshell
bracelets and anklets—all but four, one on each limb—so
she would make no sound moving, and they walked back.

"Arjuna—we are still alive!"

Majesty—every King must once behold Hell!

17: the lonely encounter

Bharata, in the morning Yudhishthira entered Krishna's tent on Kurukshetra and found him sitting with downcast eyes, immovable as a great stone, still as a lamp-flame where no wind blows.

Yudhishthira thought, "Salutations to you—
Your chariot wheels leave tracks of light;
You stand, and close the seven paths of the Wind."

Then he said, "Listen—the death-water has been poured at the river. The women have all gone, and the easy paths made by their many feet have vanished. The world is unreal and has no end, and Time is running his course. . . ."

Krishna raised his eyes and answered, "On his bed of arrows Bhishma thinks of me. He is a fire that is about to go out. Do now what must next be done."

Satyaki drove Krishna and the Pandavas across Kuru's Plain, past the hills of dead animals piled high and the smoldering pyres and the skulls with hot coals for eyes, and the carrion animals too gorged to move. The Palmyra banner still flew over Bhishma, and when Satyaki stopped at the trench they heard a bronze sword crash on a brazen shield and saw two horsemen come swiftly to face them from within, one from the Pandava army, one from Duryodhana's.

Yudhishthira jumped down and joined his hands in namaste. "Having come without weapons and in peace, we ask to enter."

"Who are you then?" asked the one with a sword.

"Yudhishthira."

The other leveled his lance. "What is your family and rank?"

"I am the Pandava king."

"Majesty, do you promise for these that they will do no treason here?"

"Yes."

"Others have also come. Pass, Majesty."

⚕

Bhishma opened his eyes and saw them all standing around him—the Pandavas and Sanjaya, Dhritarashtra and Krishna and Vyasa, Satyaki and Yuyutsu and Kripa and Vidura. They walked round him once in a right-turning circle and sat down. Yudhishthira touched his grandfather's feet with his head.

"Welcome to you, Yudhishthira," said Bhisma. "Come closer."

"I am in fear of your curse."

"Blessings, Bharata. I have no curse. Those who cannot see the North Star, or can no longer see themselves reflected in the eyes of another, have but one year to live. One who becomes pale has but six months. One who sees the full moon to have many holes like a spider's web, or who smells death in a temple, has a week. King, my time is nearer than that. You are all Pandavas. While creation lasts, again and again you shall live in the world of men. Blessed be you, let there be no fear of yours."

The Pandavas came, and Bhishma smelled their heads as he used to do when they were children, and told them, "I am the evening Sun, all covered by a halo of rays and beams streaming out." He fell silent and closed his eyes, and all there sat as still and quiet as people in a painting.

Sahadeva looked at the sun and saw it begin to turn north. "It is the solstice."

"Grandfather, I am Yudhishthira. If you hear me still, tell me what I am to do for you."

With his eyes closed, Bhishma said, "By good fortune you are all here. Goodbye, Pandavas. Goodbye, Kripa—Vidura—Dhritarashtra—Yuyutsu—Sanjaya—Satyaki—Vyasa. . . Krishna, come here."

Krishna approached.

"I told them," whispered Bhishma, "that there is truth where you are; and there is victory where truth is. Goodbye, adorable Krishna."

"Goodbye, Bhishma."

Now very weakly, barely moving his lips, Bhishma said,
"You are the sheath of the Universe;
And you hold it with love in your hands . . . "

And as Krishna bent close to hear the last words, Death also, who had been awaiting Bhishma's consent, drew near.

Through the crown of Bhishma's head, the five life-breaths fled as light, into the sky like a meteor. The arrows disappeared; the scars and wounds of war were gone from his body; Krishna lowered him gently down to Earth. All sign of battle vanished from Kurukshetra. The animals and birds went in peace to their homes; a cool and fragrant wind swept over the plain.

Spring turned in his tracks when winter's end had come, and all was repaired, and grew young again. Kama sang—

"I am the sweet Wind, the gods' messenger,
And I am Desire:
Away with the cares of the world!

"The one muttering the Veda to destroy me:
I overreach him; I become the soul of Virtue;
I become his own voice.

"Then one trying to wear me down by patience:
To him I am the strength of Truth;
He will never notice it is I.

"And the man with heavy books
Who would kill me for Salvation:
I frolic and laugh in his face!

"Away, away . . .
Away with the cares of the world . . . "

They carried Bhishma wrapped in cloth of gold and cloth of silver, and laid him on a pyre made from soft aloeswood and sandal. They covered him with solid perfumes and flower garlands and incense, and over this Yuyutsu placed a seven-tiered white umbrella, and Yudhishthira a palm leaf, and Arjuna the war-flag, and Bhima a yak-tail fan, and Nakula a helmet of white, and Sahadeva a white bow.

Vyasa covered Bhishma's holy fire and gave it to Yudhishthira. "Light it, Bharata."

Yudhishthira bowed his head and said, "The words of Vyasa must be obeyed."

The ashes were poured into the Ganges. But as they fell, the water spat and boiled, rapids surged where none had been, swift waves struck each other in turmoil and shock.

Disconsolate with grief, Ganga the beautiful river goddess rose weeping wet from her river. Every tear when it touched the water became a golden lotus floating away. She knelt on the bank, her face hidden in her hands, her shoulders trembling.

Quickly Arjuna put his dark arm around her. "Beautiful friend, why do you cry?"

"I will see him never again," said the goddess, "and who was better than he, that he should give his life to him? My son's ashes are in my mouth!"

Arjuna thought, "Maya, come back to me." He told her, "Open your eyes and swim to heaven. Goddess, remember us all, with your permission we will leave your banks."

❖

As Yudhishthira climbed the riverbank he stumbled and fell pierced with sorrow, like an elephant struck down by a hunter's spear, thinking, "This victory seems to me like a great defeat! There is only one foe and not another, and he is ignorance."

His brothers and Krishna stayed with him; the others left

for the city. Bhima held Yudhishthira's head in his lap and said, "This must not be!" But Yudhishthira only sighed again and again without speaking.

Krishna said, "Now you are like a thirsty man who will not drink; a desiring man who will not meet with a willing woman."

Yudhishthira tried suddenly to rise but Bhima held him fast. Then as suddenly he relaxed, and slowly wiped the tears from his eyes. He glanced at Bhima, and looked with compassion at the twins, and with wonder at Arjuna, and then looked long at Krishna, and none in the world could ever read the face he wore then.

"And you are like a leather bag of words and wind!" he told Krishna. "The eyes of the betrayed burn the king and strike him down. He gathers the sins of his people along with his taxes, he inherits curses and miseries along with his throne. Even when young he must walk with a staff, he grows old and dies never having stood alone. Those who are highly stupid and those who have mastered their souls find happiness here on Earth, and all others only suffer misery."

Krishna answered, "You are mild and reasonable, so men do not honor you. Do not be so anxious after doing something. Sorrow follows happiness, and happiness comes after sorrow. One man thinks that men slay others, another that they do not. This is the language of the world. But the truth is . . . "

"The truth is, that like grass and straw covering a pit, your Dharma is too often a mask for deceit. You are an unborn god, but in a hundred years I could not exhaust the tale of your felonies if I spoke day and night!"

358

"Be calm. The wind is not stained by the dust it blows away."

"I am calm!" shouted Yudhishthira.

"Oh, why do you say: *Alas, what grief!*—when it is by Time that lakes grow flowers and the forest blooms, by Time the nights become dark or lighted."

"Oh heartless Krishna,
   Only men who are like thieves
   Give counsel to a King,
   That he make war and win victory.

"See for yourselves how kings have of all men the least wits! By what right have I murdered everyone? I abandon Kurujangala, I seek the end of separate existence. Let me truly win the world. I shall wander through the forests, and though I meet cold and illness and hunger, however tired I become, the soul of Earth will walk before me, and food and drink will somehow be there. Every day I will beg for fruit from the trees—if while I stand there bowing a fruit falls I will eat it, but I will pick nothing from the tree nor from the ground. Let all creatures keep their possessions.

"I will find the excellent men who have left the world behind, I will willfully injure no creature of God, I will widen my soul and awake to discover what I am. As from a distant mountain, from far away I will see all of you wanting this and disliking that, crying over vacancy and carefully tending emptiness, holding dear what you do not have.

"As a tortoise withdraws his limbs from all sides, so I shall master my senses and desires, and find delight within my own heart. I shall fear no creature and oppress no one.

By contentment in word and deed and thought I shall behold my own soul shining. Never looking back, asking no one the way, I will go on, as Time runs always forward and never back. I will behave neither like one who is fond of life nor like one who is ready to die. If a tiger chews off one of my arms I will wish no evil to him; if an angel decks the other arm with jewels and ornaments I will not wish his good fortune. So may I find the Palace of Wisdom that is eternal and everlasting without change.

"You have not asked me what I intend, yet unasked I have told you. All of you I reject, and I repent to make good my guilt and to atone for the blood of slaughter on my hands."

Saying nothing, all went away but Bhima. In their camp Nakula told Draupadi, "He is injured. Go to him with fire and food."

She hurried to get ready, but Sahadeva said, "Take your time, go slowly. When you are there, listen when he speaks but do not answer him with words. Show that you love him without speaking, do not leave though he tells you to go."

"Stay be his side," said Nakula. "If he does not eat, keep food warm for him; if he does not sleep, take your own rest. When it is time, we will come to you there."

Draupadi's eyes filled with tears. "So much has happened," she wept.

Sahadeva put his fair hands on her dark shoulders. "Draupadi born of Shiva's fire, listen—do not doubt that he will recover. What he says—it is true, but he means otherwise than his words."

Yudhishthira lay in Bhima's arms. "I will give up all this. Isn't that right?"

Bhima sneezed. "Brother, the long wind runs across Kurukshetra. It presses down the grass; it will blow dust in your eyes if you do not turn your back on it."

Yudhishthira sat up. "Son of the Wind, you do not harangue me like the others."

"Oh, I am not good with words. I had decided to stay quiet. But no, not a palace and a kingdom, not great wealth and a wife."

"Why not?"

"I don't know, Bharata. Only to become attached to a handful of barley and a raggedy brown robe?"

"Do not doubt my intelligence."

"Madness is very clever," answered Bhima. "You cannot outmove your own image in a mirror."

Yudhishthira smiled. "If taking others' wealth were not right, the only virtue of kings would be gone! I am cruel and a coward. You be the king."

"You have forgotten your strength," sighed Bhima. "These are not the riddles of the wise; this is nonsense, with nothing in it. If the forest life of innocence led anywhere, all the trees and mountains would have gone there, because they are aloof and chaste."

"You can't think," said Yudhishthira. "All you know how to do is eat and kill."

"Dharma king, you applaud poverty but you have never looked around you. A poor man is accused of whatever may happen as he passes by, but a rich man can easily get more income, as one using an elephant can capture more elephants."

"Please shut up," said Yudhishthira.

"Now any doctor would prescribe incense by the nose, and eyedust."

"If you don't mind . . . "

"That's the cure for mental disease," said Bhima. "Who but you would regret victory? Where are you? And where is the magic land where all men are happy? Did you cry when the house of lac burnt without us?"

"Those *were* good times, weren't they? Anyone with eyes could see our victories then!"

"Remember when Arjuna the brahmana strung Drupada's bow?"

"Yes. Go on!"

"Maya's Palace of Illusion."

"Ah!"

"When you stumbled at Rishava's Hill."

Yudhishthira laughed.

"When Indra's car came down from the sky with Arjuna."

"Beautiful!"

"When you brought us all back to life by answering the crane's questions!" cried Bhima.

"The Pool of Death," said Yudhishthira softly, "but now all is unknown."

"If I've said the wrong thing," said Bhima, "be on your guard, I still hope to win." The wind flew faster by, he tore the dust from the Earth and split down the trees under the yellow sky.

Yudhishthira fell over sound asleep on the ground.

He saw himself in a dream.

With his brothers and Draupadi, all of them dressed in bark, Yudhishthira was walking north over a great desert of salt and white sand beyond the Himalya, where the sun's hollow rays had sucked up every drop of water. There were mountains in the distance ahead, but even walking quickly they drew no nearer to them.

Draupadi stumbled and fell silently to the ground. Yudhishthira knew she was dead; he did not turn to look back or break his stride. Arjuna bent over her a moment and then fell in with the others. Looking down at his feet, Yudhishthira saw a small brown dog walking panting beside him.

Sahadeva died. Nakula ran to him but softly collapsed himself and slumped lifeless over his twin. Arjuna died.

Bhima asked, "But why is this?"

"Forget all that is heard," answered Yudhishthira, "and all that deserves to be heard. Remember long ago, what you were born knowing."

"It's just as I always thought, it is so simple as that." Then Bhima fell.

Yudhishthira thought, "I know he is dead without looking. I must continue lest my death find me waiting. Had I not killed Karna, I could climb to heaven on a sunbeam. Had I not slain Bhishma, I could follow Ganga down to my death in the cool rock-built cities of the Nagas lit with jewels far underground. But here he eludes me." Yudhishthira was thirsty and tired, but he walked on. The sun stood still in the sky.

The drums of heaven thundered. Indra's chariot settled down next to Yudhishthira. The Lord of the Gods joined his hands together and said, "*Namas*. We bow to you. Get in; I've come to take you from this death-desert."

"My brothers and our wife must come with me."

"Leaving their bodies, they have gone before you," answered Indra. "Come, get in."

"Lord of the Past and Present," said Yudhishthira, "this little dog who is my last companion must also go."

"No," said Indra. "You cannot enter heaven with a dog at your heels. He is unholy and has no soul."

"He is devoted to me and looks to me for protection. Left alone he would die here."

"There is no place for dogs in heaven. They are unclean. It cannot be."

Yudhishthira frowned. "It cannot be otherwise."

"Don't you understand? *You have won heaven!* Immortality and prosperity and happiness in all directions are yours. Only leave that animal and come with me; that will not be cruel."

"Is this place some part of my kingdom?"

"It is, Majesty."

"Then I am who will decide what shall be done here. I do not turn away my dog; I turn away you. I will not surrender a faithful dog to you. Truth and a thousand sacrifices were weighed somehow in a balance, and you have heard which was heavier. Whoever comes to me from fright or from disaster or from friendship—I never give him up."

365

"I've come to take you from this death-desert"

"But I can't take him! I'll put him to sleep; there will be no pain. No one will know."

"Lord of Heaven," said Yudhishthira, "you have my permission to go."

"Your splendor will fill the three worlds if you will but enter my car alone," said Indra. "You have left everyone else—why not this worthless dog?"

"I have decided," answered Yudhishthira, "and more than that does not concern you."

Then very quickly Indra knelt on the sand and bowed his head. "My Lord Dharma!"

Yudhishthira turned in surprise. The little dog that had been lying in his shadow was gone, and in its place stood Dharma, tall and blond and grey-eyed.

"Yudhishthira, do not bow to me, my son," said the god. "Blessings to you, as a dog I followed you across this desert. You have compassion for all creatures, and that is not weak but strong, and what you believe in you have defended to heaven's gate."

Yudhishthira saw himself carried to heaven. With Indra he entered Nandana park, but when they came upon the cool river Mandakini, the heavenly branch of the Ganges, the Apsarasas bathing there were ashamed when Yudhishthira looked at them. Some plunged into the water, some into the forest groves and gardens, and others held up their clothes to cover themselves. Then Yudhishthira saw Duryodhana and Sakuni and Duhsasana seated on magnificent thrones that dazzled his eyes.

"I will share no place with them. Take me to my brothers."

Indra smiled. "Bharata, you have still your human body, so the Apsarasas shied away from you. And this is why you still feel love for the other Pandavas and why you dislike Duryodhana. But there can be no friendship or hatred with those who are dead. Only stay here and live in this place. Come and meet Duryodhana politely with me."

Yudhishthira turned his lion's eyes on Indra. "Where are my friends? Take me there, wherever it may be."

Indra answered as though soothing a child. "But King of the World, this is heaven. By pouring his body into the fire of battle, Duryodhana has earned a hero's place. Rest, and forget all the past. This is the eternal region of unending bliss that you have won. Please don't be angry. Enjoy yourself here however you wish."

Yudhishthira stood still. "I shall not even look at Duryodhana! I will see the others, this is not heaven without them."

"You are refusing my hospitality and all my good wishes."

"That's too bad."

Indra said coldly, "Great warrior, your friends are somewhere else than here. If you wish, you may go to them, of course, but I advise . . ."

Yudhishthira threw back his head. *"You take your advice and to to Hell!"*

Indra's face set like a smooth stone mask. *"No, Bharata— you go!"*

⚜

Yudhishthira slipped on something rotten in the near darkness. A cloud of stinging flies flew up in his face; he would have fallen but for the Gandharva's strong grip on his hand. A large, blind white worm fell on his arm. The Gandharva picked it off indifferently and flung it away, while he led Yudhishthira down.

Behind them ran the swift Vaitarani, a thick river of hair and steaming blood and marrow in a bed of bones. Human fat bubbled on the waves, the death-wind blew moaning in their ears. They picked their way over sharp stones, through a forest of trees whose leaves were razors that parted for the Gandharva and closed again behind them. Boiling water ran over iron rocks. Steel-beaked vultures dove screaming at them. The air was tainted and foul and dense with smoke.

Yudhishthira could hardly breathe, but still the Gandharva led him down, and the air was more fetid, and down, and the darkness increased. From behind brass thorn bushes of poison, demons with needle-mouths and huge stomachs hungrily watched them. Something smeared across Yudhishthira's leg, but he could see nothing.

He dropped the Gandharva's hand and shivered. "How far must we go on?"

The Gandharva stopped. "This far is your way. If you are tired let's turn around together; give me your hand."

Yudhishthira's mind was numb. He turned in a daze, blindly feeling for the Gandharva's hand, when a voice shaken with misery cried out: *"Do not go"*—and other voices dimly familiar called to him: "Favor us! Stay only a moment—King of Kings, you bring sweet fragrance and a breath of fresh air. While you are here the pain clears a little!"

Yudhishthira said, "Alas—how painful! Who are you?"

From all sides they answered, "I am Karna." "I am Arjuna." "I am Draupadi." "I am Bhima." "I am Nakula." "I am Sahadeva." "I am Drupada." "I am Virata." "I am Uttara."

"This is no dream, Gandharva," said Yudhishthira. "What is this perverse destiny?"

"But I am only a messenger."

In the angry voice of a king, Yudhishthira told him, "Then tell the gods from me: falling down over Dharma and Indra and all of you I send my curse! Bitterness and evil and misfortune upon you! Let dishonor and deceit fall back and crush you. Slave of sin, return and warn the god of this place: *If you do not hide from me, I will meet you here sometime and mash you like an insect!* Heavenly Gandharva, if you care for your life, be gone."

Then in his dream all was confusion—the darkness was hit by lightning that remained still where it cut, and night fell away in pieces from under his feet. Yudhishthira fell into the sun. He fell into the arms of Dharma, whose long golden hair was blinding bright. In his father's eyes Yudhishthira saw himself sleeping on Kurukshetra, with Draupadi sitting beside him.

Because by love you make him warm and whole, and yourself, so do you always protect your husband, thinking: *"How else will he take his birth in me?"*

18: pArikshita

Majesty, Yudhishthira awoke in the early dawn, alone with
Draupadi. She said, "You've been asleep since yesterday.
Are you hungry? The food is warm; whatever you see here
is all yours to enjoy."

He poured a bowl of water over his head, drank deeply
from another bowl, and smiled at her. Draupadi laughed
like a glass tree in the wind. He held her close with his face
in her fragrant hair, and she embraced him till her strength
was gone, and she relaxed in his arms.

⚜

At noon Yudhishthira saw his brothers come leading the
eight-wheeled white chariot, pulled by sixteen white bulls,
that would take him to Hastinapura.

With Draupadi by his side on the white tigerskins, with
Bhima driving and the others following behind, he entered
the Elephant City. Flowers and hanging plants were strung
over the streets; before each doorway stood a new metal jar
full to the brim with water. But the doors and the windows

of every house were closed; the streets were empty; the city was hushed and still.

Bhima stopped at the palace. Yudhishthira took flowers and incense to the city god of Hastinapura, and when he came to the inner courtyard that held the shrine he found gathered there all the brahmanas of Kurujangala, and he told them, "The war is over."

But among those brahmanas stood the Rakshasa prince Charvaka, disguised as a hermit. He held a water-pot and a rosary, and had only a tuft of hair on his shaven head. He had been Duryodhana's friend, and now he stepped out in front of the others and brought his triple staff crashing down on the flagstones.

Proud and fearless, Charvaka called out, "You have betrayed us all, you are a blight on this kingdom, Yudhishthira! You think: *I am high-born, I can do what I please, I am not an ordinary man!* Fixed and mobile, rational and irrational, all creatures curse you. You have shamefully killed your own race and family, and what will you gain by it? We all say: *Do what is right: cast away your life.*"

"I am the most excellent king that ever was, nor will anyone else ever be so good and wise," answered Yudhishthira.

"But what is this?" cried Charvaka.

"Oh, Brahmana," said Yudhishthira, "have you never heard? *To kill yourself, praise yourself; to kill the king only insult him.* Therefore I already lie twice dead, what more can I do for you?"

In one voice the brahmanas said: *"Hum"*—and as that

mantra still echoed in the court, Charvaka fell down dead, blasted to bits. And one told Yudhishthira, "Forgive our violence, but those are not our words!"

When the people of Hastinapura heard, they smiled and said, "May he stay here a hundred years." It was again a living city.

Looking east on a golden throne, Yudhishthira was made a king by the ancient Bharata rites. Dhritarashtra poured a shellful of water over his head, and brahmanas brought to him vessels filled with earth and gold, silver and gems, and set them on an altar before him, beside dishes of fried rice and milk and honey. Yudhishthira poured clear butter from a ladle of sacred fig-wood onto the fire that has burned since the first lunar king stepped down to Earth.

Then King Yudhishthira touched fresh white flowers, and the head of the most beautiful maiden in the city. Four jars of water were set before him, one made of gold and one of silver, one of copper and one of Earth. From each brimful jar he cupped water in his right hand, and with the golden water he touched his lips; with the silver water his eyes; with the copper water his nose; and with the Earth water his ears. Dhritarashtra took a conchshell netted round with gold and filled it part by part with sea water from the four directions, and again poured water over the king's head.

When it was done and his people brought him gifts, Yudhishthira gave each one back, dipping a grassblade in water, and silently saying his own secret mantra, which will never be written nor ever spoken in another's hearing. He and Dhritarashtra gave these gifts in the names of the dead, and other gifts of their own; they gave lamps, and the reward to them was clear insight; and made water-tanks, and those gifts of water would later await them after death, where it is very dry.

Yudhishthira told the people, "Treat Dhritarashtra as our father," and gave the old king a palace. To the kingdoms vacant because of the Bharata war he sent messengers to give the thrones to the wives or daughters or sisters of the fallen kings, and he put Dhritarashtra's name on the decrees before his own.

Then he walked under the flower-banners into the palace, to his private rooms, where young women with anklets and bell-girdles and golden moons on their lips helped him out of his royal robes. When he was out of the gold chains and jewels and silks and tigerskins and silver bands, Arjuna and Krishna came in.

"Well where in the world were you?" asked Yudhishthira. "I looked everywhere."

Arjuna coughed. "It's a hot day. We went swimming."

"Because I am the son of God, this honor is only fitting. What else?"

"Then we had some watermelons," said Krishna.

Arjuna laughed. "And you know the giant swings in the park? We wanted to see who could go higher with a girl on his lap, and *he* nearly fell off."

"I had the wine-jar with me, that's why," said Krishna, "and that girl kept . . . and we've brought you a present."

"Say Majesty," said Arjuna. "It's his park now, you know."

Yudhishthira sat down. "The man who hears this

incredible tale with devotion and faith . . . " But he couldn't keep a straight face. "So where's the present?"

Arjuna bowed low. "On the balcony, Sire." And there in a plain bumpy flowerpot bloomed a sweet basil with curly leaves and white flowers.

"That's a beautiful present," smiled Yudhishthira. He looked at Krishna and Arjuna. "Thank you, and have a good time."

"But how did you know?" asked Krishna.

"Majesty." said Arjuna. "I apologize for my friend's vulgarities. We're going walking to Indraprastha. Will you come?"

"Not I." Yudhishthira embraced them both. "Farewell. Tell me what you discover there; I will wait to hear."

After they had gone, your father Parikshita was born in Hastinapura. Uttarah's room was filled with everything that will destroy Rakshasas and drive them off—bright weapons properly placed, and fires, and doctors and mustard seeds and old women, and charcoal buttered and unlit, and white flowers, and water in jars. But though all this was done, Parikshita lay still and motionless when he was born, for life he had not. Struck by part of the Brahmasira weapon from a grassblade, he was not strong enough for the shock of birth.

Draupadi and Subhadra saw their son dead-born from Virata's daughter. Subhadra, fair as the embodied rays of the moon, stepped into a corner by herself and said softly,

"Krishna, what has that child-slayer done now? We pray you to make your words true, in the hearing of the whole Universe."

In Indraprastha, Krishna stopped talking to Arjuna and closed his eyes. A bright light and a rushing sound filled Uttarah's room in the Elephant City; and the newborn child began to cry. Indeed, as Yudhishthira had killed Duryodhana with words when they were the only shafts that could reach him, so again with words was your father revived. Draupadi ran to tell Yudhishthira, and the royal dreamtellers started to write what they knew of Parikshita's life in the womb before his birth.

The Bharata musicians played that song no one else ever remembers. It is very short, and they play it but one time through, and only at the birth of a first son to the king. At such a time none but the Gandharva King Chitraratha and themselves ever seem to hear it.

Chitraratha flew to Lord Indra and hummed the first few notes, but the song left his mind before he had finished. Yet the Heaven Lord knew it and smiled. "My grandson! Let's celebrate!" Indra kicked open a sandalwood box, and rummaged about through his collection of clouds and tempests.

Indra went to heaven's door, which is so hard to see, where the bar on the door is greed, and the lock on the bar is meanness. It flew open for him, and he threw out a hurricane shaken up with a storm and a cloudburst and a cyclone, with a pinch of a roaring deluge and a monsoon added for relish, and a handful of comets.

"But Lord it is winter," cried Chitraratha, "you'll mess up everything!"

"Never mind," said Indra, and opened his thousand eyes, and looked down at Earth.

Over Hastinapura and Indraprastha the racing wind tore into the heavy blue clouds and the rain spilled over. Thunders rocked the sky and shook its lace of boiling lightning, but by only looking, Indra kept the winds out of every dwelling and made the waters harmless. Not one flower or leaf was torn or crushed; no crop was spoiled nor any blossom hurt; no creature drowned in a flooded burrow or fell while flying. There were no floods, and the roads were only damp, with no sticky mud. After the storm, all the hay and straw was still dry. In Kurujangala, where a million frail lights and incense sticks burnt outdoors in thanksgiving for your father's birth, in the lashing winds and drenching rains for a day and a night, none of them went out, and no bowl of water beside the houses even overflowed.

The thousand eyes had only blinked.

And in Indraprastha, in the thick darkness, the rain soaked Arjuna's peacock-feather hat, while under a leaky tree Krishna was telling him of their past lives together. Janamejaya Raja, no one knows what lives those were. It is unknown what was said between them, and this is an ancient mystery to men, and a secret even from the gods.

❧

Yudhishthira proclaimed a fortnight festival. Bhima measured out a beautiful spot beyond the city, built broad roads on it, and made it level and smooth with uncut jewels. He built mansions of alabaster and high-columned arches of pure soft gold, red and yellow. He drew the figures of animals and birds in gold-dust on the Earth, within triangles of spice-flowers, and placed out the wooden stakes to honor the gods, and covered them with silk woven from threads of two colors. Where it was the custom to spread down grass for seats, here that grass itself was made of gold.

Yudhishthira opened the banquet with a furrow dug by a golden plow and Bhima cooked hills of food. He served eighteen kinds of barbecued meat, wild rice and sesame seeds in thirty kinds of sauce, grain boiled in milk and butter, hot candies of sugar and ginger and peppers, sour and sweet preserves, fruit fresh and dry, seventy kinds of vegetables raw and cooked, ninety-three soups, eleven stews, twenty-nine kinds of fish cooked in fifty-one ways, unleavened bread baked and refried, one hundred kinds of pie and cake; and curds, raw sugar, roots, salty fried leaves, broiled nuts, honey light and dark and in the comb, and oceans of wine and rivers of clear water and lakes of milk.

People gathered there from every nation and realm and province. By the main gate stood baskets and bins of gold and pearls, and everyone as he entered dipped his hand in where he wished and carried off what he could take.

Yudhishthira followed the last guest through the gates. The cattle and buffalo brought there for blessings, and the birds and wild animals that came to visit, were fed in their own houses full of grain and sugarcane and greens and milk. After Bhima fed each hundred thousand people he struck a hard iron gong; before the sound had died away it was time to strike it again, day after day.

King Yudhishthira gave away clothes and seed and animals and blankets and homes and medicine. Along the roads he set up fifty thousand rest-houses to give food and water to travelers. No one had heard even in story of such bounty given before, nor would future kings easily achieve such generosity. There was no carnage over precedence of rank or dignity, and no people were slaughtered through the ill-feeling of kings.

Then Yudhishthira had received everyone, all his guests were tired and happy and full, the eloquent philosophers and critics had wrangled and disputed their propositions, both synthetic and analytic, and the losers had been drowned, wealth had been given in torrents by servants wearing bright gold earrings and flowers, the crowds were quiet, resting on high beds and soft seats, the heavenly voices calling: *This is a blessed day*—had all but ceased . . . then, late on the last afternoon of the feast, a black and brown mongoose darted across the holiday clearing, dashing and running to wherever he saw flour fallen on the ground spilled over from gifts of food.

That animal rolled over and over through every pile of flour and grain that he could find, streaked through Bhima's kitchen and shot out through the picnic grounds, plunging and tumbling into all the flour dust. Then he sneezed and scampered to Yudhishthira's feet and shook himself.

The mongoose fixed his blue eyes on the king and sighed deeply. Yudhishthira saw that on one side his body and head were covered with fur of gold.

"What is it?" asked Yudhishthira. "Tell me. If I can, I will give it."

The mongoose bared his sharp white teeth and licked his lips. With a sad look he answered, "If I am not all golden now, you cannot."

"You are not," said Yudhishthira.

"I have the habit of attending every display of generosity I can discover," said the mongoose. "So I came here, and from all the talk my hopes were high . . . but I am once more disappointed, for all your celebration is not equal to a bowl of flour once given away where I live on Kurukshetra."

Yudhishthira got up from his throne and sat on the floor. "Sit on this pillow beside me. How are you disappointed, and why is half your body all golden and bright?"

The mongoose sat down on his long tail, humped his back, and crossed his paws under his elbows. He looked at the king and said, "I will tell you what I saw a thousand years ago."

Listen, Bharata—wonderful and excellent was that gift of four handsful of flour. I still live underground in the same hole as I did then.

A very old man and woman, and their son and his wife, lived in a small house made of branches tied with vines, covered with leaves and dung. They were poor and had to live on wild roots, and herbs, and what grain they could find in the fields after harvest. It was one hot late summer day on Kurukshetra, at noon; the Earth had cracked and baked into bricks, and the rain had not come. The wild plants had long before withered to death, and the forest held no food. There was famine in the land, and the king could not feed even his own city.

The family tried always to put aside enough grain to last till the next harvest, but now nothing grew, their reserves

382

had become only one bowl of coarse meal, while for a month they had eaten only dry bark and river grass and drunk water.

When they had saved that flour until they were so weakened by starvation that they could not move without trembling, then at noon a wanderer limped up to their doorway, leaning heavily on his staff. He was thin and frail and very old; he was tall and dark, wearing a wornout robe that had once been red, but was now faded and patched over and over with cheap brown cloth; his hair was long and white, he cast no shadow.

The family was glad to see a guest, and the father said, "Welcome to you." His son brought water to wash the wanderer's feet.

"I didn't expect to meet anyone here," said the stranger. "I thought this was only an empty house where I might get out of the sun to die. I am too weak from hunger to continue my way any more."

"No," said the father, "you cannot leave our home without sharing our midday meal."

"How can you have anything left to eat?" asked the stranger. "The whole world is starving."

"We are used to poverty," said the son, "and we save food by habit. Enter, and eat your fill."

The old woman led him inside and set the flour bowl before him. Her daughter said, "Eat first. We are not used to dining so early, and there is other food for our own lunch."

The wanderer had to turn his head to look at her. "Truly life is a benefit, not to be thrown away. When your own hands tremble with weakness, how can I accept this?"

"If we turned away a guest," answered her father, "we would be ashamed."

The wanderer stared softly at him, and first mixing it with water, he ate all the flour in the bowl. His hunger vanished and his strength returned. He went outside and brushed the flour-dust from his hands, then stood again in their doorway.

He told them, "I have stopped at every house where there was food. Only you were kind; no one else gave me anything. The rain has this moment begun in the south. But do you know who walks like me over the land when there is no food?"

"Yes, Lord," said the father. "We know you now."

"Hunger destroys wisdom and defeats courage," said Yama, "but you have overpowered him. Here is a car from Brahma; you will honor me by going to him as you deserve."

A chariot from the very highest, unchanging, limitless heaven came down from the sky, drawn by white swans and cranes that flew in a flower harness. It scented the air with a fresh heavenly fragrance I cannot name, and the family that had seemed so poor to me left in it, and the dark stranger disappeared before my eyes.

I was watching all this from my home. Once they were all gone I thrust out my sharp nose, laid back my ears, and cheered in a deep voice. Then I came out and rolled in the few leftover grains of meal that Yama had brushed from his hands. Wherever the powder touched me, my fur became gold, but there was very little, only enough for half my body.

The mongoose said, "Yudhishthira, that's why I run around to all kinds of gift-givings, to ascetics and kings, trying to finish the job. But I have never yet been made all gold."

Yudhishthira smiled down at the mongoose and stroked his back. "You are a simple animal, may I not give you something else? If I were you, I would not hope too much that any king's holiday could equal what you saw. That is too rare, and anything else too common."

"I don't know what else I want," said the mongoose.

"Think, there must be something."

"I don't think very much, Majesty. But I know what I like."

"Let me bring you a blue saucer of raw eggs and milk, let me give you a piece of red silk trimmed with gold for your wife to wear at home."

The animal's eyes lit up. "Thank you, Bharata, that would be fine. Thank you."

"No, thank *you* for coming to my festival and telling me your story," said King Yudhishthira. He joined his hands in namaste, and the mongoose returned the greeting.

385

"I don't know what else I want," said the mongoose

*When there is a stain, and
nothing will remove it—
Time will take it away.*

19: the timeless path

Majesty, fifteen days later Dhritarashtra sent for Yudhishthira. The old king was thin and weak; his robes were loose and his veins and nerves all visible.

Dhritarashtra said, "Blessed be you, I have lived these days very happily. By your command nobody talks of the past in my hearing. I have nothing to do for my sons who wronged you; they have died by Kshatriya Dharma. But I am now old. I will go to the forest."

"King of kings, I did not know," said Yudhishthira.

"I compare you in my mind to Duryodhana. You always consult me and obey my slightest wish. The more considerate you are, the more the contrast discourages me. Now at the eighth part of the day I eat only a little food. Gandhari knows this, but I have hidden it from my servants lest they report it to you. I sleep on the bare floor on grass, and spend my time in silent prayer with my wife."

"Who has obeyed you outwardly, but with an unwilling heart?"

With tears in his eyes Dhritarashtra answered, "I cannot

remain in the Elephant City. I kept silence so as not to cause you pain. I have lived under your protection. You have never said anything against me whatever I did; you let me give gifts and pardons as if I were still king here. You often tell everyone to see that I might not feel unhappy over anything . . . but this is beyond you."

Dhritarashtra leaned back suddenly. "Give me your permission, for by speaking long when I have not eaten, my mind is weakened."

Yudhishthira revived him with the touch of his hand. "Father, if I deserve your favor, eat something with me. I shall then know what to do. My very body is at your disposal, and all my wealth. Do not doubt it. Who has mistreated you? Who has dared to disobey me?"

Dhritarashtra sighed. "I myself disobey. I have done what I have to do. All my work is done, and it is our custom for an old king to retire from the world. Kings ought to die either in war or in the woods."

Yudhishthira bent his head, "I ask you—let us eat together for the last time; then go into the forest where you will . . . Oh Father . . ."

"Cease, my son, great has been my toil. Do not lament me. I have not the least anger against anyone. I wish to take some food, with your permission."

⚜

When they heard he would leave them, the people of Hastinapura gathered outside Dhritarashtra's home, and he spoke to them with the evening wind softly stirring through his silver hair and his white grass robes.

With Gandhari beside him, Dhritarashtra said, "I have insistently set my heart upon leaving you. Give me your permission. The good will between you and me cannot be seen in other kingdoms. I am worn down by the load of years I bear over my head. What refuge do I have but the deep forest?

"Forgive me any fault as your king, for I have not always done my best. If you consider: *He is old; he has lost his sons; he was our king*—you will pardon me that I did not destroy Duryodhana myself, though I had more than the strength to do it. But foolish as my son was, he did not oppress you. He caused a great war from pride, the death of warriors and Kshatriyas and kings, but whether this was good or bad, I do not know. I give Yudhishthira to you, and put you as a deposit in his hands. I will go away with Vidura and Sanjaya and the Queen. I bow to you all, and pray you to remember me in your hearts."

The citizens wept, covering their faces, as parents would weep over a dear son about to leave them forever. They had room in their hearts for nothing but sorrow; they said nothing, but only looked at one another.

Gradually they were able to speak among themselves. Setting their words in brief they charged a spokesman to reply for everyone. He faced the king and said, "Our answer is in my care. Listen—

"What you say is all true: there is not the slightest untruth in it. You have never broken the contract between us. The destruction of the Kurus was not caused by Duryodhana. It was not brought about by you. Such a thing could never happen without the influence of destiny. Kshatriyas especially should kill enemies and meet death in battle. Who can say anything else about this? We look on you as our preceptor, therefore in your presence we absolve your son. Cowards cannot live in the great forests . . . for all our days, we will not forget you."

Every person in that assembly said: *"Excellent, excellent"*—and took those words as his own. Dhritarashtra thanked them over and over, and with weakened strength and slow motion, he entered his home.

❧

In the morning Dhritarashtra gave parched rice and new flowers to the palace where he had lived so long, and honored his servants with gifts. Sanjaya took up the fire that the old king worshipped daily and, dressed in bark, walked beside Dhritarashtra and Gandhari and Vidura down the main street of Hastinapura. Kripa and Yuyutsu followed them to the wall and returned; then Kunti met them and led them through the gate, leading Gandhari by the hand; Dhritarashtra followed with his hand on Gandhari's shoulder.

The Pandavas were waiting outside the walls. There Bhima, slightly bending his face downwards, said, "Oh King, where do you go? Behold the reverses of Time!" Bhima sighed heavily. "When I heard you begin to speak yesterday, only with difficulty did I keep still. This is generally the way of warriors in battle, and I am devoted to war and the pride of warriors. I apologize for myself. Those who are not common do not save up the wrongs done against them, but remember only the benefits they have received."

Kunti started to walk on and told Yudhishthira, "Care for Sahadeva. Be good to Draupadi. Look after your brothers."

"But this is what you said when we left you after losing our kingdom," said Yudhishthira. "Let us return. What strange desire has caught up your mind?"

Bhima said, "We were all born in the forest. Now we have won our kingdom—or why did you bring us here at all? Why did you wish us to exterminate the Earth? Now is the time for you to enjoy with us what we have won."

"Do not wonder why," said Kunti. "Pandu's sons had been living on another's food, watching the faces of others. You were all without strength and fallen from happiness. I did not want his sons to be lost. As for myself, before this I enjoyed this land with Pandu. I want to meet him again."

By evening Dhritarashtra's party reached the Ganges far from the city. The country people lit many fires and cooked dinner for them all, and made them grass beds, and round those fires sang the old songs of ancient kings and their women, under the gold and silver moon.

Following the river, they went past Kurukshetra, where they met Vyasa, who led them to a retreat far in the forest and left them there.

Everyone in the city always talked of the old king, wondering: *"How will he live? And he is blind."* Yudhish-thira, thinking the same thing, found no pleasure in being a king, or in women, or in the study of the Veda. He would not attend to his offices at all, and never answered if anyone spoke to him.

Then Sahadeva came and told him, "We also have been standing with our feet raised for such a journey, Majesty."

Yudhishthira said to the people, "Whoever wants to see Dhritarashtra, let him come with us, properly protected." He left the Elephant City in the care of Yuyutsu, and waited outside the walls with Bhima and the twins for five days, to let the people gather for the march. They set out towards an ascetic retreat on Kurukshetra, going slowly, resting by rivers and lakes; then, crossing the plain and entering the woods, they saw from a distance Dhritarashtra's home.

The Pandavas alighted from their chariots and walked into the ashrama. All Yudhishthira's army also, and all the Kurus, and the wives of the soldiers and their children also followed them on foot. They saw the herds of deer grazing that did not run from them, and the fruit trees planted by birds, and the old king's house of straw and flowers; and they felt the unchanging peace and stood still; and they heard in the stillness the most distant birdsong and the faintest hum of life.

Yudhishthira went ahead alone. Sanjaya smiled to see him and said, "That way." By the river he found Dhritarashtra and Kunti and Gandhari bringing back jars of water, and he carried the jars for them. As they returned to the hermitage Dhritarashtra, emaciated with fasts, resembling a skeleton covered with skin, stood straight and walked confidently behind Gandhari; both of them were blind, and were led by Kunti.

Yudhishthira presented all the people, one by one, by name and race, and Dhritarashtra felt himself once more in Hastinapura. Dhritarashtra said, "Pandava King, what need I say of friends, are your foes gratified with your behavior? I hope no one has to beg in your kingdom. Are the women honored in your house? I hope your servants bring whatever you want without waiting for orders."

Yudhishthira replied, "I hope that fasts no longer give you pain. Have you found serenity from the increase in your knowledge here? Can you easily earn your food from the wilderness? I see you here without a thorn in your side. I hope your mind is pleased to be where you are, and that all of you live in peace and happiness. But where is Vidura?"

"My son, Vidura is well. He lives on air alone; he does not speak; sometimes we hear him in the forest."

"It seems to me that the end of human beings is difficult to guess."

"Bharata," said Dhritarashtra, "he who sees evil in separation must abandon union. There are three concerns above all—injure no creature; tell the truth as much as it may be told; be free from anger when you are not in danger. My life is crowned with success today, since this meeting has happened between us. Take from me these gifts of wild roots and water. One's guest must take what one takes for himself."

When Yudhishthira reached out to touch that food, he saw Vidura appear out of the forest. His hair was muddy, he had gravel in his mouth, he was perfectly naked, with dust and pollen on his body. When Vidura saw visitors he fled back, but Yudhishthira instantly followed after, though it took all his speed to keep Vidura in sight, and called out: "*I am Yudhishthira.*"

Then he lost him, until in the empty dry forest in a solitary spot Yudhishthira found Vidura leaning against a tree. He had only the general form of a man. His face was sunken and unrecognizable, but Yudhishthira knew him and asked, "Is friendship a disgrace, that you hide from me?"

Vidura eyed the king with a steadfast gaze; he entered Yudhishthira's body, part by part. First were the feet and the legs, the arms and the hands. He united his breaths with the Pandava's, in and out, in and out, and all made one. He entered his senses, one then another.

The tree held up a corpse. Yudhishthira tried to move him but he could not. The river was grey and the deep forest was black before he returned and told Dhritarashtra.

The old king said, "Sanjaya, we must bring him back. Is it already night?"

Sanjaya replied, "Here is Vyasa."

Dhritarashtra rose and joined his hands together, and Vyasa said, "No fear. Sit down. Majesty, no one will ever find that tree again, or the dark figure beneath it. That body of the one called Vidura should not be burnt, but must stay there forever, as long as Yudhishthira lives. They were always one, Majesty . . . " Vyasa turned to Yudhishthira. " . . . he is Dharma; in him is your body also; do not grieve for him at all. Your two mothers live on fallen leaves, and the Bharata race, blazing with prosperity, now rests on you."

Dhritarashtra said, "It is strange: I am sad that my brother is dead, but I am not sad. We are all very old. Our soul shows us pleasure and pain, but he is not touched more than a glass by a reflection. Yudhishthira, be mild to the peaceful, and harsh like a searing snake to the cruel. Send out your spies disguised as morons and blind men. When you meet with your ministers outdoors, do it by day, in the middle of a clearing. When you consult them at home, exclude from the room apes and birds and all other animals that can imitate human beings, lest you take wrong advice without knowing. That is all my wisdom gained from sovereignty."

"The fires are bright under Bhima's copper dishes and iron pots," said Vyasa. "The wooden trays and spoons and double ladles, the clay cups and waterjars, are all set out. Majesties, what he has done with those roots and water you will not believe."

✦

Left alone once more, Dhritarashtra and Sanjaya and Kunti and Gandhari went to the Gate of the Ganges. They made no home there, but wandered through the forest, taking food as they could find it. Once when Sanjaya had gone to get water, Dhritarashtra's holy fire tipped over in the dry leaves and grew to be a forest-fire, and Sanjaya at the river in the evening saw two sunsets through the trees, one to the west, one in the south.

Wild animals burst past them, yet Dhritarashtra and the two Queens could not move. The fire had cut them off on all sides; they met the flames in peace.

And after, Sanjaya rose from the water with the deer and bear and elephants and walked three times round where their camp had been. He poured some ashes into Ganga and went all alone up into the Hills, into the lonely Himalyas watched over by the gods.

Sanjaya's memories fell away like the dead ashes of a burnt-out fire—the bright stars of arrows in the sky, the rending sounds of the great bows, the sparks of shattered swords, the cries in the night, all were no more—and he thought to himself, "Earth my mother, how ungrateful and heartless were all those who rejected your bounty and instead chose to go to Yama. How could you appear to them as a mansion of sorrow, where no one could remain?"

"Tell me a story . . . "

20: the city of gates

In Hastinapura Satyaki told Yudhishthira, "Now I will take the Lady Subhadra to Indraprastha in Krishna's chariot. From there we will go to Dwaravati," and the king answered: *"Yes."*

When that chariot rattled its way into the other city, Majesty, such a chariot had never been seen before. It shone in the sun like a fire of bright gold, like a heap of penances.

Satyaki jumped down and embraced Krishna. Krishna looked at him and asked, "Where did you get that? What happened to my car?"

Subhadra answered him, "Coming here, we met the Asura Maya, the master of a thousand arts and maker of all ornaments."

"I know him."

"He thought it was a disgrace for someone in your exalted position to ride in that old car. His determination grew like the moon in the first half of the month."

"But I liked that old car," said Krishna. "And what exalted position?"

"That's what we asked him, too," said Subhadra. "And I told him you liked your chariot, so he asked me politely if he could just decorate it a bit. How could I have the heart to refuse? He covered the wheels with gold from the sun and silver from the moon. He covered your chariot with belts of gems, with emeralds and bloodstones and pearls, with turquoise and diamond, coral and opals and rubies, with golden topaz and garnets and amethyst and green jade."

"Am I a king, that I must put on a show and care what people think of me?" asked Krishna.

Satyaki said, "It runs like a dream. Your own flag still stands highest; your car still bears no weapon."

Krishna smiled, "If it is really the same car . . . and it is very beautiful."

"Look," said Subhadra, "here are the shiny yellow sunstones, sunshine made solid. In shade they are cool, in sunlight hot as coals. They are sharp and hard, and struck through by crossing lines. And these are moon-gems, soft and smooth, like pearls, dull in the sun and made from thickened moonbeams. Maya strung them over the chariot; when moonlight falls they glisten and glow, they become cold and moist with falling dew. Krishna, why does Arjuna never live at home?"

"His cheekbones are a little high; that is his only fault," said Krishna. "Only for this is he always on the road."

Subhadra, who could bear no flaw assigned to Arjuna, glared angrily at her brother.

But Arjuna smiled at them. "The play is all but finished. When do you leave for the sea?"

Krishna answered, "In the morning." He held Arjuna's

arms that were both covered with bowstring scars. "Wait here . . . then return, and meet me where we always were."

❧

Krishna's chariot crossed the great desert that lies between Kurujangala and the western sea; the colored banners flew and the pennons streamed from the flagpoles; the wind blew before the car, tearing away the stones and thorns. In the midst of the sands they saw the anchorite Uttanka walking through the empty dunes, and he made a sign to them to stop.

Uttanka smiled and joined his hands. "Lord of the Senses, you are coming from Hastinapura, where by your compassion you have prevented useless war between the Dhartarashtras and the Pandavas."

Krishna stared at him. Slowly he got down from the chariot and said, "Brahmana, the truth is far different; it was the work of the gods. The knot of destiny is hard to untie. Born as a man, I must act as a man. I did all I could."

"But how could you fail?"

"All my effort could not overreach the time and the place; by their own deeds bound, they called it destiny."

"That is truth," said Uttanka, "and the man who cannot see God's true form from this is a fool. I am thirsty."

Krishna brought water and said, "Whenever you need water in the desert, think of me." By silence Uttanka accepted the gift. The jewelled chariot was soon out of sight; the brahmana was again by himself in the wilderness.

Now, Bharata, it was not long before Uttanka was very thirsty and thought of Krishna. As soon as he did that, he saw approaching him a hunter dressed in rags, filthy and nearly naked, surrounded by snarling dogs, armed with a slaughtering knife clotted with blood. His tangled hair and beard were matted with animal fat and his eyes were bloodshot and wild; he came humping and stumping across the sand, gleefully smacking his lips, and courteously bowed to Uttanka.

The hunter held out a dirty waterskin. "Ascetic, shake off all inaction! Drink, I have been sent to you."

Uttanka wrinkled his nose and turned down the corners of his mouth. "It smells like it's full of urine."

"There is no help for it," said the hunter. "In the name of God, let the scales fall from your eyes. From compassion have I come to you. Drink it and live forever."

"Mock a holy man, will you!" Uttanka struck the skin from the hunter's hand. As it fell it vanished, and the man and the dogs vanished with it. Then Uttanka saw Krishna, walking by the way the hunter had come, carrying a bowl of water.

Uttanka drank. "Was that kind? What were you thinking of, to send an outcast with untouchable water?"

"But he was not what he seemed," said Krishna, "nor was the water; yet you sent him away from disregard. He loves distraction and disguise, but he is honest. We made a bet and struck a bargain together, and I have lost."

"Indra!" Uttanka looked down at his bare feet. "You thought me wiser than I am, that was your only fault. The nectar of immortality."

"When you desire water," said Krishna, "clouds will rise

over this desert for you, charged with rain. Indra is nothing but your slave, Brahmana."

And to this day, Bharata, Uttanka-clouds drop rain, now and again, on the waterless desert.

Dwaravati, the eight-sided City of Gates, touched the silver sands of the dancing sea. Under the high white sea wall were boat-gardens, and there the water was never salt, but always fresh. The city walls were of adamant, surrounded by a circular moat of sea water lined by trees and bamboo, where ducks and cranes lived and the tide never fell. Her towers were topped by blue sapphire domes that made stars of the sun by day and drew the rays of constellations by night. Her gates bore red copper stars set in bronze panels, or round brass suns set on gold, or silver moons and planets on polished steel, or spacious pearls engraved with the forgotten stories of vanished men.

Near Dwaravati was Raivataka Hill. There, in the evening, Krishna and Subhadra and the broad-shouldered Satyaki arrived from the east and saw the hill decorated for his yearly festival. Flowers and colored rice were strewn about; flags and bells trembled in the ocean wind; colored elephants kept time to the lutes and drums; lighted lamps were hung from poles and trees, making the caves and fountains and valleys bright as day. Everywhere the birds were singing and eating the rice.

There was so much noise it sounded like the hill himself was shouting and singing. When they saw Krishna, the dark-

eyed girls playing in the lotus ponds along the road embraced him with their eyes; from the hillside orchards and groves everyone came running to welcome him. Satyaki and Krishna threw loving glances and smiles at the women who surrounded their chariot.

Satyaki jumped from the driver's box and scooped up the fine copper-colored soil of Dwaravati in his huge hands. He threw a shower of dust high over his head, and most of it fell on King Ugrasena, who had walked over to meet them.

Ugrasena laughed and embraced Satyaki. Then with a quick easy motion he lifted him up and tossed him through the air to the girls in the nearest lotus pond. From the folds of his royal robes the king took Krishna's flute and threw it at him.

Krishna leapt from the chariot to catch it and landed on both feet facing the king. "Old man, don't throw people into the water like that! He's come all the way here to tell you about the great Bharata war."

Ugrasena pulled at his long white beard. "Ah yes, the war." He looked solemnly around and everyone fell silent. "Well speak up. Whoever wants to hear this charioteer's tale, say so."

Nobody said a word. Ugrasena looked at Krishna with sparkling eyes. "Maybe some other time?" He led Krishna away by the hand, chuckling to himself.

Near Indraprastha Arjuna found his way blocked by a man wearing a ratty black deerskin and a wide, flat necklace of pitted brass. He was tall and his hair was yellow and free.

Krishna leapt from the chariot to catch it

Agni said quietly, "I have already taken your chariot. Give me Gandiva bow and all the thousand arrows." When the Fire Lord touched the weapons they fell into ashes.

Arjuna sent a letter to Yudhishthira, saying:

> Khandava forest has grown up again, and Maya's magic palace lies broken in the tall grass that reaches over my head. Yudhishthira, for you it is also time.

Joined with Arjuna, Yudhishthira with his brothers and Draupadi, all wearing bark, walked into the north.

❖

In Dwaravati, one day when the wind sounded like the ocean, and the waves of the sea like the wind, the city was drowned under the salt waters. All perished but Krishna and Balarama.

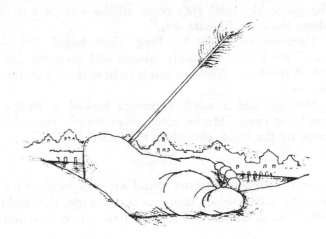

They were walking through the forests of Raivataka Hill. Krishna left his brother alone, sitting under a tree with his winejar, calmly drinking, and wandered thoughtfully by himself through the deserted wood. Sesha the endless serpent, who holds up the world, withdrew his energy from Balarama just when he had swallowed the last drop of wine: from between Balarama's eyes a jet of light entered the sea, and the body left behind fell over.

Krishna lay down in the grass, and thought, "Oh, where is Arjuna? *I have thrown my fire into the water; with uplifted arms I am crying aloud, but nobody hears me.*" He frowned. "Well tomorrow . . . " he said, "tomorrow I shall destroy the world for all its evil ways." He ran his hand through his long straight hair, clasped his dark fingers together, and fell asleep.

Just then, Bharata, Jara the hunter, searching the forest for deer, passed through Raivataka and mistook Krishna's foot for the face of a stag, and shot an arrow of grass into his heel. Jara ran up quickly to capture his kill. He found Krishna lying dead in his yellow robes, with four arms, with a smooth jewel on his breast, with an arrow slightly piercing his foot.

"How could that kill him?" wondered Jara. "I am ashamed of having done this, but what can be done about it?"

Jara cast an angry glance at the sea. It was following, rising up over the path Krishna had taken, flooding the land below. Soon it lapped against Jara's feet, and he thought, "I will never speak of it," and went far away forever.

Drowned were the sapphire towers beneath the flowing

With an arrow slightly piercing his foot

cliffs of the sea, which now stumbled against the hill-caves of Raivata.

Cherished King, Time is the root and the seed, it gives and it takes away. I bow to God, who lives in this world within us; whoever calls Him by any name, by that name does He come.

"Therefore take care with the names of God," said Vaisampayana, "and I have finished all my story."

Saunaka, the wisdom of this story, like a little flat pin to spread black dust around the eyes, opens the eyes of the searching world blinded by ignorance. As the full moon expands the night lily buds, so this romance stretches the mind. By the lamp of history is the whole mansion of nature's womb illumined.

Janamejaya said, "Oh Astika, this is a wonderful sacrifice." And from among the thousands who had gathered round Vyasa and Vaisampayana and the king, Takshaka the serpent prince rose all dressed in jewels and stars.

He saluted first the poet, then the teller, then the king, and he took Astika's arm, and they walked away into the evening. They stepped into Ganga and were gone underwater, to the Naga kingdoms far below.

Sauti said, "By Narayana's widespreading tree whose leaves are songs, on the grass plateau high on the sacred and eternal breast of Kailasa, the Players met under the colored shadows and asked: "What shall we play next?"

411

He took Astika's arm and they walked away into the evening

The long grass bends,
Oh, the long grass in the dry wind,
Oh, the wind sharp as arrows,
Cut by the swords, the long grass swords.

Here ends the Mahabharata.

notes

413

REFERENCE LIST OF CHARACTERS

Adhiratha, the charioteer who adopted Karna
Agni, the Fire God
Amba, eldest Princess of Banaras
Ambalika, youngest Princess of Banaras
Ambika, the third Princess of Banaras
Arjuna, Indra's son, Pandava
Astika, son of a Naga woman and a hermit
Aswins, twin gods
Balarama, Krishna's brother
Bharata, legendary Lunar king
Bhima, Pandava, son of the Wind; the Vidarbha King is also named
    Bhima.
Bhishma, King Santanu's son
Brahma, the Creator of the Universe, Lord of the highest heaven
    which is indestructable
Chitraratha, King of the Gandharvas, or heavenly musicians
Devi, Shiva's Wife
Dharma, Yudhishthira's father, God of Justice
Dhrishtadyumna, Drupada's son born of the fire
Dhritarashtra, the blind Bharata king
Draupadi, Drupada's fire-born daughter, the Pandavas' wife
Drona, preceptor at arms to the Bharatas
Drupada, King of Panchala
Duhsala, Dhritarashtra's only daughter

Duhsasana, Dhritarashtra's second-born son, one of the one hundred
    sons born to him from his Queen
Duryodhana, Dhritarashtra's first-born son
Gandhari, Dhritarashtra's Queen
Ganga, Goddess of the River Ganges
Hanuman, the monkey-chief, a hero of Ramayana
Indra, Lord of Heaven
Janamejaya, the Bharate King ruling when the story is told

Jayadratha, King of Sindh
Kalee, Goddess of Evil
Kali, God of Misfortune
Kama, God of Love
Karna, Kunti's first child, by the Sun
Kripa, preceptor at archery for the Bharatas
Kripi, Kripa's twin sister
Krishna, clan chief of the Yadavas
Kritavarman, kinsman to Krishna
Kunti, Pandu's first wife, mother of Yudhishthira, Bhima, Arjuna and
    Karna
Kuru, legendary King who gave his name to the Bharata people and to
    the field Kurukshetra
Lakshmi, Goddess of good fortune and plenty; heavenly consort of
    Narayana
Madri, Pandu's second wife, mother of Nakula and Sahadeva, sister of
    Salya
Manibhadra, King of the Yakshas and protector of travelers
Matali, Indra's charioteer
Maya, an Asura
Nakula, one of the twin Pandavas
Nara, the first man, the spirit of Man
Narayana, the Lord Vishnu who preserves the Universe
Pandu, younger brother to Dhritarashtra
Parikshita, Arjuna's son, Janamejaya's father
Pratipa, Bhishma's grandfather
Sahadeva, one of the twin Pandavas
Sakuni, Gandhari's brother, Duryodhana's uncle
Salwa, the heart-love chosen by Amba, a western king
Salya, King of the Madra people
Sanjaya, Dhritarashtra's charioteer

Santanu, Pratipa's son, Ganga's husband, Bhishma's father
Satyaki, kinsman to Krishna
Satyavati, Vyasa's mother
Saunaka, who listened to the story in the forest
Sauti, who told it to him
Sesha, Narayana's serpent
Shiva, the Great God whose third eye will destroy the Universe
Sikhandin, Drupada's son born a woman
Subhadra, Krishna's sister
Surya, the Sun God
Susarman, King of the Three Castles, Duryodhana's ally
Suyodhana, "good fighter," another name of Duryodhana
Takshaka, the serpent who killed Parikshita
Ugrasena, the Yadava King
Urvasi, an Apsaras
Uttara, Virata's son
Uttarah, Virata's daughter, Parikshita's mother
Vaisampayana, who told the story to Janamejaya
Vaishravana, God of Wealth
Vayu, the Wind God
Vidura, Pandu's younger brother
Virata, King of Matsya
Vyasa, the poet who composed Mahabharata
Yama, God of the Dead
Yudhishthira, eldest Pandava, Dharma's son
Yuyutsu, Dhritarashtra's son by a palace girl